THE GOLDEN RHINOCEROS

Histories of the African Middle Ages

FRANÇOIS-XAVIER FAUVELLE
Translated by Troy Tice

PRINCETON UNIVERSITY PRESS | PRINCETON & OXFORD

Original French edition © Alma éditeur, Paris, 2013
Published by arrangement with Martine Bertéa and
Patricia Pasqualini literary agencies

Originally titled *Le rhinocéros d'or*

Published by Princeton University Press
41 William Street, Princeton, New Jersey 08540
6 Oxford Street, Woodstock, Oxfordshire OX20 1TR

press.princeton.edu

LCCN 2018934178
ISBN 978-0-691-18126-4

British Library Cataloging-in-Publication Data is available

Editorial: Brigitta van Rheinberg, Amanda Peery
Production Editorial: Lauren Lepow
Text and jacket design: Chris Ferrante
Jacket and interior illustrations by Roland Sárkány
Production: Erin Suydam
Publicity: James Schneider

This book has been composed in Adobe Text Pro and Gza

Printed on acid-free paper. ∞

Printed in the United States of America

10 9 8 7 6 5 4 3 2 1

CONTENTS

NOTE ON CONVENTIONS

Except when necessary to indicate a scientific transcription, noted in parentheses, all the transcriptions from the Arabic, Ge'ez, as well as the various African languages are simplified. For the Arabic, the *hamza* and the *'ayn* are not marked, nor are diacritics, and long vowels are indicated by circumflex accents: â, î, and û. Chinese names have been spelled according to current usage in the academic literature. For personal names, I have used the English or most commonly accepted versions whenever possible. At the risk of anachronism, I have often chosen, in the chapter titles as well as the text, to locate the places and events in geography familiar to the reader: that of modern African nations. The reader is cautioned that modern political borders usually have nothing to do with those of medieval political formations. When there is a likelihood of confusion between the ancient name and the modern name, the written form follows that of the sources. Thus I use "Ghâna" and "Mâli" for the medieval kingdoms, and "Ghana" and "Mali" to refer to the contemporary countries. The adjective "Islamic" is here used to describe Islamic civilization generally. Consequently, it encompasses everything associated with the regions and populations that had converted to Islam, whether they spoke Arabic or another language (Persian, Berber, Coptic, Ethiopian, etc.), as well as everything associated with non-Muslim regions and populations, whether they spoke Arabic or not, that fell under the political sway of Islam. The adjective "Muslim" is used only in reference to Islam as a religion. The expression "Land of the Blacks" used in several chapters is a translation of the Arabic *Bilād as-Sūdān*. Unless otherwise stated, the dates are given according to the Gregorian calendar.

References marked with an arrow (↦) indicate that a subject is taken up in another chapter; readers, then, may use them as signposts to chart their own itinerary through the book; asterisks (*) indicate that the word appears in the glossary at the back of the book.

Africa in the Middle Ages

By opening this book, the reader is taking the first steps on a journey across several centuries of African history. Our first guide on this journey will be an eighth-century Chinese traveler, our last, a fifteenth-century Portuguese conqueror. Between the two we will sometimes follow merchants, diplomats, or modern archaeologists in their travels through African cities and countrysides; we will meet kings, clerics, traders, and ordinary people—individuals whom we would be honored or pleased to meet in person, and highly unsavory types it would be better never to come across; we will encounter Muslims, Jews, Christians, and people practicing nonmonotheistic religions, such as ancestor cults or cults dedicated to territorial spirits. Marco Polo and Ibn Battûtta will be our companions. We must not expect to always understand everything we see on our journey, and we must reject the certainty that our guides saw and understood things any better. For what they describe, and what we would never have known without their testimony, most often derives from what they themselves had heard or read. We must not be shocked by the geographical uncertainties about the precise location of a lost capital city or the name of a given archaeological site, the informants' contradictions of one another, or the sometimes arrogant and touristic judgment that travelers bring when they venture from one world to another. In the face of the diversity in achievements and societies we are going to encounter, we must remember Vumbi Yoka Mudimbé's and Ali A. Mazrui's warnings that "Africa" as a space of knowledge was repeatedly *invented* from the outside. We must indeed free ourselves from the image of a "uniform" and "eternal" Africa, of an Africa of innumerable and unchanging "tribes," of an Africa conceived as the reliquary of our "origins," for we are going to speak about African societies *in* history.

Eight centuries, almost a millennium, and yet so little is known. Let us confess, our attention, as readers and viewers of documentaries, turns most often to the African civilizations of antiquity: the Egypt of the pharaohs; Meroitic Nubia; Punic or Roman Africa; Aksum in Ethiopia:

civilizations whose spectacular architectural remains have long captured the imagination of all who enjoy reflecting on great civilizations. Perhaps we are also familiar with more recent centuries, when the African continent, strongly tied to the destiny of the Western powers, was supposedly "discovered," then "explored" (two rather Eurocentric terms), and most of all exploited by those who set about taking possession of it. During the last five centuries, Africans suffered the slave trade followed by colonization; finally, they confronted the violent transformations of the postcolonial present. Between these relatively familiar Africas—the antique Africa, whose splendors nourish a nostalgic erudition, and contemporary Africa, whose convulsions arouse an avid curiosity—stretch what have been called the "dark centuries" of African history.

"Dark centuries"—really? This expression was sometime used to designate a period of African history prior to the so-called Age of Discovery (inaugurated by Portuguese navigators in the fifteenth century) and colonization (inaugurated in the seventeenth century and generalized in the nineteenth), periods that produced a relative abundance of written sources. Far from seeking to denigrate Africa's ancient past, such an expression articulates a frustration with the cruel lack of available sources for recounting that past. So if there exist "dark centuries" of African history, it is only by virtue of the weak light shed by the documentation. But the case made in this book is that even if the sources relating to the "dark centuries" of African history are rare and uncertain, the period would surely better merit the name of "golden age." As far as clichés go, the latter is more accurate: our meager sources tell us that the Africa of this period was home to powerful and prosperous states, and that it integrated itself into some of the great currents of global exchange that circulated people, merchandise, and religious conceptions. It witnessed the development of cities where African princes had their palaces, where foreign merchants resided, where luxury products and slaves were exchanged, where mosques or churches were built. Africa was then a major player in the exploitation of its own resources, among which gold held a prominent place. The continent enjoyed a considerable reputation, from Europe to China, a reputation exemplified by the celebrity that Mûsâ, king of Mâli during the first third of the fourteenth century, achieved in the Islamic world and Christian Europe.

But we are not going to swap a reputation for darkness for a golden legend. It is more important to understand how the Africa of the intermediate centuries between the antique and modern periods could be a cradle of civilizations so radiant, and yet so obscured in the surviving documentation that its rediscovery seems a thankless task. What are the reasons for this apparent paradox?

The first reason for the neglect of this "golden age" is that few African societies of this period used writing or kept archives that could testify from within to their power and prosperity. It is true that a number of ancient African societies produced written texts in diverse languages and writing systems, including ancient Egyptian (in Egypt), Punic (in the Maghreb), Libyco-Berber (in the Maghreb and the Sahara desert), Ge'ez (in Eritrea and Ethiopia), Old Nubian (in today's Sudan), Greek (in Egypt, Sudan, Eritrea, and Ethiopia), Latin (in Christian North Africa), or Arabic (in Islamic North Africa, but also in some parts of sub-Saharan Africa, such as Ethiopia, Nubia, and Mali, as early as the eleventh century), among other examples. Later, beginning in the seventeenth century, some societies would produce historical chronicles (one thinks of the Sahelian communities, in particular Timbuktu, or the diverse communities of the Swahili coast), and writing would spread across the continent from the nineteenth century on. But even if writing before the modern era was geographically much more diverse and widely distributed than is generally believed, its use was considerably restricted among any given society. The African societies of the period that interests us knew about writing but, with a few exceptions (North Africa, Nubia, and Ethiopia), did not develop written traditions that could serve as sources for today's historians. That they did not do so was not the result of a lack of motivation or competence; rather, they chose not to. Indeed, another form of transmission, likewise entrusted to specialists, existed in many African societies, a transmission not of the written word but of the spoken one: what we call "oral traditions." Passed down over the generations, some stories have reached us. The question of the reliability of these oral traditions for reconstructing the distant past is a matter of heated debate among historians of Africa. Nonetheless, most among them would agree that, if oral traditions should certainly not be denied their status as historical documents for accessing the past two, three, or sometimes four centuries, their inherent limitations preclude their enabling any thorough reconstruction of earlier periods. It should not, of course, prevent us from listening very closely to African voices when they have come down to us thanks to a written document, as is the case, for instance, with the account of the rise to power of King Mûsâ of Mâli, told by the king himself to an Arab secretary in the chancery of Cairo. However, though such voices are clearly a bonanza for the historian and the reader, one should resist the temptation—rooted in both the relief of a sudden and direct access to the past and a naive attitude toward the interpretation of all things African—of taking such discourse at face value. A political statement by a Malian king of the fourteenth century is no less elaborate and finely chiseled than any diplomatic statement today, and thus it must be studied as such.

So, with few exceptions, we are left mostly with documents produced by outsiders. The outsiders, by then, were not Christian Europeans, but Muslims and sometimes Jews from the Islamic world, with whom their African partners found themselves in a closer relationship between the eighth century and the fifteenth. In fact, since the eighth and ninth centuries, Arab and Islamic powers had established themselves in most regions north of the Sahara, ruling societies that had until then been predominantly Christian, and had thus interposed themselves between the countries of "inner" Africa and the outside world. Although Marco Polo and Vasco da Gama will, at a late stage, be mentioned, it might come as a surprise to readers of this book to notice how little space is given to written European sources, which represent a very small proportion when compared with the Arabic sources (i.e., written in Arabic, not necessarily by Arab people) relative to our period. But in turn, one should not exaggerate the number and extent of Arabic sources, as contrasted with the much more substantial corpus available for Europe or the Islamic world of the time. Consider the fact that all we know from written documents in Arabic about the peoples, kingdoms, and societies of the regions today called the Sahel, stretching from Mauritania and Senegal to Chad, fits in a volume only a few hundred pages long! Why? Because information follows the same routes as ships and long-distance caravans, and because the Sahel region and the shores of East Africa were very remote from the economic and political centers of, say, Morocco, Libya, Egypt, Syria, Iraq, or Iran. Information circulates, furthermore, with merchants, individuals who are generally inclined to remain discreet about supply points, modes of transaction, precise itineraries, and personal contacts, and who, when they prove talkative, are more often than not interested only in places of commerce and powers likely to favor their business. As luck would have it, however, a few armchair geographers curious about the world, such as the Andalusian al-Bakrî in the eleventh century, and a few less scrupulous travelers, such as the celebrated Ibn Battûta in the fourteenth century, have occasionally offered the fruits of their experiences and inquiries to posterity.

But what about material remains from the past? Don't we at least have cities, palaces, various monuments, and places of worship as material witnesses to the political history of elites, the religious history of peoples, the architectural achievements of societies, their everyday life? So few, often so poorly preserved, sometimes so pathetically documented by research. Consider that we do not even know where the capital of Mâli was located at the time of its mid-fourteenth-century splendor. Is our ignorance due to a lack of research? Undoubtedly. But we should add that if the sites are lost—swallowed up by dunes, mangroves, or savanna—or if those rediscovered by archaeologists through pedestrian surveys have not retained their original significance, it is due not only to the lack of writing and the environmental changes that took place during the intervening centuries, but also to a rupture of memory. For a site or monument to retain its significance across time, it must be the subject of continual reinvestment; that is to say, it must be modified and transformed by others who take on its legacy, even if they distort it. Memory is the condition, not the negation nor the opposite, of history. Yet we should note that this continuity of memory was lacking in most of the regions where kingdoms and cities developed. Gone were the long-established foreign merchants; gone the African traders who were their longtime partners; but gone, too, were the elites and, quite often, the local population. In this book, we will sometimes visit deserted, mute places, such as the site of the likely capital of Ghâna, a brilliant kingdom of the tenth to twelfth century centered in present-day southeast Mauritania, where no urban planner would suggest having a city today. Golden centuries: not dark, but forgotten.

This forgetfulness conditions access to the distant African past, and consequently to the writing of its history. Of these forgotten centuries we have only traces, vivid but uncertain. Not even the scattered pieces of a jigsaw puzzle, for we often do not know which puzzle they belong to. A nearly worn stone inscription, a few coins, objects found in amateur or clandestine excavations, partially destroyed monuments, the terse text of a foreign author—such fragments will often be the sole surviving witnesses of a chronological slice of several centuries, of a historical context that remains, in just about every other respect, more or less inaccessible. Historians often have nothing more at their disposal than "lost items," orphaned traces. These constitute the material from which they derive their fragmentary knowledge. Let's come to terms with it: if this book presents itself to the reader as an arrangement of fragments illuminated side by side in turn, it is because I have preferred the stained-glass window to the grand narrative fresco that would have produced only the illusion of an authoritative discourse. For such an authoritative discourse on ancient Africa is impossible; the sources are hopelessly silent when it comes to entire sections of reality, such as the local economy, social organization, the family, peasants in rural areas, the daily life of women, men, and children. Yet the stained-glass window has its advantages: by carefully selecting the fragments, we can construct a history whose dominant features are the aspects best illuminated by the sources: royal power, cities, trade goods, sociability among the male members of the commercial, religious, and political elites. Even the lead joints that tie together the glass fragments are not so much a problem as a condition of a modest, perhaps frustrating, but more truthful, vision of history. The very process of putting the fragments together can transmute our frustration into an exciting challenge: that of crafting an incomplete history open to comparisons between one region and another, new discoveries, and interpretative changes.

The rarity of our sources creates an obligation—undoubtedly one of the hallmarks of the historian of ancient Africa—to consider each trace a document, be it a written text, an architectural monument, or a tiny piece of charcoal. Some might think this goes without saying. Is it really so? The historian who works on written traces from the past likes to know what they are. Their work transforms the textual fragment into a document—this is what "philology" is about. But do we really take care to apply the same techniques we use for texts to other traces from the past? The question is essential when textual sources are not the principal base for historical reconstruction, as is our case. Do nontextual traces have their philologists? Sometimes methodical excavations and exhaustive reports of archaeological operations have succeeded in turning a site into such a document through the work of cautious, systematic description of the material facts as well as the methods that brought them to light. When it comes to archaeological facts, such a document is all the more precious, as excavations efface most of what they observe. More often than we would like to admit, the excavators did not follow proper methodology or produce a meticulous report, to say nothing of the fact that, working in a colonial context, they often coerced local people to extract objects from the ground with little regard for the significance of the site to the latter or for its preservation. Occasionally some objects have likewise acquired the status of a document. But how many times has the context of their unearthing been wrapped in an impenetrable haze because of systematic pillaging that feeds the international market in cultural objects, when they do not simply disappear into private collections before having been properly described? Suffice it to say, the requirements of an investigation oriented toward the production of documents—documents useful to the recovery of the past—are not always met. Field research and erudition, from this point of view, do not always harmonize. An example, at least, has been set by the indefatigable Théodore Monod, a pioneer of document collection. Watching him at work in the 1960s in eastern Mauritania—in the most sterile quarter of the Sahara and certainly one of the most hostile environments in the world—we find him incapable, given the practical conditions of his mission, of fully documenting (as he certainly wished to) the tiny though immensely important medieval site that had been discovered only months earlier by local antelope hunters. Yet by immediately producing, in just a few hours, records of his discovery, he left behind documentation that is at once imperfect and unequaled.

In the absence of this pragmatic ideal, we must often turn to the circumstances of the discovery. This is why many stories in this book will start from a departure point situated not ten centuries ago but just one or two, in an attempt to glimpse how the site or object has come down to us. This approach takes into account the "social life" of sites, objects, and texts; it produces a social biography that reflects not only their documentary dimension but also their changing appearance and historical significance as perceived by the archaeologist or in the eyes of the local people. On this point, we will perhaps marvel that so many "treasures" unearthed from the African soil—beginning with the golden rhinoceros of Mapungubwe, which provides the title of one of the chapters and of the book as a whole—often serve as the story's starting point. "Treasures" are good documents to use in assessing the past, one might think. But we can also shift our perspective by suggesting that treasures exist only when the archaeological documentation that should have accompanied their discovery is missing. The fruits of hasty collections, of casual or selective excavations, "treasures" may sometimes be a godsend for the historian; but they also illuminate processes of elimination that have reduced all the potential documentation of a site, or indeed of a region or period, to this residual form. The "treasure" is what remains when everything else has disappeared. Any narrative history built around such traces cannot ignore its dependence on such phenomena, in Africa more than elsewhere, owing to lack of research, the violations of the underground heritage that went hand in hand with the coercion of individuals and societies during the colonial period, and the low level of awareness, until recently, of the concept of archaeological heritage on the continent.

If for no other reason than the fact that these forgotten centuries had acquired a new historical value through their coming to light, they would sufficiently warrant being called by a grand chrononym like the "Middle Ages." This expression has already been applied by a number of authors to the African past. Roland Oliver and Anthony Atmore initially titled their famous book *The African Middle Ages 1400–1800* (1981) before changing it to *Medieval Africa 1250–1800* in their revised edition (2001). But the adjustable dates of their chronological range are ample evidence that "medieval" here just meant "precolonial"; perhaps the latter word was avoided because it would have put emphasis on the changes later to be introduced by the colonizer. In his now-outdated *The Lost Cities of Africa*, Basil Davidson had a chapter on "medieval Rhodesia," the word "medieval" in this case used to counter the colonial narrative of the famous ruins of Zimbabwe as the vestiges of antique, "Mediterranean" (i.e., white), settlers. So let us admit that there can be many reasons to use the term "Middle Ages" or the adjective "medieval" that are not particularly related to the way medieval Europe is medieval. There's also a good reason not to use it; for if its usefulness resides only in designating a period of almost a millennium roughly coeval with the European Middle Ages, one could rightfully ask why we should import a label that conveys unwanted associations with medieval Europe: Christianity, feudalism, the crusades against Islam. True. But despite all this, I think that applying the term "Middle Ages" to Africa is justified. The justification concerns the scale at which we observe the Middle Ages: for one of the benefits of the current trend of historical research aiming at "provincializing Europe" (to use Chakrabarty's term) is that the European Middle Ages tends to be perceived as a province of a global world that deserves to be called medieval based only on its distinctive way of being global. This is not to say that medieval Europe has no specific characteristics. But they appear all the more interesting, or let us say more interestingly exotic, when contrasted with the background of broader phenomena like the interconnectedness of all the provinces of the medieval world, the physical centrality of the Islamic civilization within this global world, the role of specialized long-distance merchants (mostly Muslims and Jews) as connecting agents between different provinces, or the related significance of a few chosen commodities (such as slaves, gold, china, glass beads, ambergris) as evidence of an interconnectedness of a kind limited to what met the needs and tastes of the elites. In that sense, the broad picture that this book wants to draw, its fragmentary nature notwithstanding, is that Africa also deserves to be considered a province of the medieval world. Not out of a will to "provincialize" Africa in the sense of making it marginalized or peripheral, but, on the contrary, to make it part of a world made up of other such provinces.

It is beyond the scope of this book to suggest anything like precise geographical and chronological boundaries to the global Middle Ages. After all, to be a Europeanist medievalist or to read a book on medieval Europe, one needn't possess certainty about when exactly medieval Europe starts and ends. But let us only note that, just as the global Middle Ages is as much a space as a time period, so too is the African Middle Ages in this book. Let us look at the map of the areas where the histories in our book take place. We encounter a vast crescent, stretching over the entire width of the continent from the Atlantic coastlines of the Sahara and the Sahel to the Red Sea, encompassing the basins of the Niger River and middle Nile Valley. Covering the high plateaus of the Horn of Africa, it spreads from the African side of the Gulf of Aden to the eastern edges of southern Africa and Madagascar. The immensity and diversity of this space straddling the two hemispheres scarcely need emphasizing. It was home to a wide array of natural environments and a number of vastly different cultures. Yet all these diverse regions and cultures had one point in common during the period that interests us: between the eighth and the fifteenth century, they reciprocated the desire for contact expressed by merchants and clerics from different regions of the Islamic world; they contributed to the establishment of a regular system of long-distance commercial exchange across the Sahara or Indian Ocean; they were nowhere (except in part of Nubia) conquered or forced to submit to foreign rule, but willingly participated in a global political, religious, juridical, intellectual, aesthetic conversation. They were not passive partners in a vast global system into which they were slotted, but actors attentive to procuring their share of the benefits of commercial exchange, capable of negotiating the conditions of this exchange, of accepting certain social transformations—especially religious ones—and of constructing "bricolages" in order to be considered full partners. If nothing else, these vanished cities—once humming with multiple languages, the brusque cries of merchants unpacking their loads or the custom officers inspecting them, commercial arguments played out in court or before the mosque, secrets divulged in alcoves—can make us feel at once the intensity and the insecurity of their efforts to control their destiny. Of course, we should not imagine that only the societies that fell within our geographical, chronological, and documentary medieval domain had a history. If history is more *visible* here than elsewhere, it is because they appear in the documentation as active commercial partners, energetic and famous leaders: in other words, agents of historical change equipped with will, ambitions, and intentions, inevitably at the expense of those whose lower status or economic condition confined them to documentary darkness, including the innumerable slaves who were the main victims of this glorious age.

The connection between Africa and the outside world was not achieved everywhere with the same speed, nor did it have everywhere the same intensity. If partners from the Islamic world made contact simultaneously with the long Sahelian "shore," south of the Sahara, and the northern portion of the lengthy coastline extending from Somalia to Tanzania, contact with their hinterlands, as well as with the regions extending to the south of these first edges, was made only later. The fleeting images from the sources thus reveal a changing geography through the centuries, meeting points that burgeoned and declined, societies newly integrated in turn into the circle of regional systems under constant organization. Thus we see the geography deepen, the maps change. Beyond every geographer's royal market city—an already formidably exotic horizon for an inhabitant of Baghdad or Cairo—existed in its hinterland subject African populations we can scarcely perceive. Slaves and gold came from societies even farther away, of whom we catch only indistinct glimpses, absent as they are from written sources, their tenuous participation in the regional system sometimes brought to light only by archaeology. In that sense, the African Middle Ages is not only a space and a time; it is also a certain documentary regime characterized by the disparity of external written sources and the scarcity or absence of internal ones, as well as the isolated and largely incomplete nature of material remains. Moreover, texts and material traces may be sharply at odds, as when a city described in an Arabic text has no

corresponding site known in the field, or when a site well known to archaeologists cannot be related to any precise location in the written records.
This regime of documentation started to change around the end of the
fifteenth century, with the growing importance of the European written
documents. That alone would be sufficient to warrant closing the book
by this date, if the European attempts, and eventual success, at circum-
navigating the continent had not produced their enormous effects: major
disruptions of the economic circuits inside Africa; a decline in the intensity
of its exchanges with its partners in the Islamic world; the decline of the
political influence of once-major African powers such as the kingdom of
Mâli, the Christian kingdom of Ethiopia, or the city-state of Kilwa in Tanzania, which had virtually all disappeared in the early sixteenth century;
and the emergence of new African broker states along the coasts—thus
inaugurating a new, marginalized place for Africa in its relationship with
the capitalistic and imperial modern world.

This book's chapters conform to a generally chronological framework,
but one that allows for geographic zigzags and ample thematic pursuits
that lead the reader from one end of the continent to the other. The starting
points for the accounts are sometimes "classic" documents from medieval
African history; others will perhaps be more unfamiliar. Either way, all
may benefit from a new look, particularly since recently published critical
editions, the publication of long-delayed archaeological monographs, and
reopened investigations into the conditions of an object's exhumation,
or a site's excavation, or a date calibration shed new light on the scene.
Whether the document is famous or little known, rather than simply re-
treading familiar ground, I often chose to vary the scale; to bring forward
unusual sources or to hold a mirror up to documents from remote regions;
to shift perspective or to suggest a new hypothesis.

The reader will be spared the footnotes that usually clutter the bottom
of the page, but may, if he or she chooses, turn to short bibliographic essays at the end of each chapter. These essays are intended mainly to bring

together references to the primary (textual and archaeological) and secondary sources cited in the text. They are especially useful to those who would like to go deeper into the primary sources, to check the references I allude to, to have a look into how I know what I say. But they also present a selection of other textual and archaeological references, personal appraisals of the state of the documentation, or even analyses of certain aspects relevant to the context and history of the fieldwork and domain under consideration. Made within a literature in different languages, of sometimes uneven quality, which has a knack for synthesis more often than for careful attention to the sources, the bibliographical choices reflect the desire to illuminate the document itself as much as possible.

BIBLIOGRAPHICAL NOTE

Vumbi Yoka Mudimbé's work alluded to is *The Invention of Africa* (Bloomington: Indiana University Press, 1988); Ali A. Mazrui's is "The Re-Invention of Africa: Edward Said, V. Y. Mudimbe, and Beyond," *Research in African Literature* 36, no. 3 (2005): 68–82. The expression "dark ages" ("siècles obscurs" in French) is that of Raymond Mauny, one of the major founders of ancient African history in France, from the title of his *Les Siècles obscurs de l'Afrique noire* (Paris: Fayard, 1971). I have recently applied the expression "golden age" to African medieval history in my contribution "Trade and Travel in Africa's Golden Global Age (700–1500)," in Dorothy Hodgson and Judith Byfeld (eds.), *Global Africa into the Twenty-First Century* (Berkeley: University of California Press, 2017), pp. 17–26. For an illustration of the complementary, if sometimes opposite, views on oral tradition, see the various contributions in the excellent volume edited by Ralph A. Austen, *In Search of Sunjata: The Mande Oral Epic as History, Literature, and Performance* (Bloomington: Indiana University Press, 1999), which deals with the famous epic of the foundation of the kingdom of Mâli. The expression "social life" alludes to Arjun Appadurai's *The Social Life of Things: Commodities in Cultural Perspective* (London: Cambridge University Press, 1986). Oliver and Atmore's book was published by Cambridge University Press. Basil Davidson's *The Lost Cities of Africa* was initially published in Boston by Little, Brown and Company in 1959 and went through multiple editions. Dipesh Chakrabarty's book is *Provincializing Europe: Postcolonial Thought and Historical Difference* (Princeton, NJ: Princeton University Press, 2000). Reflections on the marginalized place of Africa in the global processes that took place in the modern period are based on Frederick Cooper, *Africa in the World: Capitalism, Empire, Nation-State* (Cambridge, MA: Harvard University Press, 2014).

CHAPTER 1

The Tribulations of Two Chinese in Africa

East Africa, the Eighth to the Fifteenth Century

In July 751, contingents from the Abbasid Caliphate fighting alongside rebellious Turks tore the Chinese army to pieces on the plain of Talas, near Tashkent, in current Uzbekistan. Thousands of prisoners were transported to the garrison posts of Bukhara and Samarkand, as well as Iraq, where former soldiers turned paper makers, fabric weavers, or jewelers were numerous. Among the prisoners was an officer: Du Huan. We do not know the circumstances that led him to cross the Islamic regions to return to China, but we find him in Guangzhou in 762. He wrote a book, the *Jingxingji* (Record of travels), unfortunately lost, but a few excerpts have survived in a contemporaneous Chinese encyclopedia.

One of the excerpts tells us about a certain land, Molin, where the people are black. Neither rice nor cereals grow there, nor grass nor trees. The horses are fed with dried fish. It moves on to describe the interior, a mountainous region where Muslims and Eastern Christians live. Here diarrhea is cured by incisions made on the skull. It is perhaps this latter region, if it is different from the first, that was called Laobosa, a name in which some suggest we can recognize al-Habasha, the Arabic term for the lands of the Horn of Africa, which has given us Abyssinia in English. If that is the case, Molin would refer more specifically to the low-lying coastal zones of Eritrea and Sudan. But these are only conjectures; let us simply say that they are compatible with the text. If Du Huan intended to describe what we today call Ethiopia, we would certainly not be surprised that he mentions the presence of Christians and Muslims, who lived there in neighboring communities all through the Middle Ages. But neither would we be surprised if he had actually had Egypt or Nubia in mind; or perhaps North Africa, recently conquered by the Arabo-Muslim armies, where Christian communities, in continuous decline, lived until the twelfth century; or maybe the Arabian Peninsula, where Christians, Jews, and Muslims coexisted long after the rise of Islam; or even Socotra, an island in the Arabian Sea guarding the entrance to the Gulf of Aden.

The fragments from Du Huan's account are perhaps the first testimony of a direct knowledge of Africa in China. But we should not mask their insignificance: to an uncertain geography may be added ethnological details that reveal their Sino-centric bias, and that lose almost all their value when we consider our inability to narrow down, beyond a few thousand kilometers, the region they relate to.

From the Tang (618–907) to the Yuan (1260–1368) dynasty, Chinese sources teem with indirect references to Africa, more precisely to the Horn and the African shores of the Indian Ocean. Generalizations about Chinese knowledge of Africa are often drawn from them, indeed about the incredible extension of Chinese navigation, which, some believe, rounded the Cape of Good Hope or even reached America. In addition, it is excessive to infer from the presence of shards of blue and white porcelain or Chinese coins in numerous East African archaeological sites the regular presence of Chinese merchants in these places. Judging by the form of the names of the lands that figure in the sources, when these names are recognizable, the information could have been obtained from Arab and Persian intermediaries, whose community at Guangzhou is attested from the eighth century. Chinese porcelain thus was transported to East African shores not in seagoing junks, but aboard the sambuks* of the Muslim merchants of the Persian Gulf and the Gulf of Aden. Pushed by monsoon winds flowing from the opposite direction, information about Africa made its way to China.

The oldest known direct contacts between China and Africa seem rather late: they took place only under the Ming dynasty (1368–1644). These, then, were official contacts, and they must have been quite spectacular. Indeed, between 1405 and 1433, the imperial eunuch Zheng He, grand admiral of the Chinese fleet and a Muslim, led seven naval expeditions to the Indochinese Peninsula, Indonesia, and the yet more distant Indian, Persian, Arabian, and African shores of the Indian Ocean. It has long been thought that these expeditions were peaceful. The least we can say is that they must have been very intimidating: at least a hundred junks up to two to three times larger—some even more—than the Portuguese galleons at the end of the century, carrying twenty to forty thousand men in total, the majority of whom were soldiers. Their objective was perhaps, as a specialist on the topic wrote, "to go shopping for women for the imperial harem," and to bring back perfumes and unguents, plumage and coats from exotic animals, horns and precious woods. It was also, no doubt, to record information about the sources and supply routes of these luxury items, which had reached China for centuries but were now highly sought after. Finally, it was to force local sovereigns encountered along the way to submit to the emperor, whether they acquiesced in their subordination or not, particularly by making them send emissaries and gifts.

Zheng He reached Africa twice: in 1417–1419 during the fifth voyage and 1421–1422 during the sixth. More precisely, he touched ground at Dju-bo, an unknown location perhaps situated at the mouth of the Jubba River in current Somalia; at Mu-ku-tu-shu (Mogadishu) and Pula-wa (Brava), also in Somalia; and perhaps at Malindi in Kenya. Unfortunately the official reports of these expeditions are among the many documents that have disappeared, destroyed in 1480 during factional struggles between military officers and eunuchs. However, surviving records include several personal accounts of men who served with the admiral; a large map attributed to Ma Huan, the expeditions' Muslim interpreter, depicting the coasts of the visited regions; as well as mentions in the Ming annals. More remarkable are the stone inscriptions carved as thanks by Zheng He himself in two temples dedicated to Mazu, the "Lady of the Celestial Palace," goddess of the sea and protector of sailors, near the Yangtze estuary from whence the expeditions set sail.

But, despite this near abundance, Africa is again unlucky: we learn little from Zheng He's voyages, and what we do learn does not measure up to the minor miracle of the very existence of Chinese documentation. In other words, just because they came from far away does not mean that the Chinese had any reason to leave more thorough descriptions than others. Regarding Mogadishu, for example, we are told that the houses have four or five floors, and that the inhabitants are quarrelsome and practice archery. Concerning Dju-bo: "They live in solitary and dispersed villages. The country is situated in a remote corner of the west. The walls are made of piled up bricks and the houses are masoned in high blocks. The customs are very simple. There grow neither herbs nor trees. Men and women wear their hair in rolls; when they go out, they wear a linen hood. The mountains are uncultivated and the land is wide; it rains very rarely. There are deep wells worked by means of cog-wheels. Fish are caught in the sea with nets." The description is meager, but we will have to be content with it.

But the key point lies elsewhere. Seven centuries after the voyages of Du Huan, Zheng He's expeditions brought to a close the epoch the first had opened. It was a period characterized by a curiosity averse to risking the adventure of formal contact but always concerned about keeping itself informed, albeit from uncertain sources. The expedition of 1421–1422 was the last contact between China and Africa until the modern era; above all, it signified a return to indifference. We have rambled on about the financial costs of such expeditions to explain their suppression; we have philosophized on China's withdrawal into itself. But what these relations illustrate—precisely because the improbable pairing of Africa and China, despite their geographical separation, is the manifestation of its intensity—is the force of the interconnection of the medieval Islamic world. Let us take the Chinese episodes in Africa for what they were: light contacts. But when placed in the context of increased indirect exchange between Africa and China from the eighth to the fifteenth century—as revealed through references to Africa in Chinese sources as well as archaeological evidence of Chinese artifacts on African shores—they attest to the dynamism of a universe that became the intermediary between worlds so very distant in space and culture.

Or, to put it differently, it was a universe that prospered from having made itself, deservedly, the intermediary between these worlds. For if Islam was able to connect China and East Africa, it was by creating a vast commercial system, brought together less by language and religion than by law and money.

BIBLIOGRAPHICAL NOTE

De Huan's story is told by Wolbert Smidt, "A Chinese in the Nubian and Abyssinian Kingdoms (8th century)," *Chroniques yéménites* 9 (2001): 17–28. Several Chinese sources from the Middle Ages are presented in Friedrich Hirth, "Early Chinese Notices of East African Territories," *Journal of the American Oriental Society* 30 (1909): 46–57. The short work of Jan Julius Lodewijk Duyvendak, *China's Discovery of Africa* (London: Arthur Probsthain, 1949), the text of two lectures given at the School of Oriental and African Studies in 1947, remains the best and most sober presentation of these texts in a Western language; the quotation on "shopping" is taken from p. 27, the quotation on Dju-bo from p. 30. In "The True Dates of the Chinese Maritime Expeditions in the Early Fifteenth Century," *T'oung Pao* 34 (1939): 341–412, Duyvendak had earlier established the dates and routes of the eunuch's various expeditions. The work of Teobaldo Filesi, *China and Africa in the Middle Ages*, trans. David L. Morrison (London: F. Cass, 1972), has been criticized for putting too much stock in the idea of a direct relationship between Africa and China; interested readers can easily access reviews of the book. More generally, John Shen, "New Thoughts on the Use of Chinese Documents in the Reconstruction of Early Swahili History," *History in Africa* 22 (1995): 349–358, critically analyzes available translations of Chinese sources and how historians of Africa have used them. Sally Church's entry for "Zheng He," in *The Encyclopaedia of the History of Science, Technology and Medicine in Non-Western Cultures* (Berlin: Springer, 2008), is useful. So is Geoff Wade, "The Zheng He Voyages: A Reassessment," *Asia Research Institute Working Paper Series* 31 (2004): 37–58, which recalls the military pomp of these expeditions. More recently, see Robert Finlay, "The Voyages of Zheng He: Ideology, State Power, and Maritime Trade in Ming China," *Journal of the Historical Society* 9 (2008): 327–347. For Zheng He's map, see chiefly Mei-Ling Hsu, "Chinese Marine Cartography: Sea Charts of Pre-Modern China," *Imago Mundi* 40 (1988): 96–112. On the "Sino-centrist" readings of the sources relating to Zheng He's expeditions and the hypothesis of a Chinese discovery of America in 1421, see the vigorous corrective by Robert Finlay, "How Not to (Re)Write World History: Gavin Menzies and the Chinese Discovery of America," *Journal of World History* 15 (2004): 229–242. Finally, for Arab ships and expeditions in the Indian Ocean, George F. Hourani, *Arab Seafaring* (Princeton, NJ: Princeton University Press, 1995, 1st ed. 1951) is always useful.

CHAPTER 2

In the Belly of the Sperm Whale

East Africa, Beginning of the Tenth Century

Ambergris is a marine secretion, the best variety of which comes from the Sea of Zanj. It is pale blue, pieces of it are as big as ostrich eggs, and whales that swallow it die from it. Fishermen who harpoon these animals thus obtain the precious product. At least, that is how al-Masûdî imagined the origin of this merchandise, *anbar* in Arabic, from which we get "ambergris" or "gray amber" in English (to distinguish it from amber, fossilized resin, from which beads and gemstones are made).

Similar ideas were common currency among Arabic geographers and pharmacologists. Al-Idrîsî, in the twelfth century, related that the caliph Hârûn al-Rashîd (r. 786–809) had his agents rush onto the beaches of Yemen to investigate the origins of the ambergris that washed ashore after a storm. The curious story of ambergris spurting from the bottom of the sea only to be ingested by whales in fact corresponds to a series of accurate observations: fishermen encountered ambergris floating on the sea and occasionally gathered it on the beach, but they also found it in the intestines of certain cetaceans; it seemed to be a tuber that always incorporated the remains of marine animals. In reality, ambergris is produced only in the intestines of one variety of cetaceans, the sperm whale, and among only a tiny fraction of the population. It is a concretion that forms around undigested objects, particularly the horned beaks and mandibles of the cephalopods (octopuses, squids, etc.) on which the mammal feeds. Opportunely harvested or removed from cadavers in pieces of a few dozen grams to a few dozen kilograms—sometimes several hundred—ambergris is compact and friable in texture, waxy, and of speckled gray color. Fresh, it possesses a strong fecal odor, but when exposed to the oxidizing action of seawater and air, it acquires the persistent scents of tobacco, wood, and iodine. It can be burned like incense; it can serve as an unguent. Medieval Arab authors and later Europeans were also acquainted with its medicinal and alimentary uses. Sperm whale ambergris contains various toxic alcohols, a fact that might have led to the belief among such authors that cetaceans died from it. Along with musk and civet, ambergris or its synthetic equivalent is still one of the principal animal extracts used as a perfume fixative; we still credit it with the medicinal and aphrodisiac properties first discovered by the Arab druggists of the Middle Ages.

Of all the Arab writings that evoke the lands bordering the Sea of Zanj (i.e., the portion of the East African coast extending from southern Somalia to northern Tanzania), those of al-Masûdî, active during the first half of the tenth century, are some of the few based on direct observation. Undoubtedly quite wealthy to be able to devote his life to travel, he has left us with an exceptional picture of the world as it was during the first half of the fourth century of Islam: an encyclopedic survey of geographic, natural, and ethnographic knowledge entitled *The Meadows of Gold* (*Murūdj al-dhahab*), his principal work. Certainly profiting from favorable monsoon winds during his voyage from India, he visited the land of Zanj and the island of Qambalû before returning home to Iraq.

This, then, was the land of Zanj in 916: a long band of dry lands some seven hundred parasangs (around four thousand kilometers) in length, home to populations that used harnessed oxen as mounts; cultivated millet and banana trees; hunted elephants by poisoning their watering holes; dined on millet, meat and honey, and coconut; recognized kings who bore the title of *mfalme*; and had a sovereign god whom they called Maliknajlu, "the Great Lord." They unquestionably spoke a language of the Bantu family—the mother language of the Swahili spoken today in this part of Africa—and one that had already incorporated an Arabic word, *malik* (king). Yet their society was not yet Muslim. To the south, we do not know exactly where, extended the borders of another land, called Sofala, where the Wak-Wak lived, but we do not know who they were. It was from this land that gold "and other marvels" came. But we cannot locate it: it was without a doubt the Zanj themselves who trafficked there, and in all likelihood they are the source of all the information that exists about it.

One or two days from the coast of Zanj one found Qambalû, perhaps the island of Pemba, just off the extreme northern coast of current Tanzania. There, al-Masûdî tells us, lived a mixed population of idolaters and Muslims, the latter priding themselves on their own royal family. This was certainly the early days of the Swahili civilization that would develop and spread from the beginning of the second millennium: a civilization that was at once African, Muslim, seafaring, and commercial. A Muslim traveler or merchant was certain to be warmly welcomed there, and to meet interested business partners ready to play the role of intermediaries with the continent. Is it certain that al-Masûdî visited Zanj? We cannot know for sure. But it is doubtful that he could prudently have gone without taking precautions—some tribes are cannibals, he says—or that the people of Qambalû would have been eager to let this illicit commerce take place. It was they alone, no doubt, who brought back leopard skins, supposedly the largest ever, which were used as saddles in the Arab world; tortoiseshells, more sought after than horns for the production of combs and other accessories; pieces of ivory larger than those found in India; and of course the best ambergris ever.

Al-Masûdî's account presents us with a maritime space organized into successive segments articulated with each other. Qambalû is the first articulation; the second is the border between the land of the Zanj and the land of Sofala. These articulations were borders between worlds with different cultural codes, but at the same time they were points of exchange for merchandise whose value for the other side was recognized. Gold—from a south unknown to the merchant—ambergris, ivory, and skins—from a perhaps hostile coast—thus circulated from one antechamber to the other in a system where only the gatekeepers knew one another. We should not think that a system structured in this way was frozen in place for all time. On the contrary, the segments slid together: within a few centuries, people from Qambalû would be found along the entire coast of Zanj; there were even trading posts in Sofala.

The shipowners and pilots who went to Qambalû were Arabs from Oman and Persians from Siraf. Al-Masûdî, who had set sail with some of them, mentions the names of those he had known or who had died at sea. It was they who, in this first epoch of Islamic commerce, ran trade in the Arabian Sea, that is to say, the northern Indian Ocean between the shores of Africa and India, and even as far as China. This was, in any case, the direction in which they took the ivory, which passed through Oman before being shipped to the East. In India, al-Masûdî says, they made large chess pieces, dagger handles, and sword guards from it; in China, artisans produced ivory passenger compartments for the palanquins of civil and military leaders; the Chinese also burned it as perfume on their altars. It was perhaps China that literally *oriented* this commerce by the demand it created: a demand that Asian ivory, insufficient in quantity and smaller than its African counterpart, could not meet. The same goes for ambergris, "dragon spittle" to the Chinese, which was unknown in the antique Mediterranean, and about which everything—the legends surrounding its origin, the story of the caliph—indicates that the curiosity it aroused among Arab authors was a new one. It was Chinese demand for a recent entrant into the merchants' olfactory repertoire, then, that carried ambergris from the distant shores of Africa.

BIBLIOGRAPHICAL NOTE

The most convenient collection of texts relating to the east coast of Africa is G.S.P Freeman-Grenville, *The East African Coast: Select Documents from the First to the Earlier Nineteenth Century* (Oxford: Clarendon Press, 1962). Al-Masûdî's passage on East Africa is on pages 14–17. Most authors willing to revert to the Arabic text still use the critical edition by Charles Barbier de Meynard and Abel Pavet de Courteille, *Les Prairies d'or* (Paris: Imprimerie nationale, 1861–1877), with a translation in French. There is no full edition of the book in English, but an accessible compilation is *From the Meadows of Gold*, translated by Paul Lunde and Caroline Stone (London: Penguin, 2007). Charles Pellat's entry for al-Masûdî (al-Mas'ūdī) in the *Encyclopaedia of Islam*, 2nd ed., contains all the necessary biographical details and bibliography. A very good overview on Persian navigations in the Arabian Sea, in relation to the East African

Coast, is furnished by Thomas M. Ricks, "Persian Gulf Seafaring and East Africa: Ninth–Twelfth Centuries," *African Historical Studies* 3 (1970): 339–357; but one may equally refer to George E. Hourani, *Arab Seafaring* (Princeton, NJ: Princeton University Press, 1995), pp. 61–68. A good dossier of Arab and European myths surrounding ambergris has been brought together by Karl H. Dannenfeldt, "Ambergris: The Search for Its Origin," *Isis* 73 (1982): 382–397.

CHAPTER 3

Aspects of a Border

Qasr Ibrîm, Lower Nubia, from the Seventh Century

Egypt is a gift of the Nile, said Herodotus. By rolling out a narrow carpet of greenery across the desert, the river allows civilization to thrive along its banks. Navigable from its mouth to Aswan, it made possible the cultural and political unification of this slender territory and fixed its borders. The Egyptians had certainly launched incursions to the south of the cataracts, they had even posted garrisons there, but that land was never fully Egypt: the swirling waters marked the beginning of Nubia. It is not that these cataracts are very impressive: they are only a series of rapids that make the river level fall a few meters—a few dozen meters at most—and they are spread out, with few undulations, along several dozen kilometers. But suddenly the alluvial plain gives way to an austere, mineral landscape, while the river, divided into multiple streams, makes its way across the rocky ground. The cataracts are closed doors along the river's corridor.

It is customary to number the cataracts, starting with those downstream. The first is south of Aswan; the second, upstream from Wadi Halfa. We are already in modern Sudan. Today these first two cataracts are submerged—at a depth of thirty meters—under the waters of the artificial lake called Lake Nasser on the Egyptian side and Lake Nubia on the Sudanese, a gigantic reservoir held in place by the Aswan High Dam. Four other cataracts obstruct the river along the double loop that it cuts up to Khartoum. This region of cataracts has been called Nubia since antiquity. Egypt's southern neighbor, it became Christian under that land's influence in the sixth century. There were several Christian kingdoms of Nubia that were independent until the fourteenth century, and we find mention of a few Christian communities in the sixteenth century, and indeed beyond, in northern Sudan, a land thereafter submitted to Muslim rule. (The current Christians of South Sudan stem from an evangelical movement that began in the nineteenth century.) Lower Nubia is nowadays entirely under the lake. This was the territory of the Nubian kingdom of Nobadia, briefly independent before becoming the northern province of another Christian kingdom, Makuria, whose capital, Dongola, lay between the third and fourth cataracts. Christian Nubia had little time to profit from the beneficent shadow of Byzantine Egypt: the latter fell in 642 to Arab armies, who installed a governor there. Ever faithful to their Egyptian patriarch, the head of the Coptic Church whose seat is Alexandria, the Nubians from then on had an Islamic power as a neighbor.

In 1972, excavations undertaken at Qasr Ibrîm in Egyptian Nubia, amid the rising waters of the Aswan Dam, revealed in extremis several papyrus rolls bearing on the history of Nubia. One is written in Arabic, the language of Egyptian power. The others are in Coptic, the language of the Egyptian people and possibly the administrative language of the Nubian kingdom. The Arab text dates from the month of Rajab in the year 141 of the Muslim calendar, 758 in the Gregorian calendar, or a little over a century after the conquest of Egypt. It is a letter from the governor of Egypt to the king of Nubia; it had undoubtedly been given to the Christian governor of Lower Nubia at Qasr Ibrîm, who was obliged to transmit its content to the sovereign at Dongola. The other three documents have not yet been edited; we know only that they were written by a Nubian living in Egypt, and that they all relate, either directly or indirectly, to the same question. We do not possess other versions of these documents and do not know the response of the Nubian king.

The letter of the Arab governor to the sovereign of Nubia, whom, incidentally, he addressed with the title of "lord" (*sâhib*) rather than king, displayed a very firm tone bordering on diplomatic rebuke. The sovereign was called to respect the oath that sealed an agreement, the *baqt*, between the two powers. Nubian merchants, writes the governor, were free to come and go from Egypt: their lives were safe, their freedom of movement guaranteed, their goods protected. But the Nubians, he added, have not upheld their end of the bargain: shipments of slaves (with the exception of a handful of old men and one-eyed people) that ought to have been made had not been; escaped slaves seeking asylum in Nubia had not been extradited; Egyptian merchants were harassed and their goods confiscated;

emissaries dispatched to settle the disputes enjoyed no immunity, contrary to all custom, and were imprisoned. Finally, the letter demanded the immediate and retroactive discharge of the obligations that had gone unfulfilled over the course of recent years, the restitution of goods stolen from merchants, and a return to customary good relations. The life and goods of the king of Nubia had been preserved, the governor reminded him, because he had agreed to the terms of this treaty. He concluded his missive with a thinly veiled threat: "If you do not obey, I shall have my view concerning what is between you and me, God willing."

The letter alluded to a past agreement to which the Nubian sovereign had consented. We do not have this document. Was it even put into writing? It's likely, given its restrictive character: how could one prove in retrospect that the parties had consented to the agreement, how ensure that the administrations of the two states put its terms into practice other than with the documentary support of an archive, to whose existence the papyri of Qasr Ibrîm testify? Although we do not possess this document, it is mentioned in the works of various Arab chroniclers until the fifteenth century. The situation is paradoxical: throughout the history of Egyptian-Nubian relations authors did not cease referring to this lost piece. When was it lost? When did this old diplomatic document disappear from the archives to give way among Egyptian authors to a refrain all the more pointless since its precise contents were no longer safeguarded in writing?

By the time of al-Maqrîzî, the Egyptian historian who wrote during the first half of the fifteenth century, the Christian kingdoms of Nubia were only a memory. Still, he recounted the clauses of a treaty concluded in 652 following an expedition against Dongola led by the Arab general Abd Allâh ibn Saad. It was first and foremost an armistice, in which both parties agreed to cease waging war against each other, raiding, and supporting each other's enemies, but it did not require mutual assistance in case of conflict with a third party. According to al-Maqrîzî, the document provided for the free circulation of individuals within the other party's territory, along with a law that allowed Egyptian Muslims to settle freely in Nubia. It obliged the Nubians to expel any slave or enemy of the Muslims who had found refuge in Christian territory, and arranged for the conservation and maintenance of Dongola's mosque. Finally, it called for the annual shipment, by the Nubians, of 360 healthy slaves of both sexes.

It has often been maintained, with al-Maqrîzî, that this text merely imposed a tributary status and heavy constraints on the Nubians. But modern historians have noted that Egyptians were also obligated to protect the rights of Nubians—one thinks of merchants and pilgrims—who traveled through their land. We have been tempted to interpret the text as a bilateral commercial treaty. We have sometimes viewed it as a simple attempt to codify informal diplomatic and economic exchanges. Truth be told, all these readings are possible on the basis of al-Maqrîzî's text or other sources. A mid-ninth-century author tells us, "The two parties agreed to no longer attack each other and decided that each year the Nubians would supply the Muslims with so many slaves in exchange for so much grain and lentils." Another drew up a list of the commodities furnished by the Egyptians: wheat, barley, wine, oil, fabrics. Here, commerce was regulated by imperative clauses. Another author, from the twelfth century, clarified that in addition to slaves, the Nubians had to deliver trained monkeys, giraffes, cat skins, ivory. These were the gifts of diplomacy: giraffes were always part of the diplomatic corteges accompanying African ambassadors to the sovereigns of the Islamic world.

These readings, among others, are possible, as I've said, but only when considered in turn. It is undeniable that they are not truly compatible with one another, except in the search for an improbable synthesis of a treaty of submission, a commercial contract, and an agreement guaranteeing the free circulation of people and goods. Insofar as the different mentions we have of the *baqt* can be reconciled only with difficulty, they appear, rather, to be describing different versions spread over time. We have to assume that the authors who spoke of it did not all have the original document—or did not have the *same* document—before their eyes. If the *baqt* was a treaty, perhaps it was subject to numerous amendments, juridical reflections of the evolving balance of power between the two parties over the centuries—a balance of power sometimes favorable to the Egyptians, sometimes to the Nubians? Al-Maqrîzî's version would therefore be only the belated victory roar of the Egyptian side, but precisely because of this lateness more likely to have been transmitted to us.

Across its avatars and transformations, the *baqt* has always, as far as it is possible to judge, retained two essential characteristics: on the one hand, it shielded Nubia from holy war for more than six centuries at a time when Islam was carried from Europe to China; on the other hand, it instituted a system of very asymmetrical obligations in favor of Egypt. If the indirect evidence of the papyrus of Qasr Ibrîm reflects the Islamic point of view and is perhaps biased, nevertheless we cannot deny the seriously restrictive nature of the *baqt* from the Nubian point of view. If not, how are we to understand why a mid-ninth-century Nubian prince went to the caliph in Baghdad to negotiate (and obtain) the quashing of the arrears of slave shipments, and to renegotiate the *baqt* with a triennial payment in mind? If the *baqt* had been to the Nubians' advantage, this renegotiation would have made no sense.

These apparently contradictory provisions gave the treaty between Egypt and Nubia an unusual air; in any event, it was foreign enough to Islamic law to give it a special name, *baqt*, a term derived from Latin (*pactum*) via Hellenistic Greek (*pakton*). A curious treaty indeed: one that imposed no immediate payment on the Nubians following their supposed defeat; seemed to impose tributary status on them only to get them to submit to reciprocal conditions; and declared Nubia a fertile ground for slaves but refused to take them by force . . . Would the Muslims have renounced the transient benefits arising from a victorious battle in favor of a pact valid for a virtually indefinite period of time? To declare oneself the perpetual victor in this way is always very imprudent, especially given historical contingency. But we must admit that the context of this treaty's signing, obscured as it is by the tumult of the conquest of Egypt, largely escapes us. Moreover, are we forced to accept a 652 date for the signing of the *baqt*, which several sources suggest was the result of a Nubian victory and not a defeat? In any event, there could not have been a mosque at Dongola at this time. A nice anachronism. But was al-Maqrîzî guilty of having invented his version of the document, or did he merely antedate a more or less authentic text he discovered among the chancery papers?

We are grappling, then, with an ill-tempered papyrus letter, perhaps only a facet of a juridical arrangement that adopted several forms while continuing to intrigue commentators. In the absence of the original document, its history can be only a commentary on the commentators who mentioned it. In the end, this intriguing corpus is perhaps only the sum of different perspectives on a border. It was a rather obvious border, drawn around a natural landscape that presented a profound obstacle to conquest. But another aspect of the border, the laws laid out in the *baqt* that decreed who could and could not cross it, had a more tangible effect on the local population. The right of Egyptians to settle in Nubia was not reciprocated, nor were Egyptians under any obligation to maintain Egypt's churches, unlike the Nubians with Dongola's mosque. The *baqt*'s incongruity derived from the fact that the Muslims wanted a paradoxical border, one sealed to Nubians but porous to Egyptians.

BIBLIOGRAPHICAL NOTE

J. Martin Plumley was the first to present a version of Qasr Ibrîm's Arabic papyrus. See his "An Eighth-Century Arabic Letter to the King of Nubia," *Journal of Egyptian Archaeology* 61 (1975): 241–245. A critical edition (facsimile of the original document, edition, and translation) appears in Martin Hinds, "A Letter from the Governor of Egypt to the King of Nubia and Muqura concerning Egyptian-Nubian Relations in 141/758," in *Studia Arabica et Islamica: Festschrift for Iḥsan ʿAbbās on His Sixtieth Birthday* (Beirut: American University of Beirut, 1981), pp. 9–29, and reprinted in a variorum of his articles, *Studies in Early Islamic History*, edited by Jere Bacharach,

Lawrence I. Conrad, and Patricia Crone (Princeton, NJ: Darwin Press, 1996). William Y. Adams, *Qasr Ibrîm: The Earlier Medieval Period* (London: Egypt Exploration Society, 2010), p. 245, provides insights into the author and historical context of the Coptic documents. The other sources cited or mentioned may be found in French translation in Joseph Cuoq, *Islamisation de la Nubie chrétienne* (Paris: Geuthner, 1986). See also the clarifications offered in Jean-Claude Garcin, *Qūṣ. Un centre musulman de la Haute-Égypte medieval*, 2nd ed. (Cairo: IFAO, 2005), pp. 39–43. Jay Spaulding offers a historiographical and critical approach to the relationship between Nubia and its northern neighbor, but one that seems to give little importance to the Qasr Ibrîm documents, in "Medieval Christian Nubia and the Islamic World: A Reconsideration of the *Baqt* Treaty," *International Journal of African Historical Studies* 28 (1995): 577–594. Derek A. Welsby's *The Medieval Kingdoms of Nubia* (London: British Museum Press, 2002) is, in general, the most complete work on medieval Nubia. Robin Seignobos, "La frontière entre *bilād al-islām* et le *bilād al-Nūba*: enjeux et ambiguïtés d'une frontière immobile (VIIe–XIIe siècle)," *Afriques. Débats, méthodes et terrains d'histoire* 2 (2010), available online at http://afriques.revues.org /800, offers an excellent analysis of the paradoxical character of the frontier between Muslim Egypt and Christian Nubia.

CHAPTER 4

Diplomatic Back-and-Forth at the Court of George II of Nubia

Faras and Dongola, Present-Day Sudan,
Last Quarter of the Tenth Century

The fresco is very damaged; more than half of its surface has been worn away by time. We can no longer distinguish the countenance of the larger-than-life figure facing us in the foreground. A dark-skinned hand—the figure's right—emerges in front of the chest from the embroidered sleeve of a white tunic, itself decorated with a fine yellow netting, perhaps of gold thread, and green and yellow dots, presumably precious stones. The tunic is closed with a red and yellow gold-encrusted belt. The figure wears a white cape; its hand grips a gold cross. A pendant comprising three joined yellow spheres (again, of gold) and set with green and red gems—an emblem of royalty encountered in Nubian art—hangs from the bottom of the cape. Of the figure's head, we can make out only an ear and a beard. The crown, festooned with precious stones and crosses and topped with a six-pointed star, combines a green headdress with miter-shaped hoops. Behind this figure tower a Virgin and Child wrapped in a red cloak whose folds are depicted with undulations of brown. The legend, in Greek, the liturgical language of the Nubian church, runs from one side of the image to the other. It tells us that the man thus placed under the protection of blessed Mary and her son Jesus Christ Emmanuel, the savior of the world, is King George (Georgios), son of King Zachariah. We think he was the second king of that name, and contextual elements lead us to believe that the fresco was completed around 975.

Between 1954, when the first stone of the Aswan High Dam was laid, and 1972, when the lake it created reached its maximum level, numerous archaeological missions were urgently launched throughout the region of Nubia set to vanish beneath the water. To that end, from 1960 to 1970, the "Nubia Campaign," under the aegis of UNESCO, conducted some of the most spectacular salvage operations of all time, in particular the dismantlement, block by block, of the dynastic temples of Abu Simbel and Philae and their relocation to higher ground. These circumstances spread the notion of cultural heritage throughout the world and saved some of the jewels of ancient Egypt, which quickly became major tourist attractions, from destruction. But they also provided several international teams of archaeologists with the pretext for conducting surveys and excavations, their careful work adding to the archaeological evidence available for all the Nubian civilizations that had succeeded one another over the millennia. Against this background, a Polish archaeological mission was tasked with excavating Faras in the Sudanese part of Nubia.

We have known for a long time that Faras had probably been the antique Pachoras, capital of the Christian kingdom of Nobadia, briefly independent in the seventh century, before becoming the administrative center of the episcopal remit of Maris, a province of the kingdom of Makuria. Before the Polish excavations, an enormous *kôm*, an Arabo-Egyptian term for a human-made mound, had been discovered; roughly fifteen meters in height, it was crowned with the ruined walls of an Ottoman citadel and a Coptic monastery. Once the sand and debris from later buildings had been cleared away and the ruined walls dismantled, the mound's lower levels revealed a vast religious complex dating from the eighth to the fourteenth century. It was centered on the cathedral: a triple-naved building nearly twenty meters in length made from blocks of sandstone and baked brick. Built at the beginning of the eighth century, it stood on the foundations of an earlier, mud-brick basilica. Off the southeastern end of the apse, a small commemorative chapel was built to house the remains of eleventh- and twelfth-century Nubian bishops. To the left of the cathedral's entrance, work on the site's northern section revealed the bishop's palace, the palace of the eparch (the governor), the ancient monastery, and a few houses. To the right, the southern section was found to contain the remains of another church as well as the tombs of the first bishops.

The exciting discovery of the cathedral of Pachoras was a media sensation at the time. The building had preserved practically all of its original elevations and a part of its vaulting. After its abandonment in the fourteenth century, it owed its preservation to being buried under an accumulation of sand and debris from its upper sections, a *kôm* that was soon fixed in place by the construction of new buildings at its top. Perhaps even more impressive, in any case more precious for history, the cathedral preserved its frescoes. They were studied and reproduced on-site before being detached from the wall, a process that usually uncovered earlier representations. Apart from scenes from the life of Christ (Nubian artists rarely depicted events from the Old Testament, with the remarkable exception of the "Three Hebrews in the Furnace"), the works manifested a predilection for protector figures such as the Virgin, the archangels, the saints, and the apostles. But other iconographic groups were clearly conceived as part of an official program for the preservation of the memory of the bishops of Pachoras, or even kings, queen mothers, and high dignitaries. Thus a room lateral to the church's right nave is dedicated to a few of these figures, including a bishop named Kollouthos, Bishop Peter (Petros) of Pachoras protected by Saint Peter, or even George II and the Virgin.

The cathedral was engulfed by the waters of the lake in 1964. Almost a thousand years earlier, the new Fatimid masters of Egypt had dispatched an ambassador to Nubia. The latter, Ibn Sulaym al-Uswânî, "the man from Aswan," drew on his mission, certainly undertaken around 972–973, to write a "History of the Nubians." This work is sadly lost, but extensive extracts from it have been preserved in the writings of later Arab authors. What remains constitutes the sole testimony *de visu*, from a traveler's pen, on Christian Nubia. It is full of information about the Nubian kingdom of Makuria—its geography, its territorial and administrative organization, its resources—data that the author, a spy as well as an ambassador, made it a point to put into writing.

Al-Uswânî was sent to the court of King Jirjis, the Arabic written form of Georgios or George II. He was to make two demands. First, the Nubians were to renew the commercial terms of the *baqt*, the treaty in force between the two states for more than two centuries (↦3), whose concrete application, we are lead to believe, had been disrupted for some time. The Nubians accepted, demonstrating that they felt powerful enough to accept the consequences arising from the renewal of this binding exchange—but perhaps not quite powerful enough to refuse it. Second, the Nubian king was to convert to Islam. After speaking with his advisers, the king declined and turned the demand around, inviting al-Uswânî to convert to Christianity. The ambassador had to make do with this response—a sign that the Egyptians felt powerful enough to express such a demand, but not powerful enough to make sure it was put into effect.

Coptic chroniclers piously recorded the lives of their "popes," whose see was in Alexandria. Century after century, they built up a written monument, the *History of the Patriarchs*. They sometimes incorporated into this continuous biography of the Church of Egypt—called the Jacobite Church by Muslim authors—information about the other Eastern churches under the jurisdiction of Alexandria. As a result, we sometimes come across crucial details about Christian Ethiopia and Nubia, details unknown elsewhere. Thus the author of the life of Patriarch Philotheos, head of the Coptic Church from 979 to 1003, tells us a story we can't find in any other source. It takes place a few years after al-Uswânî's visit to Dongola: the king of Ethiopia addressed a letter to Jirjis, king of Nubia—George II—asking him to intercede with the patriarch to bring the malediction against the king and his kingdom to an end. Charged with a goodwill mission, George was asked to obtain from Philotheos the consecration of a new metropolitan* at the head of the Ethiopian Church. The Nubian sovereign, we learn from the chronicle, gave a favorable response to this request and appended his letter to the Ethiopian king's. The intervention was successful: the patriarch appointed a certain Daniel, an Egyptian monk from the monastery of Saint Macarius, and sent him to Ethiopia. The matter was urgent since, following a muddled episode involving ecclesiastical usurpation and dynastic crisis, the Ethiopian monarch had been forced to hand the future of his church over to a man who possessed only one of the requirements for leading it—the totally insufficient one of being Egyptian—and whose appointment had never been confirmed by the patriarch. From then on, all succeeding patriarchs refused to accept this almost schismatic situation. For several decades, then, Ethiopian Christians lived without a canonically consecrated metropolitan. Without a leader, had priests been ordained? We do not know. In any event, at the time when the Ethiopian king was writing to his Nubian counterpart, the Christian religion, he wrote, was on the verge of extinction. What is more, a pagan queen had seized power, burned cities and churches, and spread terror in her wake. These ordeals, according to the Ethiopian, were the result of past misdeeds; through the proxy of the Nubian, he humbly beseeched the patriarch to bring them to an end.

A few years after having been commanded by the Fatimids to convert to Islam, George II thus found himself being asked to intercede between the Ethiopians and the Coptic patriarchate in Egypt. Let's suppose that there was something more to these triangular relations than the simple coincidences of "multilateral" diplomacy. Does a new power use its first diplomatic contact with its neighbor to order it to convert to its religion under the simple pretext that it costs nothing to give it a try, especially if that power does not have the means to enforce the order? And does a sovereign ask his neighbor, with whom he had scarcely any other ties, to intercede on his behalf with their common spiritual guardian to lessen its severity when he risks losing face if the severity is justified? For the patriarchs had their reasons for their touchy severity: divinely invested religious authority was not to be shared or discussed. On this point of canon law, Alexandria certainly preferred to see Ethiopia fall back into paganism rather than be freed from the strictest obedience. But it appears that in these years the king of Nubia could be impressive while facing the political power of Cairo and the religious authority of Alexandria. Did he owe this grace to the protection of the Virgin who towered over his shoulder and who caused Nubia to benefit from a divine indulgence she did not show Ethiopia? Al-Uswânî, in any case, noted that the country was prosperous: and though it was also at peace, the king took care to remind him that its armies were numerous.

In 997, toward the end of the reign of George II, a bishop from another Christian church, the "Melkite," or what we call "Orthodox," was nominated at Pachoras and set himself up in the cathedral. In the battle for influence between the two churches, the Melkites had just won an important victory. But while we don't know precisely what its repercussions were for Nubia, we can at least make out its background. A Melkite faction was scheming at the palace of the Muslim masters of Egypt: the wife of the caliph al-Azîz, and mother of his successor al-Hâkim, was a Melkite Christian; she made one of her brothers bishop of Cairo. This faction wanted to replace the Coptic Church, and the caliph certainly viewed these divisions in a favorable light, meaning that the installation of a Melkite bishop in Nubia had probably met with Egyptian approval. If the king could not be converted to Islam, the next best thing was to introduce Christian rivalry into his kingdom. Al-Azîz had learned his lesson: it was he who had al-Uswânî write an account of his embassy. As for the Coptic patriarch, could he really refuse a favor to the Nubian monarch in this context? For there was something worse than losing a church to pagans or Muslims: seeing Nubia pass into the hands of other Christians.

BIBLIOGRAPHICAL NOTE

The fresco of George II, along with the rest of the iconography of Faras, was detached from the cathedral walls before the site was flooded. It is now located in the National Museum in Warsaw; others are at the National Museum of Sudan in Khartoum. It has been frequently published, particularly in Kazimierz Michałowski's catalog *Faras: Wall Paintings in the Collection of the National Museum in Warsaw* (Warsaw: Wydawnictwo Artystyczno-Graficzne, 1974), no. 34, pp. 173–176. My presentation of the site's discovery and the circumstances of the frescoes' removal draws on this work. The Greek inscription is edited by Stefan Jacobielski in the same catalog, no. 18, pp. 291–292. The excavations of Faras have been published in either French or English in several volumes: K. Michałowski, *Faras. Fouilles polonaises 1961* [= Faras I] (Warsaw: Editions scientifiques de Pologne, 1962); K. Michałowski, *Faras. Fouilles polonaises 1961–1962* [= Faras II] (Warsaw, 1965); Stefan Jakobielski, *Faras III. A History of the Bishopric of Pachoras on the Basis of Coptic Inscriptions* (Warsaw, 1972); Jądwiga Kubińska, *Faras IV. Inscriptions grecques chrétiennes* (Warsaw, 1974); Janusz Karkowski, *The Pharaonic Inscriptions from Faras*

[= Faras V] (Warsaw, 1981); Włodzimierz Godlewski, *Faras VI. Les Baptistères nubiens* (Warsaw, 1979); Małgorzata Martens-Czarnecka, *Les Éléments décoratifs sur les peintures de la cathédrale de Faras* [= Faras VII] (Warsaw, 1982); Tadeusz Dzierżykray-Rogalski, *Faras VIII: The Bishops of Faras: An Anthropological-Medical Study* (Warsaw, 1985). A synthesis has been published in German by K. Michałowski, *Faras. Die Kathedrale aus dem Wüstensand* (Cologne: Benziger Verlag, 1967). For a recent study of UNESCO's "Nubia Campaign," see Fekri A. Hassan, "The Aswan High Dam and the International Rescue Nubia Campaign," *African Archaeological Review* 24 (2007): 73–94. We owe the identification of Pachoras with Faras to Francis L. Griffith, "Pakhoras-Bakharâs-Faras in Geography and History," *Journal of Egyptian Archaeology* 11 (1925): 259–268. A large excerpt from al-Uswânî's account has been translated into French by Gérard Troupeau, "La 'Description de la Nubie' d'al-Uswānī (IVe/Xe siecle)," *Arabica* 1 (1954): 276–288. A few details on the mission to Dongola may be found in Joseph Cuoq, *Islamisation de la Nubie chrétienne* (Paris: Paul Geuthner, 1986), pp. 56–57. For a study of al-Uswânî's embassy and the history of his account of it, along with an edition of the Arabic text of all the extracts preserved by al-Maqrîzî with English translation and commentary, see Hamad Mohammad Kheir, "A Contribution to a Textual Problem: Ibn Sulaym al-Aswānī's *Kitāb aḥbār al-Nūba wa l-Maqurra wa l-Beğa wa l-Nīl*," *Annales Islamologiques* 21 (1985): 9–72. The letter of the Ethiopian king to George II and contextual elements may be found in Stuart Munro-Hay, *Ethiopia and Alexandria: The Metropolitan Episcopacy of Ethiopia* (Warsaw and Wiesbaden, 1997), pp. 130–138. On the iconographic program of the cathedral of Faras, see most recently W. Godlewski, "Bishops and Kings: The Official Program of the Pachoras (Faras) Cathedrals," in *Between the Cataracts: Proceedings of the 11th Conference for Nubian Studies, Warsaw University, 27 August–2 September 2006*, pt. 1 (Warsaw, 2008), pp. 263–282. Godlewski designates George II as George III. The reader should note that his revision of the chronology of the Nubian kings has not engendered consensus among specialists. For his part, Martin Krause, "Bischof Johannes III von Faras und seine beiden nachfolder," in *Études nubiennes* (Cairo, 1978), pp. 153–164, has contested the reality of the Melkite episode at Faras.

CHAPTER 5

"Does anyone live beyond you?"

Central Sahara, Seventh to the Ninth Century

Later sources concerning the conquest of North Africa by Arabo-Muslim armies are notoriously unreliable. Egyptian tradition relates that Uqba ibn Nâfi, one of the Arab commanders of the conquest of the Maghreb and who founded Kairouan in 670, made several raids in the direction of the Sahara. He first pierced into the Fezzan, the Libyan desert, at some point around 642, when he was still the lieutenant of general Amr ibn al-Âs, the conqueror of Byzantine Egypt. Twenty years later (around 666–667), we find him there again; the fortified oasis cities fell to him one by one, including Germa, the antique capital of the Garamantes. Having reached the final city, the chronicler tells us, he supposedly asked the local people, "Does anyone live beyond you?" The answer was yes: the people of Kawar, a fifteen-day march to the south, in present-day northern Niger. He went there and captured all the ksour;* the local capital was the last to fall to him. Here he asked the same question: "Does anyone live beyond you?" The inhabitants had no information on this matter. So, the chronicler continues, the conqueror retraced his steps, certainly convinced that he had reached the end of the known world. In 670, Uqba subdued Ghadames, Gafsa, and Kastîliya (the region of Tozeur, in the Jerid), cities of the Roman province of Africa—that is, more or less modern Tunisia—which became Arab Ifrîqiya. He conquered Algeria and Morocco. Everywhere he went he took slaves from among the conquered Berbers. Uqba is even said, but with less credibility, to have launched an expedition into the Sous region of Morocco, a land also raided by his grandson and successor in 734, who allegedly returned with a large quantity of gold and two female captives.

These accounts are tinged with legends: water sprung from beneath the hooves of Uqba's horse, and Moroccan girls have only one breast. But the sequence of the conquest, from the steppe to the oases of the eastern Sahara, and the question itself, "Does anyone live beyond you?"—skeptical and finally dismissed in Kawar, an oasis cut off to the south and the west by the austere Ténéré—reveal that the Arab leader's journey followed little-known antique trails (themselves little traveled in antiquity) that terminated in a dead end in the middle of the great desert, far from the steppes and savannas watered by Lake Chad or the Niger River. At this initial stage, Uqba and his followers must have thought they knew that there was absolutely nothing on the other side of the arid immensity of the Sahara.

The populations encountered by the conquering Arabs, apart from the Roman and Christian elites—or perhaps we should say, the Romanized and Christianized elites—settled in the cities of the coastal plains, were Berbers, a large family of peoples established since protohistory from Cyrenaica to the Atlantic. Antique sources were acquainted with their relatively well-defined territories: the Moors in present-day Morocco and Algeria, the Numidians in Algeria and Tunisia. They were farmers, sedentary or practicing transhumance. The Libyans of Cyrenaica, the Garamantes of Fezzan, and the Gaetuli were authentic pastoralists who, while not completely unaware of the camel, introduced around the beginning of the Christian era, rode horses and oxen; they populated the vast stretches of steppe between the Mediterranean plain and the desert. It was on horseback that they conducted their raids against the Saharan oases where, as at Kawar, black farmers lived.

The Berbers were the first victims of Arab slave raids. Fiercely independent, they were at first as resistant to Islamization as their ancestors had been, a few centuries earlier, to Christianization. Once subdued, the Berbers adopted the religion of the conquerors. They thus joined the Muslim community of believers but did not give up their claim to a distinct identity, preferring the clan, the tribe, or the occasional alliance to a nation constrained by obligations and frontiers. This identity was often based around Islam itself, as the Berbers were more inclined to welcome a missionary from a breakaway sect than to tolerate the foreign rule represented by orthodox (i.e., Sunni) Islam. Consequently, Berber Africa adopted the dotrines of minority sects, especially Kharijism, a subtle way of balancing loyalty and resistance to the forms of political domination and social marginalization that resulted from the conquest. The first three centuries of Islam in North Africa thus saw a crop of dissident Berber principalities spring up and bloom before being pushed little by little toward the edges of the Sahara. Thus the Ibadi imam (Ibadism is a branch of Kharijism) of Kairouan, along with his followers, left Arab Ifrîqiya in 761 ahead of Sunnism's advance into Tunisia. Having set itself up at Tahert (near Tiaret in present-day Algeria), the theocratic community would remain active there until the beginning of the tenth century, when it moved again, this time to Sedrata near Ouargla. Tlemcen in northwest Algeria and Sijilmâsa in southeast Morocco were two other Kharijite principalities that flourished for two centuries. Ibadism is still influential today in the Pentapole of Mzab in Algeria. Elsewhere, when the fires of Ibadism began to die out in the ninth century, Berber communities would let themselves be tempted by Shiism. One downright schismatic sect, the Barghawâta, even had their own kingdom in central Morocco from the ninth to the twelfth century.

The Arab conquest profoundly transformed Berber societies, notably those whose socioeconomic conditions made them vulnerable to shifts in the ecological balance: the abandonment of certain Roman cities and the reorganization of territory brought about by the conquest weakened the frontier that had stabilized agriculture under Roman colonial administration. Once the cities were abandoned, cultivated lands receded and the way was paved for nomads who for a long time had been kept at a distance. The latter were transformed: some, those of Cyrenaica, the inhabitants of a barren desert, made the ideological as well as economic choice to specialize in camels in a symbiotic relationship with the agriculturalists. They became, perhaps before an Arab had ever set foot in their territory, the great nomads of the desert, the lords of groves of date palms and herds of camels. They thus dominated a Sahara that became what it had never been up to that point: a space unified by the need to inhabit it and the desire to control it. They conquered its bastions; they organized its regular crossing. We can track their progress south and west from Tripolitania. From the end of the ninth century, Kawar's population was majority Berber and played an important role in the slave trade that brought north slaves purchased from the *Sûdân*, the "Blacks," the inhabitants of the Sahel, the great desert's southern "shore" (Arabic *sāḥil*). While this activity and its trans-Saharan axes were being put in place, al-Yaqûbî, toward the end of the ninth century, gives us our first look at the "Land of the Blacks." A fleeting image of a world that had just been discovered: "Their dwellings are huts made of reeds and they have no towns"; it was the region called Kanem, bordering Lake Chad.

We are also introduced to a desert population in the Western Sahara: They "have no permanent dwellings. It is their custom to veil their face. . . . They subsist on camels, for they have no crops, wheat or otherwise" (al-Yaqûbî). Here, too, highly skilled breeders of camels were the masters of this new traffic, from Sijilmâsa (↦16), in southeast Morocco. Because they made themselves integral to a new economic relationship with the masters of the north, and because they in this way won freedom from the Islamic powers, these nomads did not hesitate to become good Muslims and to promote the new religion among their commercial partners in the Sahel, such as the kingdom of Gao, already converted to Islam at the end of the tenth century. Orthodox nomads, indeed rigorists; sedentary puritans, tempted by apostasy and schism: the religious routes taken by the Berbers at the dawn of the Islamization of North Africa reflect diverse strategies, but at bottom an identical choice, which the claim of independence accompanying the introduction of commerce between the Mediterranean and the Sahel firmly maintained. Was not the austere late eighth-century principality of Tahert the first northern city to undertake the almost two-month crossing of the desert, becoming the first "port" and entrepôt of a flourishing commerce? It was at this moment, writes Ibn al-Saghîr, a chronicler of the time, that "the roads to the land of the *Sûdân*," literally the Land of the Blacks, "were brought into use for trade."

The Egyptian tradition concerning Uqba ibn Nâfi is Ibn Abd al-Hakam's, recorded in the second third of the ninth century. The extracts being considered here, as well as those taken from the writings of al-Yaqûbî and Ibn al-Saghîr, may be found in Nehemia Levtzion and J.F.P. Hopkins (eds.), *Corpus of Early Arabic Sources for West African History* (Princeton, NJ: Markus Wiener, 2000), pp. 12, 21, 24. For biographical details I drew on Vassilios Christides's entry for "'Uḳba ibn Nāfi'" in the *Encyclopaedia of Islam*, 2nd ed. For a survey of the local populations of North Africa in antiquity, see the still-essential work of Jehan Desanges, *Catalogue des tribus africaines de l'antiquité classique à l'ouest du Nil* (Université de Dakar, Publications de la section d'histoire, 1962). A good general synthesis on the Berbers, covering both the archaeological and ethnographic approaches, is Michael Brett and Elizabeth Fentress's *The Berbers* (Malden, MA: Blackwell Publishing, 1996). On the Islamization of North Africa, see the essays collected in Dominique Valérian, *Islamisation et arabisation de l'Occident musulman médiéval (VIIe–XIIe siècle)* (Paris: Publications de la Sorbonne, 2011). Tadeusz Lewicki, "Les origines de l'islam dans les tribus berbères du Sahara occidental: Mūsā ibn Nuṣayr and 'Ubayd Allāh ibn al-Habhāb," *Studia Islamica* 32 (1970): 203–214, focuses more on the Sahara. For the Berbers' role in connecting the Maghreb with the Sahel, see Nehemia Levtzion, "Berber Nomads and Sudanese States: The Historiography of the Desert-Sahel Interface," in his *Islam in West Africa. Religion, Society and Politics to 1800* (London: Variorum, 1994), item X. The best, most recent study of early Tahert is that of Cyrille Aillet, "Tāhart et les origines de l'imamat rustumide," *Annales Islamologiques* 45 (2011): 47–78. On the rise of the trans-Saharan commerce that began with Tahert, readers are referred to T. Lewicki, "L'État nord-africain de Tāhert et ses relations avec le Soudan occidental à la fin du VIIIe et au IXe siècle," *Cahiers d'études africaines* 2 (1962): 513–535. My reflections on the specialized camel husbandry of certain Berber groups were inspired by G. Camps, *Les Berbères. Mémoire et identité* (Arles: Actes Sud, 2007, 1st ed. 1980). Regarding trans-Saharan commerce before the Islamic epoch, there are as many articles postulating its existence as there are denying it. In my view, the best-informed thesis argues in favor of its nonexistence during antiquity without excluding episodic contacts. See, in particular, John Swanson, "The Myth of Trans-Saharan Trade during the Roman Era," *International Journal of African Historical Studies* 8 (1975): 582–600; as well as Claude Cahen, "L'or du Soudan avant les Almoravides: mythe ou réalité?" in *Le Sol, la parole et l'écrit. Mélanges en hommage à Raymond Mauny*, 2 vols. (Paris: Société française d'histoire d'outre-mer, 1981), 2:539–545. On the Sahara as an epistemological construction and an object of history, see the excellent article by Ghislaine Lydon, "Saharan Oceans and Bridges, Barriers and Divides in Africa's Historiographical Landscape," *Journal of African History* 56 (2015): 3–22. The history of the introduction of the camel into Africa is summarized by Roger M. Blench, "African Minor Livestock Species," in R. M. Blench and Kevin C. MacDonald (eds.), *The Origins and Development of African Livestock* (London: Routledge, 2000), pp. 315–317.

CHAPTER 6

For Forty-Two Thousand Dinars

Aoudaghost, Present-Day Mauritania, Middle of the Ninth Century

What does it matter whether Ibn Hawqal lied or his memory failed? The Persian geographer (writing in Arabic) based his *Book of Itineraries and Kingdoms* (*Kitāb al-Masālik wa l-Mamālik*), which he finished in 988, on his experiences as a traveler. On several occasions, he claims to have once seen a check for forty-two thousand dinars* at Aoudaghost, when he could certainly have seen it only at Sijilmâsa. He wanted to create the impression that he had visited the Land of the Blacks, and he barely had to lie: if a check written in the southern Sahara could be cashed in the north, it is not much different from a traveler making the same journey but in the opposite direction. What is two months' travel when the distance is only between two trading posts? At the very least, this false memory tells us about the terminuses of trans-Saharan commerce in the ninth-century Western Sahara.

Our earliest reference to Aoudaghost dates from only a century before the check affair: it was a fifty-day walk from Sijilmâsa, a journey of over two thousand miles through the country of the Sanhâja nomads. Aoudaghost is an oasis; its population, we are told, lived "without religion," which simply meant they were not Muslim, and raided the Sûdân; hence they themselves were not black. If we are to judge by the situation that prevailed at the time of Ibn Hawqal—based as it is on the testimony of a later geographer, al-Bakrî, who dabbled in history—the inhabitants of this oasis, like those of the surrounding areas, were certainly Sanhâja, one of the great Berber nomad confederations. We can guess that they then became Muslims. We even know the name of the king in the 960s, a certain Tî-n-Yarûtân, who prided himself on ruling a country that extended a two-month walk in every direction, on commanding an army of one hundred thousand camels, and on having twenty black kingdoms that paid him tribute. Ibn Hawqal explains that this man, from a family that had always kept a tight grip on power, was the king of all the Sanhâja, a people of three hundred thousand tents. Who were the inhabitants of this oasis on the southern edge of the Sahara? An ancient mixed population?

An isolated community of sedentary Berbers who may or may not have driven out previous inhabitants? The residents of the capital of a vast nomadic population who had swapped their traditional tribal system for that of a hereditary kingdom? The occupants of a recently settled location? We don't know. Our sources do not offer sufficient clarity, and anyway events were shifting rapidly: three-quarters of a century after Ibn Hawqal, the city's inhabitants were already no longer the same. Those who suffered the excesses of the Almoravids, in 1054 or 1055, were Zanâta, the other great grouping of Berber nomads, and Arabs. The depredations were committed under the pretext that the city had come under the rule of one of the kingdoms of the Sûdân: Ghâna. Aoudaghost recovered but had lost its former glory.

It is thought that we have identified the site of Aoudaghost with the ksar* of Tegdaoust in Hodh, Mauritania, a transitional region between the desert and the Sahelian steppe. Excavations were carried out there between 1960 and 1976 under the direction of French archaeologists Denise and Serge Robert and historian Jean Devisse. The topographical data, the results of the excavation, are compatible with this identification. The site resembles a mound of ruins extending for twelve hectares, which seems to have once surrounded a wadi, nowadays desperately dry. It shows signs of continuous occupation from the ninth to the fourteenth century. The levels corresponding to the period for which we have written documentation revealed a city with a network of little streets, sometimes flanked with banquettes, houses made from banco* bricks or stone, depending on the occupation phase, whose walls still retain traces of white and red coating. The mosque sports a *mihrâb*,* the niche in the wall that indicates to the faithful the direction of Mecca, oriented to the south-southeast, instead of to what should be east at that latitude: an apparent aberration that seems to indicate the North African origin of the first local faithful. Some houses, moreover, have a Mediterranean floor plan with rooms distributed around a courtyard where a well might be dug. As for imported ceramics, shards of small-size pottery with a white slip or green glaze and especially hundreds of oil lamps: they were made in the Maghreb. Coin weights,* in the form of glass tokens corresponding to the weights of particular Arab coins, indicate that this was a place where things were bought and sold.

The few centuries of occupation attested by archaeology, and the barely two hundred years of great prosperity celebrated by the written sources, have left abundant remains at the southern end of the principal trans-Saharan axis. But nothing evokes the image of medieval Aoudaghost—its gardens full of date palms, fig trees, and vines; the honey pastries prepared by excellent black slaves; the young white girls with firm breasts, without a doubt also slaves, the mere mention of whom stirred al-Bakrî—better than the memory of the check for forty-two thousand dinars. We know both the sender, Muhammad ibn Alî Sadûn of Aoudaghost, and the recipient, Abû Ishâq Ibrâhîm ibn Abd Allâh of Sijilmâsa. It was a check, or, less anachronistically, a written order of payment (the Arabic term ṣakk has perhaps given us our word "check"), in brief, a bill of exchange for an extraordinary amount, just as was asserted by Ibn Hawqal, who related the anecdote to the incredulous merchants of Iraq and Persia.

As previously mentioned, there are now good reasons to believe, on the basis of internal contradictions in Ibn Hawqal's text, that he had met the carrier of the check at Sijilmâsa rather than Aoudaghost. But the significance of such an amount was barely questioned. That it reveals the trade between the two cities to be both lucrative and based on a high level of confidence is indisputable. But what exactly did it entail? It is much more likely that such a sum was meant to reimburse a down payment than to purchase goods. In any case, the investment must have been made at Aoudaghost if the check was payable in cash at Sijilmâsa; it entailed the existence of a trading company or a credit firm on solid financial footing. More likely the check was payable on the caravan's arrival, after the merchandise loaded at Aoudaghost had been sold. We know that Aoudaghost sold salt to the kingdoms to the south, which took their reserves from it;

slaves made the journey in the opposite direction. The salt for the first transaction was procured from the mine at Awlil, a month's walk from the city near the coast. How was payment made? We don't know. But the costs of this investment were certainly compensated by the resale, to the north, of other products, such as the ambergris renowned along the shores of the Indian Ocean (↦2) and which was also harvested along the Atlantic coast.

Nevertheless the check's amount would not be explained if it corresponded only to an advance of liquid assets allowing for the purchase of merchandise that was then resold, even with the 100 percent return on investments that seems to have been practiced at the time on this kind of risky long-distance trade. The written sources tell us that Aoudaghost imported copper from the north and exported gold in return. The obvious corollary is that gold was imported from the south, where it was sold for copper. But archaeology allows us to understand that this was not a question of a simple exchange of crude metals. Excavation has in fact revealed the traces of processing and manufacture. Besides the worked copper that was imported, copper arrived from the mines of Morocco in the form of the rods and ingots turned up by the excavation. Coppersmiths perhaps made luxury dishes or jewelry from them to export to the south. Powdered gold was purchased there: the same powder, we are told, used to make small purchases in Aoudaghost's market. But it was not re-exported as powder: it was cast into ingots, which would be melted down at Sijilmâsa to be struck into coins. Moreover, the excavation revealed ingot molds, although these objects could equally have been used to cast glass. From gold came the filigree used in jewelry. Goldsmiths also cast copper-alloy buckles, brooches, and rings; we have fragments of jewelry as well as crucibles and molds. In addition to being known for the oryx skins used to make shields celebrated throughout the Sahara and the Maghreb, the local ceramics and glasswork, and the beads made from seashells and ostrich eggshell, which illustrate the existence of a veritable "artisan center," Aoudaghost was already an "industrial" center that benefited from its privileged position as both entrepôt and commercial "port." It was this reality, requiring major investments, that perhaps explains the amount of the check seen by Ibn Hawqal.

BIBLIOGRAPHICAL NOTE

The editions and translations of Ibn Hawqal's book are all in Arabic and in French. The extracts evoked here are included in Nehemia Levtzion and J.F.P. Hopkins (eds.), *Corpus of Early Arabic Sources for West African History* (Princeton, NJ: Markus Wiener, 2000), p. 47 (Ibn Hawqal), p. 68 (al-Bakrî). The hypothesis of Aoudaghost's identification with Tegdaoust was first made by a French colonial officer, lieutenant Boery, in "Le Rkiss (Mauritanie). Essai de monographie locale," *Bulletin du Comité d'études historiques et scientifiques de l'Afrique occidentale française* 10 (1927): 353–367, before being taken up by Raymond Mauny, "Les ruines de Tegdaoust et la question d'Aoudaghost," *Notes africaines* 48 (1950): 107–109. The archaeological campaigns at Tegdaoust have produced several volumes: Denise Robert, Serge Robert, and Jean Devisse, *Tegdaoust I. Recherches sur Aoudaghost* (Paris: Éditions Recherche sur les civilisations, 1970); Claudette Vanacker, *Tegdaoust II. Fouille d'un quartier artisanal* (Nouakchott, 1979); J. Devisse (ed.), *Tegdaoust III. Recherches sur Aoudaghost. Campagnes 1960–1965: enquêtes générales* (Paris, 1983); Jean Polet, *Tegdaoust IV. Fouille d'un quartier de Tegdaoust (Mauritanie orientale)* (Paris, 1985); D. Robert-Chaleix, *Tegdaoust V. Une concession médiévale à Tegdaoust* (Paris, 1989). Two very good syntheses on the state of the excavations in 1970 that provide a reliable outlook on the state of the art (since only a single campaign, in 1976, took place after their publication), are those of Denise Robert, "Les fouilles de Tegdaoust," *Journal of African History* 11 (1970): 471–493; and Serge Robert, "Fouilles archéologiques sur le site présumé d'Aoudaghost (1961–1968)," *Folia Orientalia* 12 (1970): 261–278. This last article constitutes a reminder of the mission and logistical challenges that characterize such fieldwork. D. Robert-Chaleix, moreover, has given us a descriptive and typological study of oil lamps, in "Lampes à huile importées découvertes à Tegdaoust: premier essai de classification," *Journal des africanistes* 53 (1983): 61–91. Raymond Mauny, "Notes d'archéologie sur Tombouctou," *Bulletin de l'Institut français d'Afrique noire* 4 (1952): 899–918 (here p. 903, n. 1), notes that the *qibla* (the direction of Mecca as indicated by the *mihrâb* or wall niche, which must be faced by the faithful during prayer) of the ancient mosques of the Maghreb generally follow that of the mosque of Kairouan, whose *mihrâb* is oriented 115 degrees with respect to geographic north. Ann McDougall offers a history of southern Mauritania, beginning with a case study of Tegdaoust, in "The View from Awdaghust: War, Trade and Social Change in the Southwestern Sahara, from the Eighth to the Fifteenth Century," *Journal of African History* 26 (1985): 1–31. We owe the reassessment of the authenticity of Ibn Hawqal's journey to Aoudaghost to Nehemia Levtzion, "Ibn-Hawqal, the Cheque, and Awdaghost," *Journal of African History* 9 (1968): 223–233.

CHAPTER 7

A Tale of Two Cities:
On the Capital of Ghâna

The Aoukar, Present-Day Mauritania, around 1068

We must begin by stating, in order to remove any ambiguity, that the Ghâna of the Middle Ages is not the country of the same name, the Republic of Ghana, a coastal nation on the Gulf of Guinea between the Ivory Coast and Togo, which took its name from its ancient predecessor only at independence. Moreover, it is even possible that the whole history of Ghâna and its avatars is only that of a name, a ray of light that from its first appearance on the scene designated and overexposed a Sahelian political formation that we know very little about. Except that, according to al-Bakrî, before becoming the name of the capital city, then of the kingdom, Ghâna was the title borne by the country's sovereign—whose kingdom would have been called Awkâr.

Abû Ubayd al-Bakrî could have succeeded his father, the sole ruler of the modest Islamic principality of Huelva and Saltés, on the Iberian Peninsula's Atlantic coast. Given the uncertainties of political careers in the eleventh century, however, he had the good sense to make a name for himself, beginning with his exile in Cordoba, as the preeminent geographer of his day, while simultaneously acquiring a reputation as a philologist, drinker, and book collector. This erudite pleasure seeker probably never traveled outside of his native al-Andalus, but he did have access to official archives and earlier written materials since lost. It is to him, then, that we owe the magnificent, singular description—tucked away in the pages devoted to the trade routes of the Sahel in his *Book of the Itineraries and Kingdoms*—of the realm that owing to approximation and metonymy has been called Ghâna ever since; here we see the beginnings of a glorious history of African kingdoms. It was for this very reason that the British colony of the Gold Coast borrowed its name when declaring independence in 1957.

Ghâna was not the first significant African kingdom, nor was it the only one, nor even the most important of its day; but it was described by al-Bakrî. Ever the accurate author, he did not feel the need to convince his readers that Africans were inferior beings. He tells us that the current king (around 1068) was a certain Tankâminîn, who ascended the throne after the death of his maternal uncle in 1062. This custom must have surprised an Arab author: matrilineal succession did not exist in North Africa, except among an atypical Berber group, the Tuaregs, but it was common in sub-Saharan Africa. The king exported gold to Islamic lands and collected taxes on the loads of salt and copper that entered his country. His palace and dwellings were surrounded by a fortified wall. When domed-roofed houses appear in the text, one is tempted to refer to them as "huts," bringing to mind wattle-and-daub dwellings. But the text speaks explicitly of architecture made from stone and wood. We find similar residences all around the royal enclosure, as well as groves and woods. It was in these spaces forbidden to visitors that the priests saw to the local religion, what al-Bakrî called "the religion of the magi" (*madjūsīya*), and what colonial science would later disdainfully call "animism." Here were found the tombs of the kings as well as "idols," a somewhat loaded translation of a term (*dakākīr*) that certainly referred to wooden or terra-cotta statues of former sovereigns, to whom were offered sacrifices and libations of fermented drinks. Al-Bakrî's informant was a considerably talented "ethnologist," who, moreover, left his observations in the best possible hands. We recognize a familiar world in his description: an ancestor cult centered on approving or angry deities, protectors of families and lineages, whom it was necessary to appease with regular offerings made under the sheltering canopy of their sacred groves. Near the royal enclosure lay a domed room, around which were positioned ten horses cloaked in fabrics embroidered with gold; dogs, whose collars gleamed with gold and silver, were kept near the entrance. The ceremonial swords and shields held by the pages, arrayed behind the king, were made of gold, while gold was also braided in the hair of the sons of princely families, arrayed to his right. The ministers and the governor of the city sat on the ground. Drums opened the session. Petitioners prostrated themselves and threw soil over their shoulders. The royal audience could begin: its aim was to right the wrongs inflicted on the people by the king's officers.

It is easy to see that the Aoukar, a natural region of present-day southern Mauritania, derives its name from Awkâr. It is possible that Tankâminîn's land had had no other name than that. Besides, must a kingdom necessarily have a name when you already have a dynastic title, princely families who accept your legitimacy, and subjects to whom you extend your justice? In these conditions, the name of a region—like the monarch's title—can very well become, through synecdoche, that of the whole kingdom; all it takes is for a foreign visitor to have felt the need for it. But let's assume that it was indeed the kingdom's real name that would be preserved in the local toponymy. Nowadays the Aoukar is the name of a large erg* virtually devoid of human settlement. Still, the region is not entirely sterile: groundwater flows at only a few meters' depth and fosters the occasional sudden appearance of vast pastures. The sands are "alive" and could have spread to the south over the course of the last millennium.

Some scholars have claimed that the site of Kumbi Saleh, on the southern threshold of the Aoukar in the region of Wagadu, in the middle of a basin formed by massifs of fixed dunes, was the capital of the Ghâna of al-Bakrî. We are here on the ecological edge of the sedentary domain: a large pond sometimes appears during the wet season; the first agricultural village is only a few kilometers to the south. Over the past century, several surveying missions and excavation campaigns have been conducted there and have revealed architectural elements and artifacts compatible with the idea of a city in the Sahel at this point in the Middle Ages: the archaeological mound, with a circumference of almost four kilometers and a thickness of seven to eight meters, revealed squares, streets, blocks of buildings made from shale tiles, and a large mosque; as for imported artifacts: small quantities of glazed ceramics, coin weights,* and beads.

This convergence between written and archaeological sources would be sufficient anywhere else to convince us that this archaeological site is indeed that of the capital mentioned in the texts. But even though Kumbi Saleh is without a doubt the most extraordinary of West Africa's known sites, things are not that simple. Al-Bakrî specifies that the city of Ghâna was made up of two localities separated from each other by six Arabic miles (that is to say, a dozen kilometers); Muslims, by which we understand Arab or Berber merchants, lived in the first, the king in the second. The latter, as we have seen, perhaps had the appearance of a rather loose grouping of stone and wood houses around the royal enclosure where the palace and its outbuildings, dwellings, and courtyards stood. Apart from the audience chamber, a mosque was also located in the vicinity for the liturgical use of Muslims who came as merchants or diplomats. They resided in the other city, which contained twelve mosques. This was not insignificant and probably denotes a compact group of several hundred inhabitants, all surrounded by wells and gardens where they cultivated vegetables, which means that there was irrigation. Between these two poles, there were, from what al-Bakrî says, a number of villages, a sign that if the site is indeed the one we seek, then the desert has overrun it, or, rather, humans have let the desert overrun it. For neither pedestrian surveys nor aerial photography, starting from the earth wall that rings the archaeological zone, have had the slightest luck in locating even an insignificant structure within a radius of several miles.

Two cities in one, according to al-Bakrî. There are thought to be similar examples, from the same epoch, on the Senegal and Niger Rivers: an Islamic city and an African city, distant enough to avoid commingling but close enough to implement an authentic commercial articulation. But isn't the angle of observation that imposes this duality perhaps a little reductionist in turn? Once settled—or, more likely, kept at a distance—the merchants and clerics of the Muslim city were certainly inclined to approach the royal African city as the unique other pole of a system of trade relations and mutual dependence involving only elites. For in the inevitably dual logic of economic relationships, they were, by the same token, blind to the other facets of the city: the city of Ghâna was perhaps indeed a multipolar space constructed, in reality, from a fabric composed of multiple villages, a royal quarter formed from a variety of domestic, religious, and official spaces, and a residential and commercial center. Plus other spaces: for artisans and soldiers, spots for funerary or devotional practices, and then, as in any agglomeration of neglected neighborhoods, wasteland and sectors in the midst of transformation. Perhaps this was the city: an ensemble divided into "quarters" with distinct functions, containing more empty space than full, more a necessary circulation space than a densely populated area, all of which made the Arab visitor reluctant, and us even more so, to designate what should or should not be considered a "city." With Kumbi Saleh, exceptionally powerful in terms of its stratigraphy, astonishingly dense in terms of its urban fabric, we are undoubtedly looking at a major site, perhaps not without link to the Ghâna of al-Bakrî—if not with Ghâna, what else? But where were the city gardens, where were the surrounding villages, where was the royal quarter, the sovereigns' necropolis, the grove where the priests served the ancestors in secret? Only the cartography of a city virtually indistinguishable from its landscape would allow us to grasp the relationships between its sectors. This cartography, if it ever corresponded to a reality other than an idealized or sentimental one—let us admit that the cool shade of a garden contributes more to urbanity than to urbanism—was undoubtedly largely immaterial (urbanity is a quality that leaves few traces) and, in any case, at the margins of the desert, hopeless. If it were necessary to one day relaunch the quest for Ghâna, then we would have to walk first, not dig.

Before the historiographical tradition had its heart set on Kumbi Saleh, Albert Bonnel de Mézières, a French adventurer, explorer, and later colonial administrator, had surveyed the region. He certainly did not go about it in a systematic fashion, nor did he have the support offered by today's methods of surveying and description. And yet these visits enabled him to discover, within a radius of a few days' walk around Kumbi Saleh, roughly ten ancient sites where, almost as many times, and always with the same good faith and enthusiasm, he thought he had discovered Ghâna.

Al-Bakrî's text is available in a critical edition in Arabic and French by Baron MacGuckin de Slane, *Description de l'Afrique septentrionale* (Algiers, 1913). An excellent translation of the city's description as given in this chapter can be found in Nehemia Levtzion and J.F.P. Hopkins (eds.), *Corpus of Early Arabic Sources for West African History* (Princeton, NJ: Markus Wiener, 2000), pp. 79–81. For biographical details on al-Bakrî, I used Évariste Lévi-Provençal's entry "Abū Ubayd al-Bakrī," in *Encyclopaedia of Islam*, 2nd ed. For a review of the historiographical importance of al-Bakrî, see Emmanuelle Tixier, "Bakrī et le Maghreb," in Dominique Valérian (ed.), *Islamisation et arabisation de l'Occident musulman médiéval (VIIe–XIIe siècle)* (Paris: Publication de la Sorbonne, 2011), pp. 369–384. The term *dakâkîr* (singular *dakkûr*) is not Arabic and probably comes from a language spoken in the Sahel; in another instance, al-Bakrî employs it with the meaning of "idol" (*ṣanam*). An attempt at interpreting al-Bakrî's West African itineraries has been made by John O. Hunwick, Claude Meillassoux, and Jean-Louis Triaud, "La géographie du Soudan d'après al-Bakri. Trois lectures," in *Le Sol, la parole et l'écrit: 2000 ans d'histoire africaine. Mélanges en hommage à Raymond Mauny*, 2 vols. (Paris: Société française d'histoire d'outre-mer, 1981), 1:401–428 (despite the French title, Hunwick's contribution to this chapter is in English); the three authors all accept the identification of al-Bakrî's Ghâna with Kumbi Saleh, which somewhat restricts the reading of the text. In this regard, a dissident but welcome voice is that of Vincent Monteil, who in his remarkable translation and commentary of the text, "Al-Bakrî (Cordoue 1068). Routier de l'Afrique blanche et noire du Nord-Ouest," *Bulletin de l'Institut fondamental d'Afrique noire*, ser. B, 30, no. 1 (1968): 39–116, posed this question (p. 111): "If Kumbi Saleh is indeed this city [the Ghâna described by al-Bakrî], what became of the ruins of the eleven other mosques [that the author mentioned]?" It must be added, however, that only a tiny part of the site has been excavated, and that it remains possible that several mosques have yet to be discovered. On the historiographical construction of the Sudanese kingdoms in the Western imagination, see Pekka Masonen, *The Negroland Revisited: Discovery and Invention of the Sudanese Middle Ages* (Helsinki: The Finnish Academy of Science and Letters, 2000). J.-L. Triaud has delivered a detailed study of the historiographical construction of Ghâna from the Middle Ages to decolonization: "Le nom de Ghana. Mémoire en exil, mémoire importée, mémoire appropriée," in J.-P. Chrétien and J.-L. Triaud (eds.), *Histoire d'Afrique. Les enjeux de mémoire* (Paris: Karthala, 1999), pp. 235–280. The region where Kumbi Saleh is located has been very well described by Jean Devisse and Boubacar Diallo, "Le seuil du Wagadu," in *Vallées du Niger* (Paris: Éditions de la Réunion des musées nationaux, 1993), pp. 103–115. A short note based on a telegram from Bonnel de Mézières indicated the numerous discoveries he had made in the region in 1914: [Albert Bonnel de Mézières], "Notes sur les récentes découvertes de M. Bonnel de Mézières, d'après un télégramme officiel adressé par lui, le 23 mars 1914, à M. le gouverneur Clozel," *Comptes-Rendus de l'Académie des Inscriptions et Belles-Lettres* 58 (1914): 253–257. The excavations' results have been only partially published; see most recently Sophie Berthier, *Recherches archéologiques sur la capitale de l'empire de Ghana. Étude d'un secteur d'habitat à Koumbi Saleh, Mauritanie. Campagnes II-III-IV-V (1975–1976)–(1980–1981)* (Oxford:

Archaeopress, 1997). The journal *Afrique. Archéologie et Arts* has published the hitherto unseen report of D. Robert-Chaleix, S. Robert, and B. Saison. See "Bilan en 1977 des recherches archéologiques à Tegdaoust et Koumbi Saleh (Mauritanie)," *Afrique. Archéologie et Arts* 3 (2004–2005): 23–48. The same issue contains several other recent articles focusing on structures or artifacts discovered at Kumbi Saleh. Only very brief but useful archaeological syntheses exist in English: see, for instance, Timothy Insoll, *The Archaeology of Islam in Sub-Saharan Africa* (Cambridge: Cambridge University Press, 2003), pp. 228–230, as well as reviews in English of French works, such as Susan Keech McIntosh, "Capital of Ancient Ghana" [a review of Berthier's book cited above], *Journal of African History* 41, no. 2 (2000): 296–298.

CHAPTER **8**

Ghâna, One Hundred
Years Later

Banks of a River in the Sahel, between 1116 and 1154

Around 1154, the year he began his famous map of the world for the Christian king Roger II of Sicily, the Arab geographer al-Idrîsî described "the greatest of all the towns of the *Sûdân*" (i.e., the "Blacks"), "the most populous, and with the most extensive trade." "Prosperous merchants," he wrote, "go there from all the surrounding countries and the other countries of al-Maghrib al-Aqṣā,"—the "most Maghreb" or the farthest west of Islam and the known world: present-day Morocco. The king had a palace here, "strongly built and perfectly fortified, [whose interior is] decorated with various drawings and paintings, and provided with glass windows." The construction of this palace began, al-Idrîsî tells us, in the year 510 of the Hijra, that is, 1116–1117 CE, which furnishes the *terminus post quem* for the information he relates. As for al-Idrîsî's informants, the Maghrebians who traded from one side of the Sahara to the other are the most likely candidates. According to the author, they "know positively and without difference of opinion that the king has in his palace a brick (*libna*) of gold weighing 30 *raṭls* [approximately 35 pounds or 16 kilograms] made of one piece. It is entirely God's creation, without having been melted in the fire or hammered with any tool. A hole has been pierced in it to serve for tethering the king's horse. It is one of those curious objects which no one else possesses and which is not permissible for anyone else. He prides himself on it above the other kings of the *Sûdân*."

This city was called Ghâna. If all the merchants of North Africa knew it, it was certainly because it was the place in the Sahel where gold was purchased in the middle of the twelfth century. Moreover, the king did not dispense with the ostentatious displays of wealth that made it known: the anecdote about the reins of the royal mount that went through a colossal gold nugget was nothing more than an advertisement aimed at the great North African merchants. The king was richly adorned with silk, had standards carried during his official outings, and marched behind giraffes, elephants, and "other kinds of wild animals." The sequence was intended to demonstrate the domestication of the stark, brutal, and uncivilized African countryside so feared by northerners.

This king—we don't know his name—was Muslim. That was not the case a century earlier (↦7). Following conversion, the African kingdom consolidated the dominant position that it had already acquired toward the middle of the preceding century, when al-Bakrî described in detail the pomp of a king of a traditional religion, "pagan" according to the Andalusian author. We don't know when or through what process this conversion and the ascent to power of a Muslim dynasty (if the king was not of the same line as his predecessor) occurred. Nor why—perhaps as a result of troubles caused by the rise of the Almoravids, that juridical and censorious movement, which was long thought to have razed Ghâna to the ground and converted its inhabitants by force. Or perhaps it was a result of the exploitation of new gold deposits, those of Bouré, in present-day Mali. But whatever the causes, we know the consequences: the dynasty, like all dynasties, chose for itself a new genealogy, whether real or imaginary. The sovereign of a few decades prior still had at his service priests tasked with maintaining the cult of the ancestors; the present one, in contrast, chose Alî ibn Abî Tâlib, cousin and son-in-law of the Prophet, for a distant ancestor and protector. The king of Ghâna's new adherence to the Muslim faith, the affiliation with the community of believers, was a guarantee for the merchants, a guarantee of the application, in these distant lands, of a commercial law that was deemed equitable. As a result, was not the sultan reputed to be just? Twice a day, the king rode at the head of his officers "through the lanes of the town and around it. Anyone who has suffered injustice or misfortune confronts him, and stays there until the wrong is remedied."

Al-Idrîsî's description allows us to measure the religious and institutional evolution that the kingdom underwent during the decades since al-Bakrî. But we have a more serious problem: eleventh-century Ghâna was located in the Aoukar, southernmost Mauritania, where traces of it are even believed to have been found. Twelfth-century Ghâna, according to al-Idrîsî, was next to a river, and straddled its banks. Several details strengthen this version: the inhabitants "have strongly made boats . . . which they use for fishing or for moving about between the two towns," and the sultan's palace itself was built right next to the river.

On the pretext that al-Idrîsî was often unreliable, this part of his description has sometimes been dismissed, while the portion describing the kingdom's conversion, or at least that of its sovereign, to Islam has been retained. Archaeological traces of the city described by al-Bakrî would be sought after; but we have never really looked for al-Idrîsî's. Yet there are good reasons to think that it existed: for, however odd it may have sounded to him, al-Idrîsî clearly states that it was made up of two cities, situated on the two banks of a river; like that of the Aoukar it consisted of two principal entities, the commercial city and the royal city. Here the river would have promoted and maintained the capital's spatial and cultural bipolarity, all while drawing the communities set up on its banks physically closer together. Then we know the date of the construction of the palace near the river: it was recent (in al-Idrîsî's day). By itself this clue pleads for a new foundation, a royal act; in other words, for a relocation of the capital, as a new city would require a new palace. Let's call the city of al-Bakrî Ghâna I and al-Idrîsî's Ghâna II. All things considered, Ghâna II was only a few days to the south of Ghâna I, a shift from the steppe to the savanna, which would have carried the name of the kingdom with it. Nevertheless, this displacement raises a series of questions: on the bank of what river—the Senegal or the Niger—and in which areas that archaeologists have not surveyed was Ghâna located? And what became of the first? By what name was our Ghâna I then known if the capital was moved to Ghâna II? And, more importantly, what exactly was transferred from one capital to the other: a royal seat and its officials? A whole population? Or is it possible that this political transfer reflects not a physical movement, but the seizure of power, and the subsequent capture of the title of the sovereign of Ghâna, by a southern vassal from a weakened overlord? For al-Idrîsî and the Maghrebian merchants only one thing was useful to know: the greatest market of the Land of the Blacks could still be found in the shadow of the royal palace.

BIBLIOGRAPHICAL NOTE

The extracts from the text of al-Idrîsî are taken from Nehemia Levtzion and J.F.P. Hopkins (eds.), *Corpus of Early Arabic Sources for West African History* (Princeton, NJ: Markus Wiener, 2000), pp. 109–110; further bibliography on al-Idrîsî is provided in chapter 14. Nehemia Levtzion, "Ancient Ghana: A Reassessment of Some Arabic Sources," in *Le Sol, la parole et l'écrit: 2000 ans d'histoire africaine. Mélanges en hommage à Raymond Mauny* (Paris: Société française d'histoire d'outre-mer, 1981), 1:429–437, put forth the hypothesis that the transfer of the capital could have been a consequence of the Almoravid raid of 1076. However, the reality of this raid, beginning with the destruction of the city of Ghâna, has been called into question by David Conrad and Humphrey Fisher, "The Conquest That Never Was: Ghana and the Almoravids, 1076. I. The External Arabic Sources," *History in Africa* 9 (1982): 21–59, and "The Conquest That Never Was: Ghana and the Almoravids, 1076. II. The Local Oral Sources," *History in Africa* 10 (1983): 53–78. The critical opinion put forward in these articles is nowadays generally accepted, but Nehemia Levtzion, undoubtedly one of the premier scholars on the subject, and certainly not an uncritical reader of sources, made clear that he remained unconvinced. See his "Berber Nomads and Sudanese States: The Historiography of the Desert-Sahel Interface," in his collection of varia: *Islam in West Africa: Religion, Society and Politics to 1800* (London: Variorum, 2004), item X.

CHAPTER 9

The Conversion Effect

Various Parts of the Sahel, Eleventh to Twelfth Century

What happened to them all? Between the second third of the eleventh century and the first half of the twelfth, a wave of conversions to Islam swept over the sovereigns of several political formations in the Sahel, from the Atlantic to the Niger bend. First were Takrûr and Silla, two cities along the Senegal River. The inhabitants, perhaps only the most notable among them, renounced their "idols" and became Muslim in imitation of a monarch named Wâr-Djâbî ibn Râbîs, who died around 1040. At the same time, the kingdom of Malal, the future Mâli (↦28, 29), or perhaps one of the components of this future empire, suffered drought coupled with severe famine. Oxen were sacrificed, but to no avail: the rain did not fall. A Muslim named Alî was among the king's entourage. "O king," the Muslim told him, "if you believed in God (who is exalted) and testified that He is One, and testified as to the prophetic mission of Muḥammad (God bless him and give him peace) and if you accepted all the religious laws of Islam, I would pray for your deliverance from your plight and God's mercy would envelop all the people of your country and that your enemies and adversaries might envy you on that account." The king was persuaded to receive the first rudiments of a Muslim education. Alî taught him a few passages from the Koran as well as "religious obligations and practices which no one may be excused from knowing." One Friday, away on a hill, the Muslim initiated his royal disciple into prayer. Alî mouthed the incantations, while the king imitated the gestures and, throughout the night, chanted "amen." The rain began at daybreak and lasted for seven days and nights. The king's conversion was authentic, the sources tell us. It led to that of his family and his entourage, but not to that of his subjects, who basically told him, "We are your servants, do not change our religion." At Gao, Kawkaw in the Arabic sources, the king was undoubtedly Muslim from the end of the ninth century. By the middle of the eleventh century, in any case, it was the seat of a kingdom where the inhabitants "entrust the kingship only to Muslims." As for the sovereign of Ghâna (↦8), he was a Muslim in the middle of the twelfth century.

These conversions affected the top of society: the king converted first, then his entourage, while perhaps waiting for the rest of his subjects. These conversions were the work of Muslim clergymen, the ulamas, literally the "learned" well versed in the different religious sciences and capable of performing the various functions associated with preachers, scholars, and jurists. In "pagan" lands, as was predominantly the case with the "Land of the Blacks" in the Middle Ages, Muslim missionaries from the Maghreb could be found who, having entered the sovereigns' entourage, waited for, or provoked, the right moment. Conversion, we are told, was sincere; and there is no reason to doubt it. Although the "low resolution" of our sources prevents us from "zooming in" for total certitude, it appears irrevocable: no kingdom whose king had converted seems to have backpedaled during the later Middle Ages. On the contrary, wherever a king converted, this unleashed a process of elite conversion and familiarization with the new religion, even if traditional religions would remain dominant among the people until the popular movements of Islamization in the nineteenth century. In that respect, the conversion of the black monarchs of the eleventh to twelfth century was a milestone. But it was not a rupture; if adherence to the Muslim faith was sincere, it was not exclusive. Moreover, the king of Malal's apprenticeship included the basic requirements but not the interdictions of Islam. This certainly allowed the converted monarch, even if he himself rejected the idols, to listen to his subjects when they said, "Do not change our religion"—to remain, in their eyes, the protector of the traditional cults. There was no contradiction here, either for him or for the population that remained "pagan": in Malal's case, it was precisely the efficacious intercession of the God of the Muslims that allowed the king to preserve his traditional role as guarantor of the rain and the harvests. As the sovereign's legitimacy was everyone's concern, and as everyone could judge tangible effects of his piety, it was particularly important that the monarch was a good Muslim, even if Islam was not the religion of his subjects.

It has been said that the African monarchs who converted to Islam during the Middle Ages occupied an intermediate position between Islam, the official religion of North Africa, and the traditional religions of the sub-Saharan regions. This is absolutely true if what is meant here is that these kings thus fully participated in both their society and the new religion. This model must have really satisfied their subjects, and for quite a long time, for Islam certainly made only slow progress over the course of the following centuries, always confined to the cities and the political and economic elites. It would take the nineteenth-century jihadist movements to transform the lands of the Sahel into Muslim-majority territories.

The story of the conversion of the king of Malal is perhaps untrue, even if it is told with distinct details by two Arab authors. But beyond the simple fact of the conversion, it informs us about its process. Professed clerics brought it about, not merchants, and they targeted royalty, not the common people. This was surely the "strategy" of the ulamas:* convert the king to convert the kingdom. In this respect it was a failure. Their strategy, history suggests, was certainly unsuccessful in societies that were, at the time, not strongly centralized. Petty chiefdom and segmentary societies remained out of range of the new religious currents, and some were happy to keep it that way so as to maintain reservoirs of potential captives. In order to be "worthy of conversion," societies needed to appear civilized, and in order to appear civilized they needed to have kings. Islam thus offered African elites a foothold in the exterior world. This is why it was successful with them. By introducing the rudiments of a common vernacular (Arabic) to the Sahelian elites and the North African merchants, by granting access to the same spiritual references, to the same Book, to the same religious practices (beginning with daily prayers), to the same moral and juridical framework, Islam offered a shared *language* to new converts and the Islamic world alike. In this way, the king of Malal acquired all the resources that gave him access to membership in a "global" community.

Consequently, perhaps there was more to the roughly synchronous conversions among the kings of the Sahel than the mere playing out in each of the affected societies of the same sociological stimuli. Politics undoubtedly played a role. Through a simple rational calculation, a monarch's conversion to Islam—on the condition that it was publicly proclaimed with all apparent sincerity—constituted a moral and juridical guarantee to the merchants of the Islamic world, if only because it implied that religious agents active in his entourage had his ear and urged him to rule justly. News of the conversion of a king of the Sûdân carried a subliminal message: this kingdom is good for trade. In this sense, the king's conversion, because it was likely to tilt the economic balance in his realm's favor by diverting all or part of the regional trade routes, offered a decisive advantage in the competition with his neighbors. These same neighbors, jealously eying his increased political and economic clout, followed suit. The conversion effect among the region's sovereigns can be viewed as a political response to this competitive environment.

BIBLIOGRAPHICAL NOTE

The two authors who recount the story of the king of Malal/Mâli's conversion are al-Bakrî and al-Dardjînî. Al-Bakrî's extracts on Malal, as well as mentions by the same author of Takrûr, Silla, and Gao, can be found in Nehemia Levtzion and J.F.P. Hopkins, *Corpus of Early Arabic Sources for West African History* (Princeton, NJ: Markus Wiener, 2000), pp. 77–78, 82, 86–87. Al-Muhallabî, also an author who evokes Gao, and al-Dardjînî's passage on the conversion of the king of Mâli, can be found only in J. Cuoq, *Recueil des sources arabes concernant l'Afrique occidentale du VIIIe au XVIe siècle* (Paris: CNRS, 1985), pp. 77, 195. Jean-Louis Triaud, "Quelques remarques sur l'islamisation du Mali des origines à 1300," *Bulletin de l'Institut fondamental d'Afrique noire*, ser. B, 30, no. 4 (1968): 1329–1352, expresses doubts about the reality of the conversion of the king of Malal as well as about the identification of Malal with Mâli; however, he seems to minimize al-Dardjînî's testimony, which strengthens these two hypotheses. The bibliography on the process of Islamization in Africa's Sahel is vast. A good starting point is Nehemia Levtzion, "Islam in the Bilad al-Sudan to 1800," in N. Levtzion and Randall L. Pouwels (eds.), *The History of Islam in Africa* (Athens: Ohio University Press, 2000), pp. 63–91. For an essential analysis of the role of the ulamas, see N. Levtzion, "Merchants versus Scholars and Clerics in West Africa: Differential and Complementary Roles," in N. Levtzion and Humphrey J. Fisher (eds.), *Rural and Urban Islam in West Africa* (Boulder, CO: Lynne Rienner Publishers, 1987), pp. 27–43, reprinted in *Islam in West Africa: Religion, Society and Politics to 1800* (London: Variorum, 2004), item V. On archaeology, one can recommend the chapter devoted to the western Sahel (chap. 5) in Timothy Insoll's *The Archaeology of Islam in Sub-Saharan Africa* (Cambridge: Cambridge University Press, 2003). An archaeological monograph edited by R. McIntosh, S. K. McIntosh, and H. Bocoum, *The Search for Takrur: Archaeological Excavations and Reconnaissance along the Middle Senegal Valley* (New Haven, CT: Yale University Press, 2016), has recently uncovered material evidence of the early African polities of the Middle Senegal River valley, notably the Takrûr. The few reflections on the compatibility between Islam and pre-Islamic traditional religions are borrowed from Jean Boulègue who, in *Le Grand Jolof* (Blois: Façades, 1987), p. 98, expresses remarkably well the only superficial contradiction between the uncompromising faith of the sovereign and the importance of local cults: "The difference between the practices of the people and those of the royal courts perhaps simply reflects the division of social roles: since Islam was perceived to be a superior knowledge linked to power, it was intended to be primarily practiced by those in power, but in the name of all."

CHAPTER 10

The King of Zâfûn Enters Marrakesh

*Morocco and the Western Sahel, around the
Second Quarter of the Twelfth Century*

Marrakesh—Marrâkush in Arabic—the city that gave its name to Morocco in Western onomastics, was founded on the plain of the Wadi Tansift, then simple grassland, around 1070. Camp-capital become city, Marrakesh was the creation of the Almoravids. Yûsuf ibn Tâshfîn, commander of the Sanhâja Berber troops, wanted it to serve as a way station between the Adrar region of Mauritania, birthplace of the Almoravid movement, and the kingdom of Fez to the north. He provided it with a mosque, and certainly a castle, and nomads by the thousands came to join it. In 1126, his son and successor, Alî ibn Yûsuf, constructed a wall around what was then a city of tents, estimated, perhaps with some exaggeration, at one hundred thousand hearths.

The foundation of Marrakesh constituted the emergence from the desert of a religious movement that until that point had been devoted to consolidating and correcting the faith of the Western Saharan tribes. Conquerors of Aoudaghost in 1054 or 1055 (↦6), summoned the same year by the people of Sijilmâsa (↦16) to get rid of their current masters, the men of *ribât* (*ribāt*)—a fortified monastery devoted to spiritual discipline, or *al-murâbitûn*, which has given us the terms "Almoravids" and "marabouts"—took over the gold route and could not resist the temptation to spread holy war to the prosperous plains: prosperous and thus, they judged, corrupted. They began to mint money at Sijilmâsa itself, and the abundant production of gold coins fueled their war effort. The Sous and the Drâa regions of southern Morocco were taken a few years later; central Morocco, from Aghmât to Fez, fell between 1063 and 1069; the Mediterranean coast, from Ceuta to Algiers, was incorporated into the nascent empire between 1081 and 1082; finally, Islamic Spain followed in 1086.

Around 1220, Yâqût al-Rûmî, a former Christian slave from Byzantium (which is shown in his nickname, "the Roman"), compiled a dictionary in Arabic whose entries covered the geographical lore then known in Iraq and Syria. His entry for Zâfûn contains the recollection of an inhabitant of

Marrakesh, certainly drawn from another source, or else from a second-hand account. One day, a king of the Sûdân arrived in the Maghreb. En route to Mecca, he paid a visit to "the Veiled King of the Maghreb, of the tribe of the Lamtûna," the "Commander of the Muslims." "The Commander of the Muslims met him on foot, while the [King of] Zâfûn did not dismount for him." Our nameless witness recalls how the monarch looked when he entered Marrakesh: "[H]e was tall, of deep black complexion and veiled. The whites of his eyes were bloodshot as if they were two glowing coals, and the palms of his hands were yellow as if tinted with saffron. He was wearing a cut (*maqṭûʿ*) garment enveloped in a white cloak. He entered the palace of the Commander of the Muslims mounted, while the latter walked in front of him."

If the mysterious king of Zâfûn, mounted in all his majesty, here makes a unique and brief appearance on the stage of history, it is easier to uncover the identity of the king who entered his own palace on foot. The title "Commander of the Muslims" was held by the Almoravid leader, always a member of the Sanhâja tribe of the Lamtûna, from whom the empire's military elite was recruited. And if it is difficult to understand why this Berber leader rendered homage in this way—in his capital, no less—to a foreign sovereign, it's because the Almoravid Empire was short-lived, a century at most. Bending before the growing strength of a new reform movement aimed at expansion, a movement that came from the Atlas Mountains, the Almohads, it was no doubt forced, as it drew to an end, to seek support, which one could buy with homage. This hypothesis allows us to date the episode to the second quarter of the twelfth century: that is to say, the final years of the reign of Alî Ibn Yûsuf (he repelled the Almohads' first attack on Marrakesh in 1128 and died in 1143) or the years of political turmoil that preceded the city's fall to the Almohads in 1147.

Not much is known about the kingdom of Zâfûn. Although its name was corrupt in his text, al-Bakrî certainly described this same kingdom in the middle of the eleventh century: "They are a nation of Sûdân," he wrote, "who worship a certain snake, a monstrous serpent with a mane and a tail and a head shaped like that of the Bactrian camel. It lives in a cave in the desert. At the mouth of the cave stands a trellis and stones and the habitation of the adepts of the cult of that snake." This is a classic example for this region of Africa of the worship of a subterranean monster—in this case a chimerical serpent—that is brought forth from its hole by offerings of milk and fermented drinks placed in large vessels.

The death of a chief provided an opportunity for summoning the serpent. The pretenders were brought together. "Then the Snake approaches them," wrote al-Bakrî, "and smells one man after another until it prods one with its nose. As soon as it has done this it turns away towards the cave. The one prodded follows as fast as he can and pulls from its tail or its mane as many hairs as he is able. His kingship will last as many years as he has hairs, one hair per year. This, they assert, is an infallible prediction." From the perspective of our twenty-first-century rationality—imagining the pretenders brought together before such a sanctuary dedicated to a mythological creature—we cannot say how the ceremony for choosing the sovereign was actually carried out. At most, we perceive hints of an original configuration in which the accession to power, or perhaps the confirmation of the royal line, was entrusted to a deity's intervention in an ordeal, and the reign's propects were subject to augury.

That is essentially all that can be said about the ancient history of Zâfûn—or rather, its ideological atmosphere. Is it possible to say more about its location? Certainly. There are good philological arguments on that score. It corresponds to what the oral accounts of the Soninke, the inhabitants of the western Sahel and likely heirs to several of the region's political formations in the Middle Ages, know as Diafounou. If that is indeed the case, it is then necessary to place it in the region of the same name, on the upper Kolinbiné River, a tributary of the Senegal River, which it joins near Kayes. But the site corresponding to the capital of Zâfûn is still missing. Can it be assumed that there was not one or that there were several capitals, two expedient ways for predicting that one will not find what one is looking for? But if there is agreement to search first, before giving up if necessary, then one should attempt to find a ruined site whose material culture is compatible with the twelfth century: an ancient mosque since the king was Muslim; and a permanent merchants' quarter for Muslim traders, quite large since the king was powerful and rich enough to go on pilgrimage.

Based on the black king's entry into Marrakesh, it was once suggested that the people of Zâfûn had been "influenced" by the Berbers. The king was indeed Muslim, he rode a horse, and he wore a veil over his face, according to the custom, actually independent of Islam, practiced by several Saharan tribes and that we still find among the Tuaregs. This custom led medieval Arab authors to nickname them *Mulaththamîn*, literally "wearers of the lithâm" (i.e., the veil that covered the mouths of adults, both men and women). Others have seen in the same vignette evidence of a time when the blacks "dominated" the Arabs, in other words, the whites. Symmetrical vocabulary, vague judgments. These were not the aims of the kings involved, both of whom certainly needed the roles they were playing—before the same audience, who, furthermore, transmitted their content to us without weighing it down with prejudice—to revive the modes of legitimization each for his own power. It was high time for the king on foot, the descendant of the ascetic warriors of the desert, who was soon to be under siege, and who was already menaced by the rise of a new doctrine critical of secular involvement, to reestablish his links with humility. As for the mounted king, whose skin color was still rare enough in those days for our unnamed witness to notice the saffron color on the palms of his hands, he desired to show through his bearing, in this time of rigor, that one could be black and a good Muslim.

BIBLIOGRAPHICAL NOTE

Tadeusz Lewicki, "Un État soudanais médiéval inconnu: le royaume de Zāfūn(u)," *Cahiers d'études africaines* 11 (1971): 501–525, was the first to present the complete dossier pertaining to the kingdom of Zâfûn. This chapter leans heavily on his pioneering work. The translation of Yâqût's text is taken from Nehemia Levtzion and J.F.P. Hopkins, *Corpus of Early Arabic Sources for West African History* (Princeton, NJ: Markus Wiener, 2000), pp. 170–171. Al-Bakrî's account may also be found in Levtzion and Hopkins, pp. 78–79. Regarding the Almoravids, see H. T. Norris and P. Chalmeta's entry "Murābitūn (al-)," in the *Encyclopedia of Islam*, 2nd ed.

CHAPTER 11

The Rich Dead
of the Tumuli

*Ethiopia, Mali, Senegal, between the
Ninth and the Fourteenth Century*

Ethiopia certainly has more megaliths than any other country in the world. (By megalith we mean all varieties of standing stone, as well as monuments made from piled-up or interlocking stones). Sculpted or engraved steles there, which are most often funerary markers, are counted by the thousands, tumuli (sing. tumulus)* by the hundreds. Despite some initial attempts, these monuments, their typology and chronology, their spatial distribution, remain to be studied.

In the cold, basaltic uplands of the country's central and eastern plateaus, on either side of the Great Rift Valley, which flares out from here in the direction of the Red Sea—that is to say, in the mountains on whose slopes Islamic kingdoms developed from the twelfth and the thirteenth centuries—scattered tumuli may be found, often isolated on peaks of rocky spurs overlooking deeply incised river valleys, or in clusters in the center of valleys. They are often in ruins, either because they were plundered long ago—or sometimes the week prior to your visit—and abandoned to erosion, or because they have served as open-air quarries, rather practical reservoirs of raw material for the fashioning of ballast for roads and repairs to trails after the wet season. The largest of these monuments, which can reach nearly twenty meters in diameter, have been preserved. Others have survived only because they are far from current settlements or, quite the opposite, because they are found in the walls of domestic enclosures, unless their seemingly intact appearance is merely the result of stones removed from nearby fields being piled up on top of the former monument. They are cone-shaped stone structures covering a burial chamber where the dead were repeatedly laid to rest—implying that the monument was reopened several times. The dead were buried along with their weapons— iron swords, arrows—and their jewelry—silver or iron bracelets; gold or silver beads; thousands of yellow, green, orange, red, and blue glass-paste beads, as well as large, multifaceted beads made from cornelian, agate, or rock crystal; and fibulas and rings. Only a few of these monuments have been excavated; they date from the tenth to the twelfth century.

Present-day Mali on the left bank of the Niger River—from the region of Méma, which several centuries ago was irrigated by a branch of the Niger, to the riparian zone—contains hundreds of man-made buttes, some of which are 150 meters or more in diameter. They are often former settlement mounds dating from the third to the thirteenth century and testify to the existence of a once-dense population of sedentary, iron-producing farmers. Some of these buttes are tumuli. They are regularly pillaged by the neighboring inhabitants, if they have not already been "excavated," when it comes to the most remarkable of them, by French colonial officers. Few have been the object of an excavation worthy of the name or dated; those that have seem to belong to the end of the period, from the seventh to the twelfth century, the latter corresponding to the period when Islam first began to touch the region's elites. Studies of the few documented sites reveal monuments consisting of a burial chamber whose structure is a scaffold of palm trunks. The chamber, linked to the surface by a passageway, is surmounted by a thick sediment dome blocked off on top by a clay calotte, which had seemingly been baked from the inside. The excavation of the tumulus of El-Oualadji (named after the small sanctuary of a Muslim saint located nearby) in 1904 by Lieutenant Desplagnes uncovered two skeletons in a chamber situated ten meters below the surface of the monument. They had been laid to rest on a bed of branches among copious pottery shards and animal bones; weapons such as sword blades, knives, arrowheads, and the tips of spears; and jewelry including bracelets, copper rings and other ornaments, copper and jasper beads, and clay animal figurines. Archaeological remains were also uncovered on the surface of the tumulus: bones and harness fragments of horses, beads, copper and iron objects, terra-cotta animal statuettes, quite possibly the remains of offerings. This monument has been dated to the eleventh to twelfth century. The neighboring tumulus of Koï Gourey, the "butte of the chieftain" in Songhay, excavated by Desplagnes a few years later, has not been dated (although it probably dates to the same period if comparable ceramic artifacts are anything to go by). Its structure seems similar. Nearly thirty human skeletons were uncovered along with lamps, weapons and ornaments, glass beads, cowries,* and brass figurines representing a horn-bill, a lizard, and a crocodile.

In the lower Senegal River valley and, more generally, all throughout the northwestern quarter of Senegal, small, sandy mounds conceal graves; these are tumuli, initially surrounded by a circular pit that has since been filled. There are more than ten thousand of them. Several have been ex-cavated at Rao near Saint-Louis in 1941–1942. In addition to skeletons, the diggers uncovered funerary artifacts including weapons (iron swords, spearheads) and fine jewelry: gold pendants; ankle rings and wristbands made from bronze, copper, or silver; gold rings; silver necklaces and cor-nelian beads; other fragments of miscellaneous jewelry; copper plates that could have ornamented a horse's caparison; shards of pottery. Tumu-lus P, with a diameter of forty meters and a height of four meters, is the most remarkable of the group. Archaeologists discovered the remains of a young man, accompanied by a silver filigree ball necklace, gold and bronze rings, a four-lobed gold pendant, a gold neck chain, and, finally, a solid gold breastplate consisting of concentric registers of bosses, arabesques, and diamonds in filigree or twisted wire. We know of similar breastplates among the ceremonial dress of several modern African sovereigns, but in this medieval context the technique evokes an Islamic know-how. The country's oral traditions say that the kingdom of Jolof—which historians believe emerged toward the beginning of the fourteenth century, and which the Portuguese would discover (in the course of Islamization) in the fifteenth century (↦33)—was born in this region. Tumulus P is dated to around 1330. Other datings, unfortunately few in number, seem to con-firm that this type of monument belongs to the first half of the second millennium of our era.

Let us put aside a false commonality among all these monuments drawn from three regions of Africa quite distant from each other, a commonality implied in their designation as "tumuli." In fact, their resemblance to one another is superficial, limited, as it is, to their exterior profile. Apart from this, everything, from the internal morphology of the monuments to the organization of the funerary deposit, from the material used to the building techniques displayed, is different. But all the same, this similar appearance draws attention to what unites at a distance the shapes of the graves and the funerary practices: individuals who, to judge by their mode of inhumation, were not Muslims, but who evolved in a comparable historical context just prior to the presence of Islam in their region. In each of these zones, the Malian Sahel in the ninth to the eleventh century, the Ethiopian uplands in the twelfth to the thirteenth century, the northwest Senegal from the thirteenth to the fifteenth century, Islam won to its faith and cause African elites who thereafter found themselves inclined—we can imagine—to respect Islamic prescriptions concerning the inhumation of the dead, even if they were of a high rank, and to abandon at death the ostentatious manifestations that they might have displayed while alive.

But while we can easily understand that Islam's arrival suddenly modified funerary practices and caused tumuli to be abandoned in favor of tombs more in accordance with the humility demanded of Muslims, how do we explain the apparent convergence of different regions, whereby tumuli multiplied during the centuries *preceding* the arrival of Islam's influence in such and such region of Africa? Let us clarify that certain tumulary traditions, such as some of the Malian monuments, clearly predate the seventh century. But what is interesting is the apparent strengthening of various funerary traditions of a tumulary type in several regions of Africa during the centuries between the birth of Islam and the arrival of its ideas and prescriptions in these regions.

In each of these cases, the tumuli are imposing monuments whose realization required a massive amount of labor. (The largest Senegalese tumuli are estimated to have required twenty-five thousand man-hours.) This is an indication of an important social status that allowed for the accumulation of riches and a lavish lifestyle to which the grave goods bear witness. The number and distribution of these monuments, scattered over immense territories, argue in favor of the formation of aristocratic or seignorial elites, already differentiated from the rest of society, but not yet centralized. For royal dynasties do not leave behind mounds in the landscape; averse to dispersal, the spatial representation of political fragmentation, they usually gather their dead in compact necropolises. It is thus rather tempting to see in these still-multiple elites the political matrices of the more concentrated and uncontested powers that would soon develop in these same areas. Some of their traits were already perceptible. Here were individuals who desired to go to their final resting place with all the trappings of the mounted warrior, but who wished to be buried among objects signaling that they owed their rank to their economic power: beads faceted with translucent rocks probably produced in India, beads of Egyptian or "Indo-Pacific"* glass, cowrie* shells from the Indian Ocean, pieces of Islamic gold work, all in a new abundance revealing the existence of organized commerce. Long before they became Muslim, local elites benefited from long-distance trade—through multiple intermediaries—with the expanding Islamic world. The tumuli are the markers of the initial shock wave caused by this commercial encounter with Islam. In short, these archaeological vestiges are a snapshot of a brief historical moment that has left only a few other traces: a moment that passed between the early connections of each of these African regions with the Islamic world and the first effects of Islamization.

Toward the middle of the eleventh century, the Andalusian geographer al-Bakrî described the funeral of one sovereign of Ghâna: "When their king dies they construct over the place where his tomb will be an enormous dome of sâj wood. Then they bring him on a bed covered with a few carpets and cushions and place him beside the dome. At his side they place his ornaments, his weapons, and the vessels from which he used to eat and drink, filled with various kinds of food and beverages. They place there too the men who used to serve his meals. They close the door of the dome and cover it with mats and furnishings. Then the people assemble, who heap earth upon it until it becomes like a big hillock and dig a ditch around it until the mound can be reached at only one place. They make sacrifices to their dead and make offerings of intoxicating drinks."

BIBLIOGRAPHICAL NOTE

A brief but good overview in English of Ethiopian megalithism can be found in Niall Finneran, *The Archaeology of Ethiopia* (London: Routledge, 2007), pp. 243–248. On the specific subject of the steles, the work of Roger Joussaume is indispensable. See in particular R. Joussaume (ed.), *Tiya, l'Éthiopie des mégalithes* (Chauvigny: Association des publications chauvinoises, 1995) and *Tuto Fela et les stèles du sud de l'Éthiopie* (Paris: Éditions Recherche sur les civilisations, 2007). The most recent work concerning the tumulus culture of Ethiopia is François-Xavier Fauvelle-Aymar and Bertrand Poissonnier (eds.), *La culture Shay d'Éthiopie. Recherches archéologiques et historiques sur une élite païenne* (Paris: De Boccard, 2012), of which the main results and interpretations were presented by the same authors in "The Shay Culture of Ethiopia (10th to 14th century AD): 'Pagans' in the Time of Christians and Muslims," *African Archaeological Review* 33, no. 1 (2016): 61–74. For the Malian tumuli, see the assessment of Raymond Mauny, *Tableau géographique de l'Ouest africain d'après les sources écrites, la tradition et l'archéologie* (Dakar: Institut français d'Afrique noire, 1961), pp. 92–111, especially pp. 96–97 for the El-Oualadji Tumulus, and pp. 95–96, 106, for the Koï Gourey Tumulus. Desplagnes's excavation does not escape criticism as a destructive archaeological intervention, but the two tumuli he excavated in the Goundam region are among the rare, significant monuments whose excavations have yielded published results. See Louis Desplagnes, *Le plateau central nigérien* (Paris: Émile Larose, 1907), pp. 57–66; "Étude sur les tumuli du Killi dans la région de Goundam," *L'Anthropologie* 14 (1903): 151–172; and "Fouilles du tumulus d'El-Oualadji (Soudan)" [edited and annotated by R. Mauny], *Bulletin de l'Institut français d'Afrique noire* 13 (1951): 1159–1173. The brass animal figurines of Koï Gourey have been studied by Laurence Garenne-Marot, Caroline Robion, and Benoît Mille, "Cuivre, alliages de cuivre et histoire de l'empire du Mali. À propos de trois figurines animales d'un tumulus du delta intérieur du Niger (Mali)," *Technè* 18 (2003): 74–85. The Desplagnes Collection, made up of artifacts collected during his digs, is in the Musée du Quai Branly. These studies should be read in conjunction with the survey reports, which offer a clearer picture of the magnitude of the megalithic phenomenon in Mali. On this subject see Michel Raimbault and Kléna Sanogo (eds.), *Recherches archéologiques au Mali. Les sites protohistoriques de la Zone lacustre* (Paris: Karthala, 1991), as well as the article by Téréba Togola, "Iron Age Occupation in the Méma Region, Mali," *African Archaeological Review* 13 (1996): 91–110, which provides an overview of current research on Méma as well as a report on the excavation of Akumbu. Readers should consult appendix 1 in Raimbault and Sanogo for a table of the very numerous datings that have been carried out. The excavation of Rao in Senegal is described by Jean Joire, "Archaeological Discoveries in Senegal," *Man* 43 (1943): 49–52; and "Découvertes archéologiques dans la région de Rao (Bas Sénégal)," *Bulletin de l'Institut français d'Afrique noire*, ser. B, 17, nos. 3–4 (1955): 249–333. The radiocarbon dating (1300 ± 50) is mentioned in Bruno Chavane, *Villages de l'ancien Tekrour* (Paris: Karthala, 1985), p. 46, which also gives a rapid summary of more recent excavations. I haven't been able to identify where this dating was originally published. Susan Keech McIntosh and Roderick J. McIntosh, "Field Survey in the Tumulus Zone of Senegal," *African Archaeological Review* 11 (1993): 73–107, presents the results of more recent surveys; the estimates of the number of tumulary monuments in Senegal as well as the man-hours required to make them are both taken from this article. The essential work on the history of Jolof remains Jean Boulègue, *Le Grand Jolof (XIIIe–XVIe siècle)* (Blois: Façades, 1987). Al-Bakrî's text is found in Nehemia Levtzion and J.F.P. Hopkins (eds.), *Corpus of Early Arabic Sources for West African History* (Princeton, NJ: Markus Wiener, 2000), pp. 80–81. Although they are not mentioned in this chapter, it is worth citing work conducted on the tumuli of other regions. Archaeologists have conducted several excavations at Durbi Takusheyi, a site east of the city of Katsina in northern Nigeria, whose tumuli are remarkable for their grave goods. Dated to the fourteenth century, they are contemporaneous with other tumuli discussed in this chapter and share a similar context: subsequent to the first links with regions participating in Islamic commerce, but prior to the Islamization of local elites. See Detlef Gronenborn (ed.), *Gold, Sklaven & Elfenbein. Mittelalterliche Reiche im Norden Nigerias / Gold, Slaves & Ivory. Medieval Empires in Northern Nigeria* (Mainz: Verlag des Römisch-Germanischen Zentralmuseums, 2011), pp. 72–107. A similar, albeit earlier, archaeological context is the one described by Sonja Magnavita's work at Kissi in Burkina Faso, which incidently also provides the first significant evidence of pre-Islamic exchanges through the Sahara; see in particular Sonja Magnavita, "Initial Encounters: Seeking Traces of Ancient Trade Connections between West Africa and the Wider World," *Afriques* 04 (2013), http://afriques.revues.org/1145. Informed by the ethnographic literature on West Africa, D. Gronenborn's article in German, "Zur Repräsentation von Eliten im Grabbrauch: Probleme und Aussagemöglichkeiten Historicher und Ethnographischer Quellen aus Westafrika," in Markus Egg and Dieter Quast (eds.), *Aufstieg und Untergang* (Mainz: Verlag des Römisch-Germanischen Zentralmuseums, 2009), pp. 217–245, constitutes a remarkable theoretical explication of sumptuary funerary practices and grave goods as instruments and signs of social distinction.

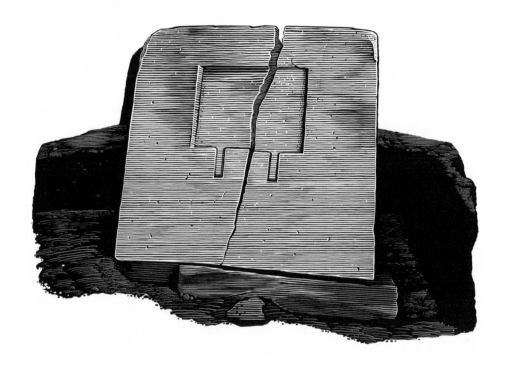

CHAPTER 12

Aksum, the City
That Made Kings

Northern Ethiopia, around the Twelfth Century

In 1906, a German archaeological mission discovered an ancient throne-base at Aksum, the antique Christian city of northern Ethiopia. Dozens of them are known in the current city, but their precise function remains mysterious; the designation "throne-base," moreover, is totally conventional: no throne capable of being properly fit into the notches on the supposed bases has ever been found. One side of this block bears two inscriptions (we will refer to them as I and II) and a fragment of a third, of which only a single word remains (III). A fourth inscription (IV) on another stone lying nearby must have originally belonged to the same monument. The stones are still in the same spot today, but exposure to humans and weather has made deciphering their inscriptions practically impossible.

The inscriptions are in Ethiopic syllabic script; their text is in Ge'ez, the language of the Ethiopian Church from antiquity to the present. One would generally expect these four texts to be contemporaneous; but that doesn't have to be the case. The writing of inscriptions III and IV is slightly different from the others (no vowel is marked), their engraving is regular, and the text uses a specific vocabulary. All this makes it quite possible that they belonged to an earlier, certainly ancient, iteration of the "throne." Inscriptions I and II, attributed to the "Post-Aksumite" Period—another conventional term denoting a High Middle Ages of which we know very little—would therefore have been engraved on a support that had been reemployed for something different from its original use, and in any case was already damaged. There is a reuse here that should be carefully studied in light of the inscribed texts.

Inscriptions I and II are incomplete and difficult to interpret, but even so we can extract some information from them. They begin with an identical formula: "In the name of the Father, Son and Holy Spirit." The author, therefore, is Christian; he is called Daniel (Danə'el in Ge'ez), son of Debre Ferem. In inscription I, he tells how he subdued the local potentate, a certain Karuray, from whom he plundered, unless he took them from someone else—the sentence is not entirely clear—10,000 cows and 130 bulls, before raiding the lands of his other enemies. In the second, he glories in having defended Aksum against the people of Welqayit, from whom he obtained colts and steers. These two texts, which express different intentions—one celebrating the legitimacy born of conquest, the other praising the defender of the conquered land—seem to be evidence of two political moments; here we see two different and successive inscriptions demanded by one and the same author.

Because Debre Ferem could be the name of a community of monks, it has been assumed that Daniel's inscriptions were less a celebration of his biological filiation than of a spiritual one with his monastery of origin; he was therefore a sort of warrior monk. It has also been assumed that his capital was in a locality called Kubar mentioned in the ninth and tenth centuries by a few Arabic sources. All this is quite possible, but is of limited relevance since we don't know where Kubar was located or what power structure prevailed between the collapse of Aksumite kingdom and the abandonment of Aksum in the seventh century, and the reappearance in the sources of a Christian dynasty in the eleventh. There remains the matter of the title Daniel gave himself, incidentally the same borne by the potentate subdued by him: *hatsani* (Ge'ez *haṣani*). One recognizes here the title borne by Lalibela (↦23), an Ethiopian sovereign at the dawn of the thirteenth century, which, lacking a better case, has been used to argue for a contemporaneous dating. Also related to the same word are the titles *hatsé* and *atsé* (Ge'ez *ḥaśe, aṣe*) or *qât* (Arabic *qāṭ*) employed by the Christian and Muslim rulers of Ethiopia, respectively, from the fourteenth century, while Arab authors used hadâni (*ḥadāni*) or hâtî (*ḥāṭī*) to designate the Christian sovereign. But that *hatsani* was an ancestral term designating royalty is perhaps not enough to convince us that Daniel is the ancestor of a royal line. Is it even certain that he was king in the sense that this term would cover later?

Thus, on a modest stone in an ancient capital that has since become a town of straw huts, Daniel left two victory inscriptions to posterity. But if it is difficult to know their meaning and historical context for want of other contemporaneous documents, all the consequences of the very existence of these inscriptions have not, as it happens, been drawn out. For the documentary exception that they represent for these obscure centuries implies not only that no one else, including the defeated adversary—who, nonetheless, lived among the ruins where droves of inscribed monuments were still visible—left such traces; but also, and vice versa, that Daniel didn't leave any such traces anywhere other than at Aksum. In short, there were compelling reasons for this conqueror or some cleric from his entourage, steeped in a culture of power that valorized writing as proof that an act was authentic, to inscribe the memory of his raids on a block of stone reused for the purpose. It stood alongside others (twenty in this same locality), which recounted, in Ge'ez or Greek, the acts of the Aksumite sovereigns from the fourth to the sixth century, and, even more ancient, those of the "pre-Aksumite" monarchs almost a thousand years earlier. This was thus the third time in history—and it would not be the last—that Aksum made kings. In sum, Daniel's visit to the city provided him with the occasion to participate in a tradition whose antecedents were before his very eyes; a tradition that entailed at the same time proclaiming his victorious acts, safeguarding their memory in writing, and installing a monument to be their frame. More than his name, which tells us nothing, or his laconic title, it was the will to inscribe his acts in the stone of Aksum, an open-air archive, that reveals Daniel's royal status or aspiration.

BIBLIOGRAPHICAL NOTE

Detailed archaeological reports of excavations made in Aksum have been published in the journals *Annales d'Éthiopie* (mostly in French) and *Rassegna di Studi Etiopici* (mostly in Italian). For comprehensive monographs, I recommend Stuart Munro-Hay, *Aksum: An African Civilization of Late Antiquity* (Edinburgh: Edinburgh University Press, 1991); and David Philippson, *Archaeology at Aksum, Ethiopia, 1993–7* (London: British Institute in Eastern Africa, 2000). A very good overview is provided by D. Phillipson, *Ancient Ethiopia* (London: British Museum Press, 1998), chap. 3. For a more recent and wider synthesis by the same author, see his *Foundations of an African Civilization: Aksum and the Northern Horn, 1000 BC–AD 1300* (Oxford: James Currey, 2012). The Deutsche Aksum-Expedition discovered and copied Daniel's inscriptions in 1906; their results were published by Enno Littmann, *Deutsche Aksum-Expedition*, 4 vols. (Berlin: G. Reimer, 1913). The facsimile, transcription, and German translation appear on pp. 42–48 of vol. 4: *Sabäische, Griechische und Altabessinische Inschriften*, nos. 12 to 14. (D. Philippson, *The Monuments of Aksum: An Illustrated Account* [Addis Ababa: Addis Ababa University Press, 1997], is a very useful English digest of the German Deutsche Aksum-Expedition's very rare four volumes.) A new edition of the inscriptions, but without translation, has been made by Étienne Bernand, Abraham J. Drewes, and Roger Schneider, *Recueil des inscriptions de l'Éthiopie des périodes pré-axoumite et axoumite, t. 1—Les Documents* (Paris: De Boccard, 1991), nos. 193 and 194. My numeration follows that of the latter edition, with the exception of inscription IV, which is edited under the number 194. The photographic plates, despite being almost unreadable, appear in volume 2 of the same work. Stuart Munro-Hay and Denis Nosnitsin's entry for "Danəʾel," in Siegbert Uhlig (ed.), *Encyclopaedia Aethiopica* (Wiesbaden: Harrassowitz, 2005), vol. 2, offers a useful assessment of the state of the art and bibliography. Bertrand Hirsch and I have written an article on the royal uses of Aksum from the Middle Ages to the modern era: "Aksum après Aksum. Royauté, archéologie et herméneutique chrétienne de Ménélik II (r. 1865–1913) à Zärʾa Yaʿqob (r. 1434–1468)," *Annales d'Éthiopie* 17 (2001): 57–107.

CHAPTER 13

The Treasures
of Debre Damo

Northern Ethiopia, until the Twelfth Century

Debre Damo will not be the object of an attentive inspection anytime soon. Not only are women forbidden in the monastery; we also have to climb twenty meters by rope just to reach the summit of the *amba*, the flat-topped mountain where we find two permanent churches and clusters of huts for the monks. Furthermore, as is the case everywhere in Ethiopia, the testy Christian clergy and the rural communities attached to their churches are resistant to all investigation, which they view as intrusive. We must wait patiently to be shown a hidden part of the church or a manuscript, and some, not having this patience—which is, moreover, rarely sufficient—have on occasion resorted to unsavory maneuvers to penetrate the sanctuaries and lay their hands on the sacred objects.

The history of Debre Damo is as obscure as the apocryphal traditions of its origins are numerous. At most, we know from the acts of Ethiopian saints and the accounts of European travelers that a continuous monastic tradition existed here from at least the thirteenth century. And we assume, based on the presence of architectural elements (notably stone columns and capitals) reused in the principal church that it was preceded by a building from the ancient Aksumite (↦12) period. (The church is dedicated to Za-Mikael Aregawi, one of the country's evangelist saints, who first climbed the mountain thanks to a serpent who let himself be used as a rope.) As for when it was built, whatever restoration it may have undergone thereafter, the chronological criteria are so uncertain that specialists oscillate between the seventh and the sixteenth century, with some of them appearing to agree to place it around the tenth.

Antonio Mordini, head of the colonial ethnographic service of Italian Africa, had the chance to visit Debre Damo several times during his country's brief occupation of Ethiopia (1936–1941), a political context that, one can hazard, contributed to reducing potential resistance from the local people. Oral tradition among the "Ethiopianist" community maintains that the same Mordini, an Italian military intelligence officer during the war, found refuge at Debre Damo, which he knew well, while being pursued by a British counterpart. Whatever the case may be, we owe the principal observations of the site's natural history and archaeology to him. The least we can say is that these observations revealed to the outside world the existence of exceptional treasures right at the moment they were about to be—or even worse, had just been—pillaged. Some of the ancient textiles found at Debre Damo were then sold on the illicit antiquities market at Cairo. Mordini discovered others in 1939 in the sacristy of the church as well as in a completely forgotten cache containing thousands of parchment leaves; there were pieces of Islamic fabric, some bearing Arabic inscriptions embroidered in silk, datable to the ninth to eleventh century. After the rains washed away the soil on the *amba*, monks frequently found gold or silver Arabic coins, which the community's treasurer hurried to melt down. Mordini discovered numerous others during a small excavation he undertook in the community's former cemetery: there were dirhams* and dinars* struck with the names of Umayyad and Abbasid caliphs (seventh to ninth century).

Early in 1940, a monk of Debre Damo stumbled upon a new treasure among the shreds of a small, gold-plated wooden coffer hidden in the crevice of a wall covered with earth in a cave located near the smaller of the site's churches. The prior of the monastery, scarcely more alert than his treasurer to the historical value of such a find, took it to a goldsmith in Asmara, the administrative capital of Italian Eritrea. The goldsmith bought it, only to sell it in turn to an "informed" customer who told Mordini about it. That is how the latter was able to examine, before it disappeared on the collectors' market, a batch of 103 gold coins bearing the names of Kadphises II, Kanishka I, Huvishka, and Vasudeva I. These were not Ethiopian kings, but sovereigns of the Kushans, a people of Greco-Buddhist culture, who ruled over an empire that covered large swaths of present-day India, Pakistan, and Afghanistan from the second to the beginning of the third century of our era.

Coin hoards have a paradoxical interest for the historian: they often come from the peripheries of the economic zone under consideration and not from its center (Roman coins more often come from Great Britain, Bulgaria, or India than from Italy). They testify less to the motivations behind economic exchange than to the motivations, which can be completely irrational, behind hoarding money; the occurrence they mark was not economic activity at its peak but its decline or its cessation. Thus they are less an illustration of the rule, the way things ordinarily functioned, than the exception, the contingent, and their meaning is that much more difficult to discern. But beyond the difficulty, in the present case, of interpreting the presence of Kushan or Arabic coins at Debre Damo, the conditions of their discovery have erased, as is often the case (one thinks of the weekend pillagers in the countryside of developed countries), most of the information that would have been useful to us. From the moment the find constituted a "hoard," its material value (the weight of its metal) and its face value (for the collector or even the researcher) overtook its contextual value. We would have loved to inspect the coins' hiding place and the cave, to examine and analyze what remained of the coffer, to radiocarbon-date the wood, to collect the ceramic fragments that, Mordini tells us, were associated with it. We would have loved to view the Kushan coins that Mordini saw and catalog them, which was never done. We would have loved to visit the storeroom containing the fabrics and the manuscripts; to visit it when it had just been opened, before its treasures were dispersed to experts and philologists—who could speak only about what had come to them. We would have liked to know the precise inventory of the monastery's manuscripts, but it appears that they were destroyed in a fire in 1996. We would have liked to possess the layout of the excavations that uncovered the Arabic coins, to know what other remains (graves, ceramics, building elements, jewelry, etc.) were associated with them, what was the extent of the zone of the finds. We would have liked to survey the *amba*, to carry out archaeological testpits there, visit its cavities freely, and take samples for analysis.

Lacking all this information, and until more emerges, we are condemned to keep reexamining the meager observations that have come down to us, the scattered and incomplete pieces of a puzzle whose contours remain obscure. At the very least, the questions that can be asked help define some of the problems brought up by the site's history: why, out of so much evidence for diverse periods present on this mountain, is so little of it attributable to the period from the fourth to the seventh century, which saw the hegemony of the kingdom of Aksum not only over the lands of northern Ethiopia and Eritrea but also over the coastal regions of both sides of the Red Sea? And what are we to make of the presence of Islamic coins and luxury goods in a country where Christianity had been present since the fourth century? Do they argue in favor of prolonged and regular contacts between the community of Debre Damo and the Coptic patriarchate of Egypt (which found itself under Islamic rule from the seventh century on), or are they evidence of a Muslim community in the vicinity of the monastery?

But most of all: why had so many treasures—Mordini's, and how many others whose discovery did not have a Mordini for a witness—been buried at Debre Damo? To which we hasten to respond that if so many treasures have been *found* in this place, it's because just as many were *forgotten* as soon as they had been dropped or hidden there. The results of memory gaps, these discoveries undoubtedly illustrate Debre Damo's checkered history over the course of the first millennium of our era, much more than the long-distance relationships (first with the Indo-Iranian world, then with the Islamic) about which we know so very little. Are not these successive discontinuities, which have buried treasures all over Debre Damo, better testimony to the status of this high place than the treasures themselves?

BIBLIOGRAPHICAL NOTE

The pages that David Phillipson, *Ancient Churches of Ethiopia* (New Haven, CT: Yale University Press, 2009), pp. 51–64, devotes to Debre Damo are a good introduction to the subject. The first collection of archaeological data at the site was undertaken by the Deutsche Aksum-Expedition and was published by Enno Littmann, *Deutsche Aksum-Expedition* (Berlin: G. Reimer, 1913), 2:168–194. A second collection, more systematic and implemented during a restoration campaign on the principal church there in 1948, was carried out by Derek Matthews. Most of the data collected independently by Mordini and Matthews have been conveniently brought together as a monograph: D. Matthews and A. Mordini, "The Monastery of Debra Damo, Ethiopia," *Archaeologia* 97 (1959): 1–58 and 15 plates. The information about the discovery of the Kushan coins comes from Antonio Mordini's Italian article "Gli aurei kushāna del convento di Dabra Dāmmò," *Atti del Convegno Internazionale di Studi Etiopici (2–4 avril 1959)* (Rome: Accademia Nazionale des Lincei, 1960), pp. 249–254. Mordini describes some of the fabrics in "Un tissu musulman du Moyen Âge provenant du couvent de Dabra Dāmmò (Tigrai, Éthiopie)," *Annales d'Éthiopie* 2 (1957): 75–79. The parchment has been briefly studied by Carlo Conti Rossini, "Pergamene di Debra Dammó," *Rivista degli Studi Orientali* 19 (1940): 45–57.

CHAPTER 14

One Map,
Two Geographies

Horn of Africa, before the Middle of the Twelfth Century

First clime, fifth section. Here is a page of the atlas of al-Idrîsî, completed in the late 1150s. It comes from a manuscript—a copy, the original is lost—today in the Bibliothèque nationale de France in Paris. In the Arabic cartographic tradition, which both drew on and transmitted the cartography of the second-century Greek astronomer and geographer Ptolemy, the spherical world was projected onto a plane, which was then divided into grids. The longitudinal bands were called "climes"; the latitudinal bands, "sections." The intersection of the fifth section with the first clime brings us to the edge of the known world. The equator serves as the southern limit, which, as is often the case with medieval Arabic maps, features on the top of the page. The river that starts beyond the line and runs to the north (i.e., toward the bottom of the page) is a tributary of the Nile. To the left we can make out the bottleneck of the Red Sea that forms the Bab al-Mandab Strait, and, to the south, the Indian Ocean. The points in the shape of rosebuds are localities. We should be on familiar ground here: this map comprises what al-Idrîsî knew about the region that for us constitutes the northeast corner of Africa.

And yet we recognize almost nothing. Has human geography changed so much that only the names Allâqî, a mountain in southeastern Egypt known for its gold mines; the Beja, a pastoral people of Sudan and Eritrea; and Abyssinia still mean anything to us? Or is the information on this map simply fantastical? It is true that al-Idrîsî, a cartographer of Andalusian and Maghrebian ancestry in the service of a Latin Christian sovereign, Roger II, Norman king of Sicily, and who had certainly never traveled farther than Spain, Morocco, or, perhaps, Provence and Italy, was not necessarily well informed about these remote regions. It has often been noted, with regard to other regions, that he relied on sources that were one or two hundred years old; it has even been thought that some of the mangled toponyms on his maps were borrowed from Ptolemy. Be that as it may, provided that we are in a position to date these borrowings, we are curious to know to which reality the names on the map and in "the Book of Roger" (*Kitāb Rujār*), which is in a way its libretto, corresponded. Two zones are particularly interesting: first, the region between the river and the mountain, where the names of several localities appear; and second, the coastal fringe of the Gulf of Aden with its string of ports. Obviously, if we succeed in finding the key to this map, there would be sufficient material to bring a little clarity to this region (basically what we today call the Horn of Africa) that, in this period (let's say from the eleventh to the middle of the twelfth century), is more or less completely obscured from us.

But it's rare, as far as historical documents are concerned, for there to be a unique key, or even some intellectual tool that is truly able to act as a key. Failing that, let's attempt to force the lock. On the right side of the page, two parallel sets of mountains define three regions arranged from north (bottom) to south (top), which correspond to the eastern Egyptian desert, the plain from Sudan to Eritrea, and finally "Abyssinia," a vague term. However, the presence of a river delineating the northern horizon of the latter region and flowing to the west leaves little doubt that we are on the high central plateau of Ethiopia, precisely inclined toward the west and serving as catch basin to the Nile. We should perhaps not draw too much attention to the lake and deserts mentioned beyond the equator, fictive evocations. Moreover, no locality is identified on the left bank of the river that, given the map's apparent logic, is certainly not the Sudanese Nile or the Blue Nile, but more likely an evocation of the upper Takkazé, a powerful river whose waters carved the continent's deepest canyon and which continues into Sudan where it joins the Atbarah River, a tributary of the Nile. Had we been dropped blind into this part of al-Idrîsî's map, we would thus find ourselves in the Tigray Region of Ethiopia and neighboring districts to the south and east. But we don't know any more than that. It's a shame, for it should be acknowledged that the information transmitted by the geographer from Palermo originated during the period of Ethiopia's dark centuries.

Of the string of ports that spread from Zâligh in the direction of the ocean, not one is named (on the map) or described (in the libretto) in such a way as to evoke for us a precise place. However, we are at least following the coast of present-day Somaliland, the northern part of the Horn, where each rosebud, equidistant between the ones preceding and following it, seems to evoke the stopovers of a maritime itinerary. This means that al-Idrîsî's informant, unlike whoever informed him about the highland, would have been a sailor. But are we really where we think we are? In place of Zâligh, the commentators wanted to read Zeyla, which was not yet the great commercial port it would be between the thirteenth and the nineteenth century, and which today is a sleepy shantytown at the end of the Gulf of Aden. A convenient identification if we wish to focus only on the two common letters in the names of these cities and their identical position on the bottleneck of Bab el-Mandeb.

Even so, there is still something not quite right: in the text that accompanies the map, the Zâligh of al-Idrîsî is sometimes clearly situated on the edge of the Red Sea, in the land of the Beja, and from this "maritime city of Abyssinia" it was a two weeks' journey to the uplands, which is strictly impossible from present-day Zeyla. In order to resolve these contradictions, Zâligh must be split in two and the information that has been associated with it disassembled. We are thus dealing with two localities, close enough in name and distance for the geographer to have confused them. The first is our Zeyla, the initial stopover on the voyage into the Indian Ocean in the direction of the equator. The other belongs to the geography of the Red Sea and the spaces that unfold from Egypt to Abyssinia; perhaps it's Dahlak, an archipelago off the Eritrean coast, or else some littoral harbor from where one could then reach the Ethiopian interior, that is, the Abyssinian highland.

Two distinct geographies meet on this map: one is the area around the Red Sea, a sort of distant annex of the Mediterranean; the other, past the Bab el-Mandeb bottleneck, is another world entirely. When these two geographies were mentally stitched together, two ports on the borders of their respective worlds found themselves conflated in the seam.

BIBLIOGRAPHICAL NOTE

The pages of the atlas decorate the chapters of the work called "the Book of Roger" in the subsequent Arabic literature, but initially titled *Nuzhat al-muštāq fī iḫtirāq al-āfāq* (A diversion for the man longing to travel to far-off places) in Arabic; this manuscript, copied around 1300, is in the Bibliothèque nationale de France in Paris under the shelf number Ms Arabe 2221. It has been translated into French by Pierre-Amédée Jaubert, *Géographie d'Édrisi*, 2 vols. (Paris: Imprimerie royale, 1836–1840). His translation of the sections of the text relating to the western part of the map (Africa and Europe) have recently been revised by Annliese Nef, in Henri Bresc and A. Nef (eds.), *Idrîsî, la première géographie de l'Occident* (Paris: Garnier- Flammarion, 1999). The critical edition of the Arabic text is al-Idrīsī, *Opus geographicum*, 9 fasc. (Leiden, 1970–1984); this is the "Naples" edition, so-called because it was produced by learned scholars at the Istituto universitario orientale di Napoli. The map is available on CD-ROM: *La géographie d'Idrîsî. Un atlas du monde au XIIe siècle* (Paris: Bibliothèque nationale de France, 2000). The most recent biographical treatment of al-Idrîsî is A. Nef, "Al-Idrīsī: un complément d'enquête biographique," in Henri Bresc and Emmanuelle Tixier du Mesnil (eds.), *Géographes et voyageurs au Moyen Âge* (Nanterre: Presses Universitaires de Paris Ouest, 2010), pp. 53–66. For the canonical interpretation of al-Idrîsî's information on the Horn of Africa, see Carlo Conti Rossini, *Storia d'Etiopia* (Bergame: Istituto italiano d'arte grafiche, 1928), pp. 324–326. Regarding Zeyla, see the article by Bertrand Hirsch and myself, "Le port de Zeyla et son arrière-pays au Moyen Âge. Investigations archéologiques et retour aux sources écrites," in F.-X. Fauvelle-Aymar and B. Hirsch (eds.), *Espaces musulmans de la Corne de l'Afrique au Moyen Âge* (Paris: De Boccard, 2011), pp. 27–74.

CHAPTER 15

The Case of the Concubine

*Aydhâb, Berbera, Present-Day Coastal Sudan
and Somaliland, December 1144*

Late in 1144, an embarrassing affair rocked the port of Aydhâb. On 19 December, the twenty-first day of the month of Tevet of the Hebrew calendar, a Jewish merchant back from India, Abû Saîd Ibn Jamâhir, appealed to the Muslim chief of police to demand justice. He said he had been falsely accused by a certain Sâfî, the powerful representative of the head of the *yeshiva*, the Jewish high council, in Cairo. Despite his influence, Sâfî was juridically a slave, perhaps of Ethiopian origin (his name, Ṣâfî, means both "the sincere" in Arabic and "the scribe" in Ge'ez). Ibn Jamâhir produced witnesses: his Muslim associates. The chief of police moved swiftly to defuse the situation; he had Sâfî publicly flogged, threw him in prison, and released him only after the slave paid him in cash.

There were, however, other Jewish merchants in the city, who had a different take on the matter. They neither affirmed nor denied Sâfî's accusations; they merely highlighted Ibn Jamâhir's eagerness to quash them. They certainly knew details about the truth behind the accusation, but they were satisfied with redacting a memorandum on the events in Aydhâb so that the case could be judged in Cairo before the Jewish tribunal. It is this document that comes down to us. It is written in Arabic using Hebrew characters. It is not signed, evidence that it was never produced in court, perhaps because a settlement had been reached that, if it could not redress the harm done to Sâfî, at least cleared him of defamation. Like every written document bearing the name of God—and every document containing a salutation or oath bore the name of God—it could not be destroyed. It was kept, therefore, along with tens of thousands of others, in a room known as the *geniza* in the synagogue of the "Palestinian" Jews (as opposed to the Jews of Iraq or Persia, the "Babylonian" Jews) of Cairo. They were rediscovered only in 1890, when the old synagogue was razed so that a new one could be built. The documents were bought by collectors and libraries and today are dispersed among Cambridge, Oxford, New York, Philadelphia, Budapest, and other places. Private and official correspondence, judicial acts, contracts, accounts, and other business documents open a window not only on Jewish society, but on medieval Mediterranean society more broadly (for the most part, the documents date between the eleventh and thirteenth centuries), particularly an area we would know very little about without them—trade with India. The Jews played a prominent role in this trade. The papers of the *geniza* show us the buying and selling of textiles, dyes, medicinal plants, spices, perfumes, scented resins, copper, and tin. Their commercial universe stretched from the western shores of the Mediterranean to the southwestern coast of India; the central pivot was Cairo.

Whatever compromise had brought an end to the affair, a crime had been committed that was likely going to go unpunished: precisely the one Sâfî denounced. It was this accusation Ibn Jamâhir sought to counter by playing the outraged victim. What was the core of the accusation? The authors of the petition took care to put it directly in the accuser's mouth: "You had a slave girl, made her pregnant, and when she bore you a boy, you abandoned her together with her boy in Berbera." It is safe to assume the slave was Indian, and that the unfortunate girl was abandoned during a stopover between India and Aden, or Aden and the Red Sea. She had, for her part, offered the exotic pleasures of foreign travel to a merchant far from home. If she was left behind, whether by ruse or by force, on the coast of Somaliland—an unsavory back alley where men went to acquire cat skins, with little hope of turning a profit on the trinkets that were traded there—it was because Ibn Jamâhir did not want her disrupting his domestic universe at Aydhâb. Not that Cairo wasn't already far enough away: a two weeks' journey across the desert to the Nile at Aswan or Edfu, then more than a month downriver by felucca. But Aydhâb was a threshold between the East and the Mediterranean. And Ibn Jamâhir returned home.

We don't know what had irritated the Jewish merchants of Aydhâb: was it that Ibn Jamâhir had kept a concubine when the rabbinic law forbade such relationships; that he had left her on a beach; that he had abandoned a newborn baby, his own son; that he had unjustly accused his denouncer?

But it is understandable that the affair had caused a sensation. If it was barely possible to hide a crime carried out in secret in a harbor in Somaliland—in other words, at the ends of the earth—it was because Aydhâb was a noisy crossroads where merchants of all religions, men from East and West, mariners and businessmen, not to mention the usual port crowd, came into contact. Aydhâb was also where the *kârim*, the annual maritime convoy between India and Cairo, landed. And it was through Aydhâb that North African and West African Muslims passed on their way to the Islamic holy sites. The writings of one such pilgrim, Ibn Jubayr, have come down to us: "It is one of the most frequented ports of the world," he writes of Aydhâb, "because of the ships of India and the Yemen that sail to and from it, as well as the pilgrim ships that come and go." The man from whom our pilgrim rented his lodgings for his three-week stay was an Abyssinian; few people owned houses or boats in the city. Everything was imported, including the water. The local population, the Beja, "closer to wild beasts than they are to men," dove for pearls, but mostly made their living by exploiting pilgrims. They charged exorbitant rates for passage to Arabia and reserved the right to load the pilgrims, "like chickens crammed in a coop," into their *jalba*, skiffs made from palm planks sewn together with cord made from coconut fiber. In an environment where the boats often ran aground on reefs in shark-infested waters, their owners were eager to make a single crossing profitable. Often the boats wound up on even less hospitable shores—if that's possible—leaving their pilgrim passengers at the mercy of the austere environment and unscrupulous bandits. "Not seldom pilgrims will stray on foot through the wayless desert and, being lost, die of thirst," wrote Ibn Jubayr. "Those who survive and reach Aydhâb are like men quickened from the shroud. While we were there we saw some who had come in this manner, and in their ghastly shape and changed form was 'a portent for those observed carefully' [Koran 15:75]." Our author's opinion of the region? "This is the country of Islam most deserving a *hisbah* [flagellation], and the scourge employed should be the sword."

From the very beginning of Islam, Aydhâb allowed for the exportation of gold and slaves from its hinterlands. From the eleventh to the thirteenth century, it was, if not the hub between Africa and India—a role reserved for Aden, where the firms and the entrepôts were located—at least the hub where goods passed from ships to caravans, where customs and the obligatory contribution to the Beja were paid. Today the site of the city is largely forgotten; it lies in the Hala'ib Triangle, a disputed zone between Egypt and Sudan. The few scholars who have passed through it over the last century have seen the ruins of small stone houses and cisterns; ground covered with pieces of Chinese porcelains; and, especially, thousands of Muslim rectangular tombs made from large blocks of coral limestone—the final resting places of pilgrims who never made it to Mecca or never came back home. There is still a small police station.

BIBLIOGRAPHICAL NOTE

The study of the exceptional material that is the Cairo *geniza* was the life's work of Shelomoh Dov Goitein, to whom we owe the magisterial *A Mediterranean Society: The Jewish Communities of the Arab World As Portrayed in the Documents of the Cairo Geniza*, 6 vols. (Berkeley: University of California Press, 1967–1999); two of the volumes were published posthumously. The memorandum detailing the case of the concubine is treated in the same author's *Letters of Medieval Jewish Traders* (Princeton, NJ: Princeton University Press, 1973), no. 79 (pp. 335–338); I have taken all details concerning the case from this book, with the exception of the hypothesis on Sâfî's Ethiopian origins. Tim Power's excellent article "The Origin and Development of the Sudanese Ports (Aydhâb, Bâdi', Sawâkin) in the Early Islamic Period," *Chroniques Yéménites* 15 (2008): 92–110, covers the early history of the ports on Sudan's Red Sea coast, while Jean-Claude Garcin, "Transport des épices et espace égyptien entre le XIe et le XVe siècle," in *Actes des Congrès de la Société des historiens médiévistes de l'enseignement supérieur public, 7e congrès* (Rennes, 1976), pp. 305–314, studies Aydhâb's role in medieval Egyptian trade. Among the reports of people who have visited Aydhâb, consult G. W. Murray, "Aidhâb," *Geographical Journal* 68 (1926): 235–240; and, more recently, David Peacock and Andrew Peacock, "The Enigma of 'Aydhâb: A Medieval Islamic Port on the Red Sea," *International Journal of Nautical Archaeology* 37 (2008): 32–48. The latter offers a brisk summary of the documentation and suggests locating Aydhâb's harbor twenty kilometers southeast of the main site. But we should consider this a temporary, revisable hypothesis, as the observations made from satellite images have not received full confirmation on the ground. Regarding the *kârim*, see S. D. Goitein, "New Light on the Beginnings of the

Kārim Merchants," *Journal of the Economic and Social History of the Orient* 1 (1958): 175–184. But it is Éric Valet's study, *L'Arabie marchande. État et commerce sous les sultans rasūlides du Yémen (626–858 / 1229–1454)* (Paris: Publications de la Sorbonne, 2010), pp. 471–539, that outlines the state of the art on this matter. Ibn Jubayr visited Aydhâb in 1183. For an English translation of his travel accounts, see R.J.C. Broadhurst, *The Travels of Ibn Jubayr: Being the Chronicle of a Mediaeval Spanish Moor Concerning His Journey to the Egypt of Saladin, the Holy Cities of Arabia, Baghdad the City of the Caliphs, the Latin Kingdom of Jerusalem, and the Norman Kingdom of Sicily* (London: Jonathan Cape, 1952). The excerpts cited here are from pp. 63–66.

CHAPTER 16

Sijilmâsa, Crossroads at the Ends of the Earth

*Southeastern Morocco, from the Twelfth
to the Fourteenth Century*

Judah ben Joseph ha-Kohen was the head of the Jewish merchants in Cairo. In 1145, we find him in a very bad state: a pirate attack left him stranded in Bharuch (or Broach) in Gujarat, in northwestern India. We don't know how he escaped the pirates' clutches, but he had lost his cargo and was, inevitably, penniless. A letter he received must have been a comfort to him: God would compensate his losses. If he needed gold, his correspondent wrote to him, Judah could borrow it from a close confidant in a nearby city. Perhaps he would be glad to know that his share of the proceeds from the sale of a shipment of silk had been used to buy pepper. And, not least of all, he was invited to make haste for Mangalore, where a boat waited to take him to Aden. The author of these reassuring words was a certain Mahrûz ben Jacob, a shipowner. It is not incidental to clarify that Judah was the husband of Mahrûz's sister. In Jewish families involved in long-distance trade, judicious marriage alliances could offer both assistance and consular services. Judah ben Joseph ha-Kohen's own sister was married to the representative of the Jewish merchants in Aden. As for his surname, "the Sijilmasian" (*Sijilmāsī*), it probably indicates that Judah was born in Morocco, undoubtedly because his father had contracted such an alliance for himself, although in the opposite direction from his son's, in the extreme west of Africa. Sijilmâsa, Aden, Mangalore, these were the furthest reaches of the commercial universe of contemporaneous Jewish merchants.

Sijilmâsa: did this city located in a palm grove in southeastern Morocco really deserve to be mentioned in the same breath with the most famous ports and entrepôts of the time? A doubt could worm its way in if Ibn Battûta, the most famous Arab traveler of the Middle Ages, hadn't implied as much about Sijilmâsa, which he visited in 1351. Hosted by one of the city's jurists, a certain Abû Muhammad al-Bushrî, Ibn Battûta pointed out that he had met his host's brother in China. And he exclaimed somewhat disingenuously, "How far apart they are!" Never mind that Ibn Battûta had probably never traveled into the interior of China; the encounter is said to have taken place at Qanjanfû, a city located on the coastal plain not far from Canton. The brother, who had arrived in India as a youth, with an uncle, had become a rich, respectable man in this city, where he conducted business among a colony of Muslim merchants and clerics; he was all the more honorable in the eyes of the famous traveler in that he offered him four slaves—two men and two women. We don't know whether the brothers were business partners, but the logic of it reinforces the probability: one brother, in Morocco, was well positioned for the gold trade; the other, in China, for the silk trade.

If the large commercial firms, Jewish or Muslim, placed a family member in Sijilmâsa, it was certainly because it seemed worthwhile. From the end of the ninth century, when the ancient trail joining the Niger River with Upper Egypt was abandoned owing to lack of security, to the end of the fourteenth century, when other routes took over from it in central Sahara, Sijilmâsa was the staging ground for most of the caravans that set out on the great crossing: fifty days "through solitude and deserts," eighteen hundred kilometers as the crow flies to go from the pre-Saharan steppes to the sub-Saharan Sahel. And it was to Sijilmâsa that they returned with their loads of gold and their long lines of slaves. In the days of al-Masûdî and Ibn Hawqal, in the tenth century, coins were struck there from gold brought from the "Land of the Blacks," and Sijilmâsa contributed almost half of the taxes levied by the Fatimid sovereigns over the whole of the Maghreb.

Nothing is known about the origin of this route, a development that perhaps began around the middle of the eighth century. But we can guess what was needed for it to take shape: a willingness to take risks, a certain stubbornness, an entrepreneurial spirit, a collective organization, and a cohesive community. Slowly but surely, one of the Zanâta nomads' seasonal pasturages was transformed into a trading post—indeed, an international trading post, endowed with all the facilities and social structures necessary for the trans-Saharan trade. The requisite skills for effecting this transformation were honed among society's social marginals: dissident Muslims and Jews. We thus see the introduction, in the ninth and tenth centuries, of an articulated system in which Kharijite Berbers organized trade between Sijilmâsa and the Sahel, while the Jews took over between Sijilmâsa and the Mediterranean. This ecumenical synergy would not survive the advance of Sunni orthodoxy from the eleventh century or the episodes of religious fanaticism in the following centuries (↦32).

Since profit is inevitably followed by censure or taxation, the rise of this commercial crossroads couldn't help but arouse envy. In the middle of the eleventh century, the Almoravids, zealous followers of a religious brotherhood turned dynasty, captured Sijilmâsa and installed an emir there. A century later, the Almohads—bloody, puritanical reformers who denounced their predecessors' tepidity—did the same. In an epoch that saw Muslims massacred on the pretext of heterodoxy or moral deviance, the Jews suffered the flames of persecution. From Cairo, Shlomo ha-Kohen sent a letter to his father, the aforementioned Judah, whom it reached in Aden in 1148, detailing—based on the testimony of survivors—the executions and forced conversions that accompanied the capture of Sijilmâsa two years earlier. Between the mid-thirteenth century and the mid-fifteenth, a third Berber dynasty, the Marinids, succeeded in unifying Morocco. In 1255, they captured Sijilmâsa before turning toward Marrakesh. The paradoxical situation of Sijilmâsa was that it was both a political outpost and a formidable cradle of riches; hence it was simultaneously a rear bastion and refuge of Moroccan powers, and the "bank" for every project of conquest that would eventually undermine those same powers.

It was certainly at the beginning of the thirteenth century that Sijilmâsa enjoyed its greatest prosperity. This is how Yâqût described it in 1220: "The city is crossed by an important river, on whose banks were planted gardens and palm trees as far as the eye could see." A river? It was a wadi, that is to say, sometimes it was a torrent carrying melted snows from the High Atlas to the Sahara; at other times it was nothing more than a dry riverbed. It was the Ziz, and, according to al-Masûdî, Sijilmâsa extended a half day's walk along its banks. Yâqût claimed that its people cultivated a unique grape and numerous species of dates. The women produced colorful wool fabrics that were always in high demand. He confirmed that "the inhabitants of this town are among the richest of men." One of Yâqût's contemporaries, al-Sarakhsî, paints a portrait for us of the Almohad governor of Sijilmâsa, grandson of the dynasty's first monarch, a ruler not given to the summary punishments imposed by his ancestors, but who at the same time was not afraid to harshly reprimand his subjects. He was a "good-looking man, highly experienced, and had an admirable command of the Arabic and Berber tongues." Al-Sarakhsî depicts him receiving the news that one of the kings of the "Blacks," namely, the sovereign of Ghâna, had forbidden small merchants from the north to ply their trade. He threw them in prison, perhaps after having established a tax for the right to trade in his kingdom. Our governor redacted a sententious letter, in which we suddenly find him acting the part of the defender of religious tolerance and free enterprise: "We [the kings] ought to have good relations, even if we are of different religions. . . . Rendering justice is one of a king's foremost obligations, a matter of good policy; injustice is the prerogative of vile and ignorant souls." By suggesting that what was being done to the merchants was unjust and, consequently, the action of a vile soul, he pleaded in favor of the free circulation of commercial agents, which would only be profitable to the population. The conclusion of the moral syllogism: "If we wanted to, we too [at Sijilmâsa] could imprison your subjects whom we find in our land. But we would never do it. It would not at all be dignified for us to condemn such actions only to then commit them ourselves."

Other witnesses to this benevolent period include the Maqqarî, five brothers of an old Arab commercial family who "made a partnership by which all had equal shares in what they possessed or might possess." In the modern Western world, this would be the surest path to quarrels or bankruptcy. But at that time, firms were subject to the least fallible of loyalties: that of family. Two of the brothers, Abû Bakr and Muhammad, established themselves in Tlemcen, in the extreme northwest of modern Algeria; two others, Abd al-Wâhid and Alî, departed for Oualata, in Mauritania, at the southern edge of the Sahara (↦26). They were the youngest, a necessary condition for taking local women and laying down roots. Abd al-Rahmân, the oldest, that is to say, the most experienced, settled in Sijilmâsa, which became the company's "headquarters." According to the chronicler, it was there that orders were given and information was centralized: "The Tilimsânî [i.e., the ones established in Tlemcen] would send to the Sahrâwî [i.e., the ones established on the other side of the Sahara] the goods which the latter would indicate to him, and the Sahrâwî would send to him skins, ivory, nuts (*jawz*), and gold. The Sijilmâsî was like the tongue of a balance, indicating to them the extent of rise or fall in the markets and writing to them about the affairs of merchants and countries. And so their wealth expanded and their status grew." Where the brothers chose to settle had nothing to do with chance: their network hugged the commercial route that linked the Sahel with the Maghreb and, from there, the Mediterranean world. Like the Kohen family's marriage alliances, the Maqqarî's sibling-based business reflects a strategy that aimed to extend the geographical range of the family network while at the same time ensuring that family links played the role of insurance against risk.

Once these six or seven prosperous centuries had passed, often punctuated by warriors and censors, the city of Sijilmâsa faded before the growing prominence of the villages of Tafilalt, an oasis of tamarisks and palms whose name had been rarely mentioned up to that time. The urban concentration that had allowed for intense economic activity and the accumulation of wealth came undone when they declined. The "world"-renowned urban center was then succeeded by what had without a doubt preceded it: a crop of small, fortified, villages built of rammed earth,* namely, ksour,* anonymous oasis dwellings on the Ziz wadi. Not far from one of them, Rissani, the ruins of Sijilmâsa are miraculously preserved. In the seventeenth century, marabouts, or holy men, walked the grounds and did not hesitate to declare themselves prophets or messiahs. At first, people gathered to receive their benediction; soon they would chase them away. From this holy place a new dynasty would emerge, one that reigns in Morocco to this day. The local tradition will point out to you the former city's mosque. Before the saints and the kings was the time of the true heroes, the merchants.

BIBLIOGRAPHICAL NOTE

The information on Jewish merchants in this chapter comes from Shelomoh Dov Goitein, *Letters of Medieval Jewish Traders* (Princeton, NJ: Princeton University Press, 1973), pp. 14 (and n. 12), 62ff., 203 (n. 6). The story of Ibn Battûta is found in Nehemia Levtzion and J.F.P. Hopkins (eds.), *Corpus of Early Arabic Sources for West African History* (Princeton, NJ: Markus Wiener, 2000), p. 282. The hypothesis of the impossibility of Ibn Battûta visiting China has been formulated several times; see the article by Bertrand Hirsch and myself, where we compare the voyage to China with the voyage to Mâli: "Voyage aux frontières du monde. Topologie, narration et jeux de miroir dans la *Rihla* de Ibn Battûta," *Afrique & Histoire* 1 (2003): 75–122. The expression "through solitude and deserts" takes us back to al-Yaqûbî, one of the first authors to describe this route, around 891; see Joseph Cuoq, *Recueil des sources arabes concernant l'Afrique occidentale du VIIIe au XVIe siècle* (Paris: Éditions du CNRS, 1985), p. 48. The citations from Masûdî, p. 61, Yâqût, p. 186, and al-Sarakhsî, pp. 178–179, are from the same work. The translation of al-Sarakhsî's has been modified according to that in Henri Pérès, "Relations entre le Tafilalet et le Soudan à travers le Sahara du XIIe au XIVe siècle," *Mélanges de géographie et d'orientalisme offerts à E.-F. Gautier* (Tours: Arrault et Cie, 1937), pp. 409–414. On the Jews of Sijilmâsa, see Nehemia Levtzion, "The Jews of Sijilmasa and the Saharan Trade," in Michel Abitbol (ed.), *Communautés juives des marges sahariennes du Maghreb* (Jerusalem: Institut Ben-Zvi, 1982), pp. 253–264; it is this article that evokes Shlomo's letter to his father. An excerpt from the letter is translated in Paul B. Fenton and David G. Littman (eds.), *Exile in the Maghreb: Jews under Islam, Sources and Documents* (Lanham, MD: Rowman & Littlefield, 2016), pp. 50–51; the author indicated that around two hundred of Sijilmâsa's Jewish inhabitants fled before the city was captured. They took refuge in the Draa valley of Morocco, but there had been no news from them since then. Among those who stayed or couldn't flee, 150 had been massacred after several months of being under orders to convert. The others converted, following the example of a rabbinic judge (who would later return to Judaism). The source for the Maqqâri brothers is Ibn al-Khatîb, in Levtzion and Hopkins, *Corpus of Early Arabic Sources*, pp. 307–308. For the history of Sijilmâsa, see Michel Terrasse's short, but otherwise excellent entry "Sidjilmāsa" in the *Encyclopedia of Islam*, 2nd ed. On the site of Sijilmâsa from an archaeological point of view, consult the reports of the archaeological work that has been carried out there, notably Ronald A. Messier, "Sijilmasa. Five Seasons of Archaeological Inquiry by a Joint Moroccan-American Mission," *Archéologie islamique* 7 (1997): 61–92, and the historical-archaeological synthesis recently published by Ronald A. Messier and James A. Miller, *The Last Civilized Place: Sijilmasa and Its Saharan Destiny* (Austin: University of Texas Press, 2015). Among more recent archaeological results produced by my own team (presenting a significantly different interpretation of the archaeological excavations), see F.-X. Fauvelle-Aymar, L. Erbati, and R. Mensan, "Sijilmâsa: cité idéale, site insaisissable? Ou comment une ville échappe à ses fouilleurs," *Études et Essais du Centre Jacques Berque* 20 (2014): 1–17. On the reason why previous archaeological publications should be read cautiously, and their results considered overinterpreted, see my review of Messier and Miller's book (cited above) in *Journal of Islamic Archaeology* 4, no. 2 (2017): 251-255, and "African Archaeology and the Chalk-Line Effect: A Consideration of Mâli and Sijilmâsa," in Toby Green and Benedetta Rossi (eds.), *Landscape, Sources and Intellectual Projects of the West African Past: Essays in Honour of Paulo Fernando de Moraes Farias* (Leiden: Brill, in press). A fruitful approach to studying Sijilmâsa in its rural landscape is that of Dale R. Lightfoot and James A. Miller, "Sijilmasa: The Rise and Fall of a Walled Oasis in Medieval Morocco," *Annals of the Association of American Geographers* 86 (1996): 78–101.

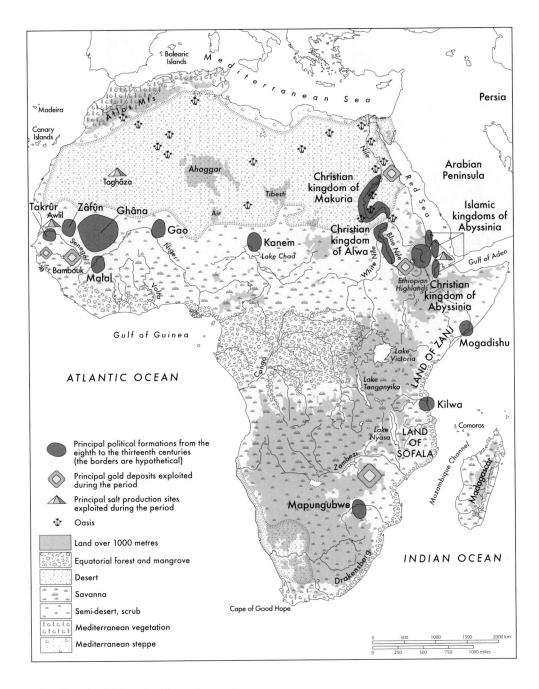

Africa from the eighth to the thirteenth centuries.

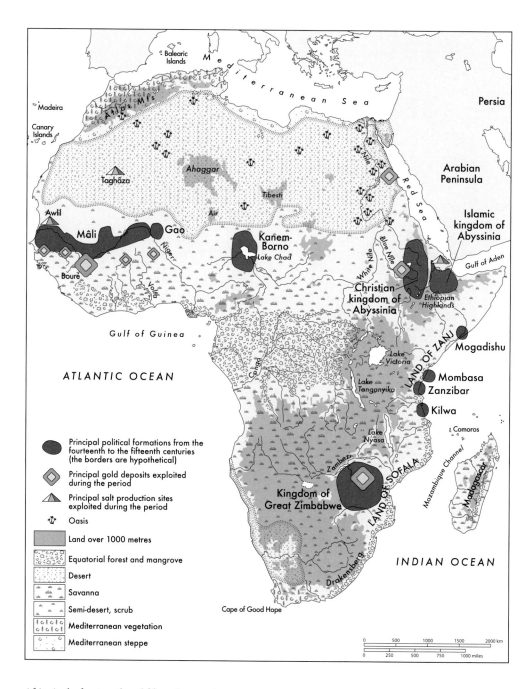

Africa in the fourteenth and fifteenth centuries.

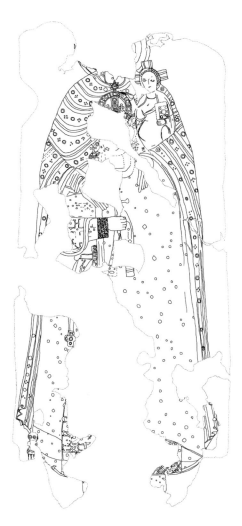

Fresco removed from the walls of the Nubian cathedral of Faras before its submersion under the waters of Lake Nasser. Despite its damaged state, the fresco bears a Greek inscription, and enough detail remains to reveal a king named George (probably George II) protected by a Virgin and Child who stand behind him. Height of the fresco: 2.52 meters. Source: National Museum of Warsaw (inventory: 234032).

Facsimile of the fresco of George II of Nubia. Here we can clearly make out the richness of the clothing, the baby Jesus to the monarch's left, as well the latter's crown. Source: Facsimile kindly made available by Magdalena Wozniak from her "Iconographie des souverains et des dignitaires de la Nubie chrétienne: les vêtements d'apparat" (doctoral thesis, University of Paris 4—Sorbonne, 2013). Used with permission.

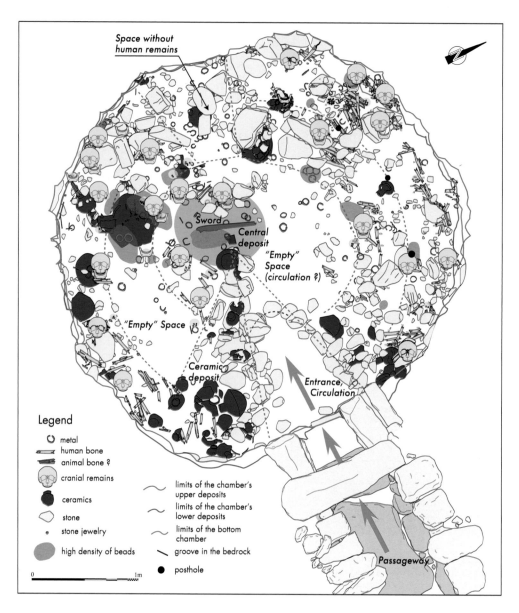

Layout of the Tätär Gur Tumulus, Ethiopia, showing the distribution of human remains and artifacts in the burial chamber. This collective grave contained the remains of several dozen individuals buried over the course of several successive phases, accompanied by intact pottery and jewelry, notably bracelets and thousands of beads. The monument was probably in use between the ninth and eleventh centuries. The excavation was undertaken by B. Poissonnier in 2002; the results are published in Fauvelle-Aymar and Poissonnier 2012. © Régis Bernard and Bertrand Poissonnier.

Grand pectoral en or

3

Musée de l'Institut Français
d'Afrique Noire, Dakar

Golden breastplate from Tumulus P, Rao, Senegal, around 1300. The excavation was undertaken by J. Joire between 1941 and 1942. The solid gold object is 18.4 cm in diameter and weighs 191 grams. The production of filigree and hemispheric decorative heads is typical of Islamic goldsmiths; but the motifs are still frequently encountered in modern West African jewelry where they are generally created using the repoussé technique. IFAN Museum of African Arts, Dakar, Senegal.

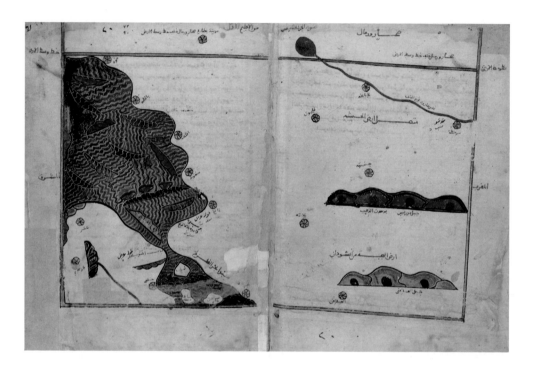

Page from the atlas of al-Idrîsî, middle of the twelfth century. It is one of sixty-eight that make up the map. It represents the intersection of the first clime and fifth section. North is at the bottom of the image. The bodies of water to the left are the Red Sea (bottom) and the Indian Ocean (top). Bibliothèque nationale de France, manuscrit arabe 2221.

Grand mosque of Kilwa, Tanzania. The monument, built from blocks of coralline limestone, dates mostly from the fourteenth century. This view of the interior, oriented toward the mihrâb,* illustrates the very fine architecture; the gently pointed arches support cupolas. © François-Xavier Fauvelle.

The Church of St. George, Lalibela, Ethiopia. As with all the complex's churches, the monument is sculpted from a single block of solid volcanic rock standing in the middle of a courtyard that has itself been hollowed out from the rocky massif. The church's interior has also been hollowed out and sculpted to imitate a built church. © Claire Bosc-Tiessé.

Catalan Atlas, 1375. Detail. Surrounded by icons representing Timbuktu and Gao, the sovereign of "Guinea" (Ginyia or Gineua) enthroned in majesty and holding a golden orb in his hand. The caption is in Catalan. Bibliothèque nationale de France, manuscrit espagnol 30.

CHAPTER 17

The Land Where Gold Grows like Carrots

The Sahel, from the Tenth to the Fourteenth Century

Around 951, a Persian geographer, al-Istakhrî, claimed that Sijilmâsa was located not far from a gold mine. "It is said," he adds, "that no other mine is known to have more abundant or purer gold," but he makes it clear that "the road there is difficult." If this latter assertion is certainly an enfeebled echo of the realities of trans-Saharan commerce whose function was to carry gold to Sijilmâsa, the mine, on the other hand, poses a certain problem: there is no gold deposit in the city's immediate vicinity. The geographer was ill informed, even for his own time. A half century earlier, al-Yaqûbî had already asserted that the mines were situated in the kingdom of Ghâna, on the other side of the Sahara. It was, if we may say so, a little truer, although still false: there was no gold mine in the southern region of Mauritania where the African kingdom was located (↦7, 8). Our authors must have conflated the production sites with the sites where their informants purchased their gold.

For a long time little more was known. In the middle of the fifteenth century, a Genoese merchant, Antonio Malfante (↦32), the first Latin Christian whom we know to have visited the Sahara, recounted for his Italian partners what his Muslim patron had told him about where the gold came from: "I was fourteen years in the land of the Blacks, and I have never heard nor seen anyone who could reply from definite knowledge. That is my experience, as to how it is found and collected." Even if this man, also a merchant, had some reason to lie to his interlocutor, we can believe him: no contemporaneous voyager or geographer obtained better information than this: gold is not produced in the land of the black merchants that the caravans visit; it comes from still farther away.

To the ignorance of its origins were added marvelous stories about its collection. "In the country of Ghâna," wrote one early tenth-century author, "gold grows in the sand as carrots do, and is plucked at sunrise." In the middle of the fourteenth century, the secretary of the chancery of Cairo, al-Umarî, recounted without batting an eye what he had been taught on the subject. Two types of golden plants were harvested. "One is found in the spring and blossoms after the rains in open country. It has leaves like the najîl grass and its roots are gold. The other kind is found all the year round. . . . There are holes there and roots of gold are found like stones or gravel and gathered up." It has been thought that such accounts constituted a screen of legends artificially maintained by the West African and Muslim powers to keep their North African commercial partners from seeking to control the mines directly in the event they came to know their location. But apart from the screen's principal effect of arousing curiosity, it is likely that if the Sahelian powers were better informed than their northern partners on the gold networks, they probably had no direct access to the mining areas, nor did they have the ability to exert influence over the supply. To be better convinced of this, let's listen to what al-Umarî had to say on the subject: each year the sultan of Mâli was brought the fruits of the harvest of the yellow metal from the land of gold, with which he had a treaty of friendship. "If the sultan wished he could extend his authority over them but the kings of this kingdom have learnt by experience that as soon as one of them conquers one of the gold towns and Islam spreads . . . the gold there begins to decrease and then disappears. . . . When they had learnt the truth of this by experience they left the gold countries under the control of the heathen people and were content with their vassalage and the tribute imposed on them." An avowal of powerlessness turned around with diplomacy. We should say that the Sahelian powers' knowledge of the gold-producing areas was as indirect as their political suzerainty over them was nominal.

But how, one wonders, did the commercial network around so precious a commodity function when its zone of extraction was pushed back beyond the horizon not only of the buyers, but even of their suppliers; when its exploitation does not seem to have been completely mastered? For the vendors Islamic merchants encountered in the Sahelian trading posts were themselves intermediaries. They had a name: the Wangâra, first an ethnic group from the edge of the Sahel, whose name was later given to a class of professional traders who spread throughout West Africa, and who would be found under different collective designations up to the Dyula of today. They formed a network of peddlers, indefatigable pedestrians accompanied by a slave or two, Muslims and conveyors of Islam, displaying strong bonds of solidarity. It was they whom the merchants, coming out of the desert, encountered in the markets of Ghâna and Mâli, contact points between two symmetrical commercial networks.

We can infer from sometimes-confused information transmitted by Arab authors that the Wangâra's settlements were on the banks of the Niger River, toward what is called the Inner Niger Delta (a network of lakes, distributaries, and pools inundated during the annual flooding), or perhaps throughout the whole region between the Niger and Bani Rivers, which certainly corresponds more to the designation of "isle" given in the sources. But it was not a gold zone. The geography of the large deposits— Bambouk, between the Senegal River and its tributary the Falémé; Bouré, between the upper Senegal and the upper Niger; Lobi on the upper Volta, in Burkina Faso; or even the Sirba valley in present-day Niger—delimits the range of the Wangâra network in the savanna zone. It was a regional network that drew a thin net over all the mining zones, or rather covered them one after another as one deposit dwindled and another was developed, and that also funneled gold toward secondary markets, which the itinerant merchants in turn siphoned off toward the capitals of the Sahelian kingdoms. The role of the latter, then, was in no way to organize the trade; it is known that they had only a modest capacity to intrude into the gold-deposit zones. These were not merchant states that purchased goods from the south to resell them in the north; they were broker states that brought two commercial systems into contact and made trade possible by guaranteeing its security and integrity. Their revenue was not a capital gain, such as would have been made from the purchase and resale of the precious metal; it came instead from taxes levied on goods in transit: gold in one direction, salt in the other.

This long-distance relationship between two foreign worlds, this confrontation between partners who did not know of which world the other was the intermediary, this meta-interaction: the authors of the period sought to understand its mechanisms. They often describe it as Masûdî did in the middle of the tenth century: "[The Islamic merchants] bargain with [the "Blacks"] without seeing them or conversing with them. They leave the goods and on the next morning the people go to their goods and find bars of gold left beside each commodity. If the owner of the goods wishes he chooses the gold and leaves the goods, or if he wishes he takes his goods and leaves the gold. If he desires an increase he leaves both gold and goods." Or as Yâqût did at the beginning of the thirteenth century: "They strive onwards with much suffering until they reach the place which separates them from the owners of the gold. When they arrive there, they beat great drums which they have brought with them, and which may be heard from the horizon where these people of the Sûdân live. . . . When the merchants know that those people have heard the drum, they produce whatever they have brought of the aforementioned wares and each merchant lays down his own. . . . Then they go away from that place a distance of one day's travelling. Then the Sûdân come with the gold, put a certain amount of gold alongside each kind, and withdraw. Then the merchants come after them and each one takes the gold which he finds beside his merchandise. They leave the merchandise and depart after having beaten their drums."

How to meet when the land is unfamiliar? How to establish communication when the same language isn't spoken? With the aid of drums. How to adjust supply and demand on this improvised market? How to settle the terms of trade to the satisfaction of each partner if neither uses the same measures or currency? By successive increases. What passes for security in this unregulated trade, which has no common law as Islam does on such matters? The stripping and deposit of clothing. This "silent trade," often encountered in the sources but which probably never occurred, is a story that responds to all the questions that contemporaries could have posed. It is a story that, much like the marvelous tales about the "harvesting" of gold, obscures the concrete, material circumstances of the gold trade in the Sahelian markets of the Middle Ages, but which also lays bare the intrigue of the gold trade and the preoccupations of the northern merchants who took part in it.

BIBLIOGRAPHICAL NOTE

The excerpts cited in the text are taken from Nehemia Levtzion and J.F.P. Hopkins (eds.), *Corpus of Early Arabic Sources for West African History* (Princeton, NJ: Markus Wiener, 2000), p. 28 (Ibn al-Fakîh—on gold growing as carrots do), p. 32 (Masûdî), pp. 169–170 (Yâkût), pp. 262 and 267 (al-Umarî). On the "Letter from Tuat" of Antonio Malfante, see chapter 32 of this book. The hypothesis identifying the Inner Niger Delta as the land of the Wangâra was suggested by Susan Keech McIntosh, "A Reconsideration of Wangara/Palolus, Island of Gold," *Journal of African History* 22 (1981): 145–158. On the circulation of gold between the West African savannas and North Africa, see F.-X. Fauvelle and C. Robion-Brunner, "Les routes de l'or africain au Moyen Âge," in C. Coquery-Vidrovitch (ed.), *L'Afrique des routes* (Arles: Actes Sud, musée du Quai Branly Jacques-Chirac, 2017), pp. 82–89. On the Wangâra, see Andreas W. Massing, "The Wangara, an Old Soninke Diaspora in West Africa?" *Cahiers d'études africaines* 158 (2000): 281–308. Finally, Paulo Fernando de Moraes Farias, "Silent Trade: Myth and Historical Evidence," *History in Africa* 7 (1974): 9–24, is the best analysis of the problem of silent trade.

CHAPTER 18

Phantom Mines

Present-Day Zimbabwe Highlands and the
West African Savanna, around the Thirteenth Century

During the "gold rush" that struck the regions then known as Matabeleland and Mashonaland (the lands of the Ndebele and the Shona), between the Limpopo and Zambezi Rivers, in the 1880s, European prospectors often encountered the shafts of abandoned mines. For them, that was the first sign of an underground vein. Mining rapidly became mechanized, but it was still common for mining company engineers to notice the presence, under the drills and buckets of the machines, of filled-in shafts and tunnels. Men had found gold and extracted it long before the colonial era. No one was really surprised by this: colonists, Christian missionaries, or simple travelers who expropriated and exploited the Africans liked to believe that prestigious predecessors had already made these same territories their own. Whether Phoenicians or Hebrews, Egyptians or Sabeans, by belonging to the ancient Mediterranean world, they were offered a privileged place in the cultural memory of a colonial society that proclaimed itself the standard-bearer of a civilizing mission. Invisible ancestors, they made the African countryside familiar; they passed their claim to it on to their "descendants."

Today we know of some four thousand sites that were previously exploited on the plateau of Zimbabwe alone. There are open-air mines, systems of tunnels as well as shafts that made it possible to access and exploit auriferous quartz veins. But, with few exceptions, hardly anyone today believes that these deposits in the heart of southern Africa are the land of Ophir, where King Solomon and his associate King Hiram of Tyre sent a fleet that brought back gold, gems, and wood that was made into harps and beams for the Temple at Jerusalem. These sites, which essentially consist of holes in the ground accompanied by piles of rubble, are the coarse vestiges of mines that were in operation across various periods from the twelfth century. They were still there when the Portuguese came from the Mozambican coast in the seventeenth century, and they are still there today. Iron chisels were used to cut into the rock; fire, stone, and wood wedges to break up the compact parts of the vein; grindstones and rock grinders to crush the ore; crucibles to melt the metal. Sometimes these objects are found; and we can radiocarbon-date their use from pieces of charcoal discovered alongside them. Ceramics found at the bottom of the shafts are compared with those from better-known sites. Scholars have noticed that many of these locations are situated within the perimeter of ancient "stone houses" or *zimbabwe* in the Shona language, fortified complexes that date from the thirteenth, fourteenth, and fifteenth centuries (↦31). It is understood that a power—whatever it was, but we can well imagine a centralized power like a "kingdom" or, indeed, an "empire"—had control over the exploitation of these gold deposits, that is, control as much over a complex technique as over a territory and population. But did this power really have to be exercised by a king rather than an aristocracy or even a merchant class? It is impossible to say, in the absence of written sources.

We know of several deposits that were once mined in the savanna of West Africa, where there was certainly never a power that could have directly controlled them. The geology there is different: mostly detritic or alluvial formations. Gold panning is practiced in the rivers, or else holes are dug in the goldfields on ancient river terraces: tiny yellow flakes are encountered at a few meters under the laterite crust, in contact with the bedrock. On the surface, we can spot the mines on aerial or satellite photographs, sometimes even from our computer screens, by the parallel alignments of the entrances of the vertical shafts; underground, the hollowed-out sections sometimes form connected cavities held up by pillars carved into the rock. Often the shafts were fitted with notches to make them practicable for ascent or descent. Here too we find dolerite or granite grindstones and grinders, crucibles, shards of ceramics, of little use for establishing a chronology since we do not possess clear reference collections.

But the sites sometimes also reveal shells with a porcelain-like shine called cowries,* imported since the Middle Ages, bowls and tubes of clay smoking pipes, which accompanied the spread of tobacco from the seventeenth century, modern coins, and the like, clues that, when taken together, point to these mines' long history of exploitation.

It was these mines that, from around the twelfth century in southern Africa, the eighth or the ninth century in West Africa, furnished the gold that African intermediaries would then sell in turn to the merchants from the central regions of the Islamic world. These gold mines, or rather their vestiges in the midst of the bush; their spatial distribution; the techniques whose use they demonstrate; the meager finds made when the site has not been destroyed through reexploitation—all these specifics in themselves provide little information about the societies in which the mining took place. And even if, by a stroke of inestimable good luck, we had found female skeletons in a caved-in tunnel, would we infer that extraction was a feminine activity allowing women to augment their individual incomes; or that a sexual division of labor reigned in the mines, where women were given the most difficult, riskiest tasks; or else that exploitation was familial or communal work, and that the women that day paid the ultimate price?

Because we don't really have other solutions for responding to the questions raised by these archaeological sites, we are often forced to appeal to the resources of the colonial archives and ethnographic investigation into modern populations. The tools, the gestures, perhaps the intentions of the medieval miners will be recovered in this way. Or so we may hope. For this comparative or ethnoarchaeological method has a drawback: the assumption that African societies possess unchanging elements that remain petrified in tradition. It would be wrong, however, to deprive ourselves of an approach—as open to criticism as any other—that involves comparison with the present; perhaps it is enough to remember that such an approach cannot answer every question. In the case of the female skeletons in the caved-in tunnel, for instance, what can we conclude about the social structures of these societies given that today women don't toil at the bottom of the shafts?

More fixed, perhaps more durable, than the techniques, representations, or social structures are the environmental conditions that field surveys allow us to observe. In southern Africa as in West Africa, mining is only an off-season activity. During the rainy season everyone works in the fields. Once the harvest has been gathered, the dry season—from November to June in West Africa, from May to October in southern Africa—frees up more time for work. It is also the period when the water table gradually subsides to its lowest level, drying out the bottom of the shafts or allowing for digging in them to recommence, during a mining season that effectively lasts from three to four months. Another constraint: the weak yields of traditional mining exploitation. Before the era of mechanized extraction and the chemical treatment of ore, a man's labor never yielded more than a minute quantity of gold (less than a gram per day) and that at the price of a collective effort, an abundance of energy and risks (as skeletons found in tunnels testify). The revenues from this activity were certainly so meager that it never threatened the viability of the agricultural economy of the societies that practiced it, and furthermore it was because mining had a place in the cycle of the seasons that it could be a durable activity and procure the extra revenue that was expected of it. Gold did not provide for these societies; it complemented the revenue of those who could already provide for themselves. It was a supplement that one could turn into jewelry or sell. But let's adjust the focus: at the scale of entire regions that for centuries knew how to attract merchants, drops of gold turned into rivers.

BIBLIOGRAPHICAL NOTE

The classic study on Zimbabwe's ancient mines is that of Roger Summers, *Ancient Mining in Rhodesia and Adjacent Areas* (Salisbury: National Museums of Rhodesia, 1969); however, one should not put too much stock in the author's hypothesis that the mining techniques were of Indian origin. A more recent synthesis is given by Duncan Miller, Nirdev Desai, and Julia Lee-Thorp, "Indigenous Gold Mining in Southern Africa: A Review," *South African Archaeological Society*

Goodwin Series 8 (2000): 91–99. The archaeological examples relating to Zimbabwe are taken from this work. See also A. Hammel, C. White, S. Pfeiffer, and D. Miller, "Pre-colonial Mining in Southern Africa," *Journal of the South African Institute of Mining and Metallurgy*, January/February 2000, pp. 49–56. For West Africa, consult the references provided in the previous chapter. Jean-Baptiste Kiéthéga mixes archaeology and ethnoarchaeological investigation in his approach to the gold deposits of the upper Volta Basin; see his *L'Or de la Volta noire* (Paris: Karthala, 1983). Philip D. Curtin offers a very good economic analysis of another West African gold deposit, Bambuk, in "The Lure of Bambuk Gold," *Journal of African History* 14 (1973): 623–631. I have borrowed from Curtin the paradox, slightly reformulated, of a source of wealth produced in the context of poor returns. Curtin presents it in a different, perhaps more radical, fashion: "By a curious paradox, then, Bambuhu [Bambouk] came to have a reputation for great wealth because it produced gold, but it produced gold because it was too poor to do anything else" (p. 631). On the importance colonial myths had for the interpretation of archaeological remains of southern Africa, see my *Histoire de l'Afrique du Sud* (Paris: Le Seuil, 2006), chap. 3 ("Les pouvoirs et le territoire"). King Solomon's mines are mentioned in the Bible, 1 Kings 9:28, 10:11–12.

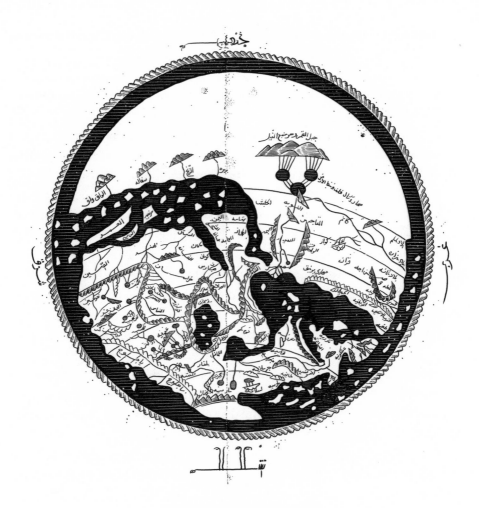

CHAPTER 19

The Land of Sofala

Coasts of Present-Day Tanzania and Mozambique,
End of the Thirteenth to the Beginning of the Fourteenth Century

Ibn Saîd al-Maghribî, born near Granada (in present-day Spain) in 1213 and who died in Tunis (capital of today's Tunisia) in 1286, made the pilgrimage to the holy places of Arabia at least twice. His travels took him to Iran. He was the continuator of a family summa, a sort of geographical anthology, which, unfortunately, is mostly lost. As for Abû l-Fidâ (1273–1331), he was a prince of the Ayyubid family and governor of Hama in Syria in the time of the Mamluk sultans. A learned connoisseur of geographic knowledge, he skillfully compiled the writings of past authors whose manuscripts he was able to procure. We owe large extracts from the works of Ibn Saîd to Abû l-Fidâ, who dutifully cited them in his own encyclopedia, but not before correcting, for better or worse, what he had judged to be his predecessor's aberrations.

Ibn Saîd and Abû l-Fidâ: Whom should we praise? Whom should we incriminate? They have transmitted to us the knowledge of fine, learned men like themselves regarding the African coast of the Indian Ocean. But this knowledge, as it has come down to us, has remained almost incomprehensible. Let's start with the closest feature—already quite remote for men from the central regions of the Islamic world—Bab-el-Mandeb at the southern end of the Red Sea. Here first is the land of Berbera, which extended from west to east, opposite the south Arabian coast, before turning off toward the south, marking the profile of the Horn of Africa (as we say today, using an image that was not used by medieval cartographers). We recognize the name Khafouny or Hafouny: it's Cape Hafun, a promontory known by all the region's sailors since antiquity. We recognize Maqdishû: it's Mogadishu. Once we have passed the arid coast of modern Somalia, we find ourselves in a more pleasant region, the land of Zanj. The only city names given to us are familiar: Malindi and Mombasa, two ports on the southern coast of Kenya (↦34). Next comes a desert, and then we arrive in the last known segment of the eastern coast of Africa: the land of Sofala. But this time, in spite of the names, we recognize nothing: a city named either Batyna or Banya; the capital of the people of Sofala, which is called

Seyouna; an important port, Leyrana, whose inhabitants are Muslims; and finally the last stopover, Daghouta.

It was from this land, where people dressed in leopard skins, that the Zanj merchants bought the gold that they resold farther north to Muslim traders. The region had changed since al-Masûdî's day in the ninth century (↦2): the land of Sofala, once a mysterious horizon far beyond the Coast of Zanj, had become more familiar. Now in the late thirteenth and early fourteenth centuries, we find entire communities that had converted to Islam. It is even known to some Arab authors that gold came from a land in the interior where it was harvested in tunnels dug like those of ants.

It is frustrating to be reduced to conjecture to place these names on the map. Our authors, however, took care to aid their readers by providing each place's geographical coordinates, the distances in degrees from one port to another. But in fact, by positioning the points on a grid, we can only draw a horizontal coast stretching from Malindi to Kenya, all in longitude, barely crossing the equator by twelve degrees and seeming to link up with Southeast Asia. This is not what Africa looks like; so it must be said that our geographers believed that Africa's eastern extremity connected to China, that the Indian Ocean was a closed sea. How are we to trust information inscribed in geography so manifestly erroneous? Or rather, to put it differently: how are we to use such precise geographical information inscribed in cosmography so manifestly different from our own?

And yet, a quarter turn clockwise, the longitudes change to latitudes; the profile of the land of Sofala becomes familiar: when it is superimposed on the coastal profile of Tanzania and the northern half of modern Mozambique, they match to a very accurate degree. Nevertheless, it is not any easier to identify cities or, say, the stopovers in question over vast distances. But at least we can locate them in the coastal segments. The last segment, angled to the southeast, which Abû l-Fidâ imagined being the farthest east, and which for us is the farthest south, outlines the coast of Mozambique between the Island of Mozambique and Beira at the mouth of the Pungwe

River. It was here two centuries later that the Portuguese coming from the south, eager to harness the flood of gold from the Zimbabwean plateau for their own profit, erected a fort that they named Nova Sofala.

BIBLIOGRAPHICAL NOTE

The Arabic edition of Abû l-Fidâ's text was published by Joseph Toussaint Reinaud and William McGuckin de Slane, *Géographie d'Aboulféda* (Paris: Imprimerie royale, 1840). For English readers, the essential texts on the East African coast are brought together in G.S.P. Freeman-Grenville, *The East African Coast* (Oxford: Clarendon Press, 1962).

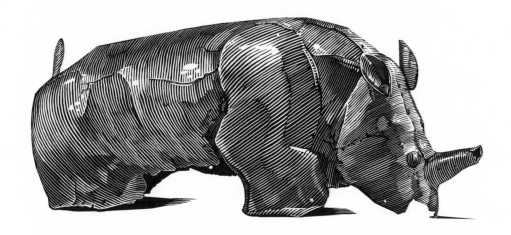

CHAPTER 20

The Golden Rhinoceros

Northeastern South Africa, Thirteenth Century

The waters of the Shashe River join those of the Limpopo close to where the borders of South Africa, Botswana, and Zimbabwe converge. Nearby, on the right bank (on South African territory) sits the Greefswald farm. It is the property of the Republic of South Africa, and its "cultural landscape" has been inscribed on UNESCO's World Heritage List. As for the natural landscape, it is high savanna, home to the thorn tree and mopane,* covered with grass in the rainy season and dotted here and there with enormous baobab trees. Mapungubwe, the "hill of the jackals" in Venda (a language of southern Africa), is a steep-sided sandstone outcrop that gives its name to a collection of archaeological sites in the vicinity dating from the tenth to the thirteenth century. During apartheid, this site was one of the battlefields over the country's past (the skirmishes were fought among white academics, it goes without saying): was it possible, the whites asked, that black Bantus were responsible for Mapungubwe, or was it necessary to invoke some other population with a more noble pedigree? Was it possible that the Africans who had lived and prospered here were the ancestors of the black South Africans then confined to Bantustans,* or "reserves," and townships*? Was it possible that civilized natives had preceded white colonists on ground where the latter believed, or gave the impression of believing, that they were the first occupants?

As befits a place that is today considered the "capital" of the first South African kingdom, the objects discovered there have become the country's "crown jewels," and the history of their transmission to our own time, an archive. From the moment of its discovery, a story developed that gave prominence to white heroes—as could only be expected of a site for which the colonial elite was both the discoverer and the exegete—just as elsewhere colonial settlers and Western readers were fond of a white queen of the Atlanteans. As is often the case when *lieux de mémoire* are at stake, this intrigue transformed a banal story of pillage into an allegory that romanticizes the circumstances of the objects' discovery.

It is therefore a story of mystery and friendship, which perhaps really happened in the way it's been told, but is no less mythical for it. In his youth, Francois Bernhard Lotrie had served as guide to missionary and explorer David Livingstone; he had been a gold prospector and elephant hunter. At the beginning of the twentieth century (he died in 1917), Lotrie settled in the Soutpansberg massif not far from Limpopo. Here, we are told, the eccentric, solitary old man gave an African friend, Mowena, an ancient piece of terra-cotta pottery. It was said that he had taken treasures from a sacred hill he had discovered. Around 1930, a group of young men went for a weekend hunt in this same region. Of course, they were whites, for only whites could freely cross the property of other whites. While looking for water, they came across an old man, an African, who diligently and respectfully offered them refreshment. The old man was Mowena. One of his young guests, Jerry Van Graan, a student of history at Pretoria, was intrigued by the vessel to which he put his lips: the celebrated terra-cotta. Returning in December 1932 with a group of his friends, he managed to identify and climb the hill on the Greefswald farm. There they discovered tombs, and they spent days disturbing them, laying hands on a small rhinoceros made of gold foil. Completed much later from scattered data, the retrospective inventory of three disturbed tombs (out of around thirty) reveals that they were shallow graves, perhaps surmounted by stone slabs, where the dead were buried in a sitting position, unless the skeletal remains had initially been buried elsewhere before being reburied there. The graves contained several golden animals, the gold casing of a "scepter" or a cane as well as a headrest, gold filigree jewelry, thousands of gold beads, tens of thousands of glass beads, and both intact and broken pottery.

Seized with misgivings, the young man would later write to Leo Fouché, his former history professor, to inform him of his discovery. Fouché, a liberal Afrikaner, immediately had the farm bought by the state, purchased objects coming from the site that had not already been dispersed or melted down, and launched the first excavation campaign. It was learned that other clandestine visitors had climbed the hill during the 1920s. Since then numerous structures have been excavated, a remarkable series of objects have been discovered, but of course information we would like to have about the disturbed graves themselves is lost forever. The golden rhinoceros is nothing more than a recovered stolen document, except that a stolen archaeological artifact will always remain lost—even if it is rediscovered: it will always be missing the associations its original context would have allowed us to observe.

The archaeological research carried out over several decades at Greefswald has revealed stratigraphic deposits several meters thick, not only at the top of the hill but also at its base, as well as at several other sites within a radius of few dozen kilometers from the hill. The sequence of occupation illustrates an increase in population size and social differentiation between the tenth and the thirteenth century. Social differentiation is especially noticeable toward the summit of Mapungubwe, an area occupied by a new elite from the end of the twelfth century, and toward the upper end of the stratigraphic deposit, corresponding to the last occupations a little before 1300, when high-ranking individuals had themselves buried there with their wealth, thereby denying it to the living. But can we refer to them as kings without presupposing the nature of a political formation we can apprehend only very imperfectly through the prism of archaeology? Let's stick with kings, if the golden objects are to be taken as royal symbols or evidence of royal status, but only if we don't forget the other dimensions of the society the archaeological data shed light on. Here medieval societies were distinctly pastoral. At the excavated sites, domestic spaces were spread out around a vast central corral, a sign of the important place cattle occupied not only in the economy and diet, but also, more generally, in all social transactions, notably matrimonial ones, as was the case in the societies of southern Africa in later centuries. The numerous clay animal figurines, particularly of cows, that come from this region further reinforce this point.

To better grasp Mapungubwe's significance, we must zoom out to measure the regional synchronies while also honing in on the elements of material culture. That the rise of the sites on the right bank of the Limpopo is linked in one way or another to the development of mining on the plateau on the other bank (↦18), in current-day Zimbabwe, is very probable, partly because, as far as we know, gold was not exploited on the South African side until the colonial era. That strong social distinctions and spectacular evidence of the accumulation of gold begin to appear in this fluvial region at exactly the same time as the oldest mentions of a gold trade with the south coast of East Africa is equally remarkable. A triangular relationship thus took shape about which we can be even more precise. The minute glass beads, found in the thousands during the excavation, likely originated in Arikamedu, near Pondicherry, in southeast India, unless they came from another atelier in the "Indo-Pacific"* production zone. Like the cowries* from the Maldives (↦27), or the fragments of Song dynasty greenware, "celadon," these beads bear witness to the trade nourished by the commercial zone of the Indian Ocean. In exchange, did the little "kingdom" of Mapungubwe export elephant ivory (we have found bracelets whose standardized form and technique suggest serial production); the skins of cats and other carnivores, if we are to judge by the bones of genets, civets, leopards, servals, and lions that show signs of cut marks, and which have nothing to do with food waste; and gold? Perhaps, although only gold objects (beads, jewelry, objects finished with gold leaf) have been uncovered, not ingots, which would soon have been melted down. But it's not necessary: Magpungubwe Hill could have traded in several directions with its new regional partners without necessarily being their intermediary. It could have profited from this trade by amassing a treasure out of goods that the other regional partners bought or sold for their weight value. Symbolically, a golden rhinoceros was something more than a gold nugget or a dinar.*

The little rhinoceros is perhaps, in its way, evidence of the existence of a network of contacts even more complex. Reassembled, then restored, the object measures a little more than fifteen centimeters long. It is solid in appearance; the neck looks more "robust" than that of the real animal. But its compact appearance, the projection of its shoulder line, and its lowered head reinforce the feeling of power that emanates from the figurine. Lines of small, regular perforations indicate that the hammered foil was riveted to a wooden core, which is corroborated by the gold pins found during the sieving of the sediment from the graves. The animal's tail is a thin, solid gold cylinder, the ears delicately cut out-turned ovals, the eyes two small half-globular "upholstery nails," the horn a gold foil cone. The horn? It has long been pointed out that unlike the African rhinoceros, which has two horns, the golden rhinoceros of Mapungubwe has only one. Its excavators, custodians, and restorers were categorical on this point: it had never had a second horn. We can see here a simple stylistic feature or the representation of an Asian species, the Indian rhinoceros (*Rhinoceros unicornis*) or the Javan rhinoceros (*Rhinoceros sondaicus*), both of which have a single horn. For this reason, some scholars have considered the rhinoceros, emblematic of the site and the history of South Africa as a whole, an imported object. That is unlikely for its golden carapace; studies done on the geochemical fingerprint of the metal from several gold objects found at Mapungubwe point to a regional provenance. But it remains a possibility for the object's missing part: its core, certainly made of wood, which began to slowly disintegrate as soon as it was buried. Only a meticulous excavation could have yielded fibers whose analysis might have revealed its species and age.

We will thus stick with the hypothesis that the wooden figurine was perhaps made elsewhere than Africa, and was gilded on the banks of the Limpopo as a sign of its appropriation by royalty. At any rate, this hypothesis is not even necessary if one simply wants to illustrate the emergence of a power capable of harnessing the political benefits of a commercial relationship with unknown worlds. For Mapungubwe, with its society based on a traditional agricultural economy, was situated both beyond the horizon of regular Islamic trade—probably even beyond the limits of the land known to the coastal African merchants—and at a good distance from the goldfields of the Zimbabwean plateau.

BIBLIOGRAPHICAL NOTE

The Order of Mapungubwe, established in 2002, is the highest distinction awarded by the Republic of South Africa; its insignia incorporates the golden rhinoceros. The account of the site's discovery is taken from Sian Tiley, *Mapungubwe: South Africa's Crown Jewels* (Capetown: Sunbird Publishing, 2004), which catalogs the objects kept in the museum dedicated to Mapungubwe at the University of Pretoria. The original excavations by Leo Fouché were published in *Mapungubwe, Ancient Bantu Civilization on the Limpopo* (Cambridge: Cambridge University Press, 1937). The Mapungubwe Cultural Landscape was added to the list of World Heritage sites in 2003. For a presentation of the site as a "cultural landscape," see Jane Carruthers, "Mapungubwe: An Historical and Contemporary Analysis of a World Heritage Cultural Landscape," *Koedoe* 49 (2006): 1–13. Andrie Meyer, "K2 and Mapungubwe," *South African Archaeological Society Goodwin Series* 8 (2000): 4–13, delivers an excellent synthesis of the stratigraphic sequence. For a retrospective inventory of the tombs' contents and an updating of the anthropological data based on unpublished photographs, see Maryna Steyn, "The Mapungubwe Gold Graves Revisited," *South African Archaeological Bulletin* 186 (2007): 140–146. Some samples of gold from Mapungubwe have undergone a spectrometric analysis; see B. Grigorova, W. Smith, K. Stülpner, J. A. Tumilty, and D. Miller, "Fingerprinting of Gold Artefacts from Mapungubwe, Bosutswe and Thulamela," *Gold Bulletin* 31 (1998): 99–102. Linda C. Prinsloo, Nigel Wood, Maggi Loubser, Sabine M. C. Verryn, and Sian Tiley, "Re-dating of Chinese Celadon Shards Excavated on Mapungubwe Hill, a 13th Century Iron Age Site in South Africa, Using Raman Spectroscopy, XRF and XRD," *Journal of Raman Spectroscopy* 36 (2005): 806–816, offers a new dating of Chinese greenware fragments that enables us to determine when the site's sequence of occupation ended. Finally, a study of glass beads has recently been done by Marilee Wood, "Making Connections: Relationships between International Trade and Glass Beads from the Shashe-Limpopo Area," *South African Archaeological Society Goodwin Series* 8 (2000): 78–90, from which is borrowed the hypothesis of an Indo-Pacific origin. The animal data come from Elizabeth A. Voigt, *Mapungubwe: An Archaeozoological Interpretation of an Iron Age Community* (Pretoria: Transvaal Museum, 1983). Two new gold foil figurines— one a humpbacked bovine, the other a cat—were reassembled from fragments in 2009 and are on display in the Mapungubwe Museum in Pretoria. For a vigorous perspective on the various historical interpretations of Mapungubwe, see Munyaradzi Manyanga, Innocent Pikirayi, and Shadreck Chirikure, "Conceptualizing the Urban Mind in Pre-European Southern Africa: Rethinking Mapungubwe and Great Zimbabwe," in P.J.J. Sinclair, G. Nordquist, F. Herschend, and C. Isendahl (eds.), *The Urban Mind. Cultural and Environmental Dynamics* (Uppsala: Uppsala

University, 2010), pp. 573–590. The University of Pretoria has published a compendium of numerous documents relating to the history and institutional environment of the excavations at Mapungubwe: S. Tiley-Nel (ed.), *Mapungubwe Remembered: Contributions to Mapungubwe by the University of Pretoria* (Pretoria, 2011). Among the reproductions of important documents are Van Graan's letter to Fouché and the transcript of an interview in which the aged Van Graan recounted the circumstances of the discovery.

CHAPTER 21

The Stratigraphy of Kilwa, or How Cities Are Born

*Coast of Present-Day Tanzania,
from the Tenth to the Fifteenth Century*

Deep inlets along the coast, marking the mouths of two southern Tanzanian rivers, have formed Kilwa Bay, a basin closed by reefs. Small, meandering rivulets of seawater penetrate the local mangrove cover. An island rises from the middle of the bay, a protected space that also controlled access to the continent. A crop of archaeological sites bear witness to the fact that this bay was a privileged zone of human occupation for a millennium. The current city of Kilwa is on the continent. The most important ruins are on the island: Kilwa Kisiwani, "Kilwa-on-the-island," in Swahili.

The first thing one sees through the thick curtain of mangrove trees is the massive remains of a vast palace complex. Located atop a cliff in the middle of the open cove that demarcates the northern side of the island, the site is called Husuni Kubwa, or the "large castle" in Swahili. (We recognize the borrowing of the Arabic word *hisn*, "fortified enclosure.") Among the recently restored leveled-off walls, which have not kept their roofs, one first notices doorways to small rooms arranged along the four sides of a vast, closed courtyard; it brings to mind a trading station, both entrepôt and marketplace, framed by shops and storehouses—this was the commercial space. The complex includes several other open-air spaces whose exact functions remain uncertain, but which were undoubtedly suitable for meetings—this was the political space. It is hard to escape the suspicion that this architectural ensemble was intended for the various aspects of the public life of local and foreign elites: receptions, audiences, symbolic exchanges, commerce, taxation, deliberations. Bordering the top of the cliff like a rim; dominating the sea; soberly decorated, although we do note alcoves and moldings; its architecture robust even if the vision of its original elevations is lost to us—this "castle," whose dedicatory inscription names Sultan Hasan ibn Sulaymân as its builder, was considered the gateway to the Zanj coast. Perhaps it replaced an earlier complex whose ruins are visible immediately to the east of Husuni Kubwa.

The grand mosque was some fifteen hundred meters from the palace, in the extreme northwest corner of the island. With the exception of that of

Timbuktu (↦28), it is certainly the largest ancient mosque in sub-Saharan Africa, in any case of those that have come down to us in a recognizable state. It is a vast ensemble whose stone walls retain their original height, and whose roof is made up of alternating rows of cupolas and barrel vaults. Doorways and windows are molded. The interior is a forest of pillars linked by gently pointed arches that give this architecture its fine appearance. Although the building went through multiple transformations up to the eighteenth century, the mosque is contemporary with the palace of Husuni Kubwa; its floorplan has not been altered since the fourteenth century. At the end of the prayer room, behind the *mihrâb* oriented to the north in the direction of Mecca, we discover another room that also has a *mihrâb.* This is the former mosque, which undoubtedly became too small and was integrated into the walls of its successor.

Neville Chittick, the British archaeologist who excavated Kilwa between 1958 and 1965, designated the archaeological levels associated with the mosque's enlargement and the construction or reconstruction of the "large castle" as "period III." This period corresponds to the fourteenth and fifteenth centuries. From the archaeological point of view, this monumental architecture marks a sharp break from the former periods. Most of the city, however, consisted of rectangular wattle-and-daub dwellings on wooden poles sunk into a foundation made from blocks of coralline limestone. Most of the coins found on-site date to this period, silver dirhams* and bronze divisional coins (dinars* were rare) struck by a dynasty of sultans called the Mahdalî. The excavations also revealed an abundance of imported glass beads, while Chinese porcelain, the classic blue and white and greenware, predominated among foreign ceramics. The beginning of this period is equally marked by a clear shift in the assemblage of local pottery; the underlying archaeological levels in fact reveal a production almost entirely distinct, notably a type of red-painted open bowl common on the Swahili coast. The levels corresponding to period II (thirteenth century) contained bronze coins, plus a small number of silver ones, issued by a previous dynasty called the "Shirazi." (It is not necessary to see in this anything other than a mythical link with the city of Shiraz in Persia.) The original mosque is evidence of a significant Muslim community. We have even found distinctly Muslim tombs. The material imported in this period included Islamic ceramics from the Persian Gulf and silverware made from chloritoschiste, a soft rock from Madagascar. Madreporic limestone masonry blocks cut into fossilized coral, as well as the use of lime as mortar and flooring, were developed over the course of this period. Crucibles indicate that copper was worked there, probably imported.

No solid construction exists from the earlier archaeological phases, grouped together as period I. Nor was there a mosque, although if a mosque was ever erected in wattle and daub,* it probably would have escaped the attention of archaeologists. Still, no evidence for the existence of an established Muslim community has been found. Which doesn't mean there were no Muslim individuals, foreigners established more or less permanently, or even local adherents; on the contrary, a stone fragment bearing an Arabic inscription indicates their presence in period Ib, around the eleventh and twelfth centuries. At that time cornelian beads were imported from India. But the site, where the remains of only wattle-and-daub dwellings have been detected, on the whole shows few signs of intense commercial activity—at least with overseas trading partners. Fragments of tuyeres and slags bear witness to an iron industry of limited scope. The iron ore certainly had to be imported, but from the neighboring continent. The large number of cowries* found in these levels is perhaps evidence of an industry whose products were intended to be sent in the opposite direction. The same is true of marine shell beads whose local production is attested by the remains of sandstone polishers. The island's inhabitants grew and ground sorghum, but it is their taste for mollusks that has left the most traces. The shell middens are the best snapshot we have of the economy practiced by the island's ancient occupants, perhaps from the ninth century: mixed with shards of local ceramics, they make up the bottom of the stratigraphic sequence, right where it meets virgin sand. Kilwa's inhabitants thus were simple fishermen. But as pleasant as the environment may be, it does not on its own explain why people settled here. Perhaps one should add that shards of so-called Sasanid pottery—more rightly designated as Islamic (Abbasid)—with its typical lead glaze, were found, though in small quantity, in the deepest archaeological strata. It therefore can't be said that there was settlement here long before the connection with the Islamic world. Indeed, settlement began at the same time the area was experiencing the first shock waves of this merchant activity. There can be no trade, however modest it may be at the beginning, without people going onto the beach to take part in the exchange. It was these encounters, and the opportunities they created, that made it possible to establish the settlement and delimit its function: commercial contact.

The accounts of the founding of Kilwa, of which we possess versions from the seventeenth century on, are half history, half legend. They insist on the foreign origin of the city's royal and commercial elites. This is, of course, an elite point of view. The archaeological data have often intensified the importance of this foreign character, a flaw explained by the role imported objects, generally luxury goods, have played in the chronological assignment of the different archaeological periods identified in the site's stratigraphic deposits. But archaeology also tells us another story, a story about a population of fishermen that was capable of ironworking. The latter skill was the mark of Bantu-speaking agricultural societies, which disseminated metallurgy in the southern half of the continent during the first millennium of our era. At that time, the inhabitants of Kilwa still looked to the continent: they exported there. It was only at the dawn of the second millennium of our era, then decisively in the thirteenth century, that the islanders, or a group of them, turned toward the open sea and catalyzed long-distance commerce. The evolution of their role in this commerce has left traces: first the simple evidence of arriving merchandise—Kilwa was a remote stopover for ships from all over the Arabian Peninsula, indeed, from even farther still. Traces, of an archaeological nature, of course, but which need to be interpreted as markers of identity, indications of which were not only imported as material goods but also adopted in practice and ideas: permanent architecture that made use of locally available materials; the Muslim religion; the use of luxury dishes; coins struck with the names of kings, the sole sub-Saharan example from the Middle Ages. Here indeed are witnesses to a repertoire of values, tastes, and beliefs that took root among local elites and allowed them to recognize themselves in others of their status, to communicate and culturally join with them. They constituted the features of a culture that created the sense of belonging to cities before cities existed.

BIBLIOGRAPHICAL NOTE

An inventory of the Kilwa Bay archaeological sites, with observations on the recent restorations, has been published by Stéphane Pradines and Pierre Blanchard, "Kilwa al-Mulûk. Premier bilan des travaux de conservation-restauration et des fouilles archéologiques dans la baie de Kilwa, Tanzanie," *Annales Islamologiques* 39 (2005): 25–80; the article is accompanied by a rich iconographic dossier, notably high-quality maps and cross sections. It can be used in conjunction with John Sutton, "Kilwa: A History of the Ancient Swahili Town, with a Guide to the Monuments of Kilwa Kisiwani and Adjacent Islands," *Azania* 33 (1998): 113–169. The archaeological publication of reference on Kilwa is Neville Chittick's monograph, *Kilwa: An Islamic Trading City on the East African Coast*, 2 vols. (Nairobi: British Institute in Eastern Africa, 1974). The information about the stratigraphic levels presented in this chapter derives from this work. For a remarkable architectural study of the built remains of Kilwa, including high-quality maps and layouts, see Peter Garlake, *The Early Islamic Architecture of the East African Coast* (Nairobi: Oxford University Press, 1966), passim. Derek Nurse and Thomas Spear comment on the stratigraphy of several Swahili sites in *The Swahili: Reconstructing the History and Language of an African Society, 800–1500* (Philadelphia: University of Pennsylvania Press, 1985), pp. 16–22, which rightly insists on the important transformations that occurred in the thirteenth century in the architectural techniques and urban plans of Swahili cities. By distinguishing the Mahdalî from the Ahdali, a name that seems to belong to another regional dynasty, I part with Chittick and subscribe to the opinion put forth notably by Mark Horton and John Middleton, *The Swahili* (Malden, MA: Blackwell Publishers, 2000), passim. From an abundant literature on the site of Kilwa, we should mention the study by S. Pradines, "L'île de Sanjé ya Kati (Kilwa, Tanzanie): un mythe shirâzi bien réel," *Azania* 41 (2009): 1–25, which, despite espousing a heterodox point of view on the beginning of the site's stratigraphy, offers a very useful overview of the state of the art.

CHAPTER 22

The Camels of Madagascar, or Marco Polo's Africa

Somalia and Madagascar, End of the Thirteenth Century

It is well known that the island of Madagascar, separated from the continent by the Mozambique Channel, has no lions, zebras, monkeys, giraffes, antelopes, or any of the other common species of large African mammals. Yet regarding "Madeigascar," our Madagascar, an island with a perimeter of four thousand miles (or so he estimates), Marco Polo had this to say: "In this Island they eat no flesh but that of camels; and of these they kill an incredible number daily. They say it is the best and wholesomest of all flesh; and so they eat of it all the year round."

Marco Polo never went to Madagascar. Captured by the Genoese in 1298, he related his adventures to a fellow prisoner, a certain Rustichello, who wrote them down in Old French. Marco Polo likely learned about Madagascar during his long journey home from China, a journey that obliged him to take the maritime routes dominated by Muslim sailors. When it came to these remote regions, he couldn't help but talk about the bird called the roc, a creature of the *One Thousand and One Nights*, "so strong that it will seize an elephant in its talons and carry him high into the air, and drop him" to kill it and feast on the carcass. Moreover, Marco Polo claimed to have seen a roc feather in China; it measured ninety spans in length. Of course, we have some trouble believing this; Marco Polo had no such difficulty. The amusing thing about all this is that the legend of the roc attests to the presence of elephants on the island when none were found there or had ever been found there. Nor, for that matter, had camels. But it doesn't matter. What Marco Polo says about the size of the island and the existence of a southern current, "so strong towards the south that the ships which should attempt it [i.e., going beyond Madagascar] never would get back again," could apply only to Madagascar and the Mozambique Channel. It is a fitting tribute to the Venetian, therefore, that the name of Madagascar, found for the first time in his writings, has established itself over the other names given to it across history, al-Qumr by Arab authors, Saint Lawrence by later European navigators.

We have known for a long time that the rest of the information contained in the chapter on "Madagascar" in the *Description of the World* derives from the East African coast, more specifically from Mogadishu, whose name Marco Polo had simply confused with the island's. Power there was shared among four *esceqe* (i.e., sheiks, an Arabic word meaning "chief," "leader," "elder"), who are said to "govern the whole Island." Let's put aside the island, for Mogadishu is on the continent. From Mogadishu, merchants exported "red sanders" (perhaps an aromatic wood), ambergris (↦2), elephant tusks, and boar tusks (certainly warthog ivory). The list of animals—leopards, wolves, deer—probably corresponds to the skins that were sold there: cats, hyenas, antelopes. As for what was purchased there, it was brought by merchants. "Many traders and many ships go thither with cloths of gold and silk, and many other kinds of goods, and drive a profitable trade."

Marco Polo never went to Mogadishu either. Indeed, he tells us nothing of local society other than that the inhabitants "live by trade and handicrafts," and that they have "rather large herds"—but of what? We do not know. The reported information betrays the world of Marco Polo's informants: merchants accustomed to the quays where they loaded the cloths and unloaded the African products, but ignorant of just about all local customs.

One could say that Marco Polo's description is an unfortunate mixture of information about two different regions: Madagascar, the large island off the southeast coast of Africa, and Mogadishu, formerly a trading post, today the capital of Somalia. But truth be told, there isn't even a mixture: the two categories of information separate as easily as oil and water. The geographical information pertained to Madagascar; the commercial to Mogadishu. For Muslim navigators, Mogadishu was the first stopover, the northern port of commerce in the lands of Zanj and Sofala (↦19). In the thirteenth century, Swahili—the Bantu language, with trace elements of Arabic vocabulary, which would become the lingua franca of Kenya and Tanzania in the modern era—was already spoken there. The trading post frequented by foreign merchants was perhaps anterior to the tenth century, but it was only starting in this period that there developed a local elite strongly oriented toward trade, and which acted as an interface between the continent and the ocean. The oldest Arabic inscriptions from the region date from more than two centuries before Marco Polo. The dedicatory inscriptions of Mogadishu's ancient mosques, sure indications of the existence of a local community of believers, date from his century. Forty years after Marco Polo, the great Arab traveler Ibn Battûta described the city in this way: "We sailed on from there [Zaila] for fifteen nights and came to Maqdashaw [Mogadishu], which is a town of enormous size. Its inhabitants are merchants possessed of vast resources; they own large numbers of camels, of which they slaughter hundreds every day [for food], and also have quantities of sheep." The city was no longer run by a small senate of dignitaries but by a king, whom the traveler was obliged to visit and to whom he was expected to give homage. "He is by origin of the Barbara," said Ibn Battûta (i.e., Somali), "and he speaks Maqdishû" (i.e., Swahili), "but he knows the Arabic language," the language of trade and the Muslim religion. So sophisticated were the commercial mores that at the approach of each ship small sailboats, sambuks,* were sent to welcome the new arrivals, offering them food and lodging.

At the other, southern, extremity of the Indian Ocean universe, lay Madagascar. Persian and Arab sailors were familiar with it from at least the tenth century. Speakers of Austronesian languages coming from Borneo and Africans from the continent had been settling on the island for centuries, and it was undoubtedly visited more or less regularly by Malay pirates and merchants. We are familiar with several Muslim settlements along the northeast coast of the island; but since the powerful crosscurrents mentioned by Marco Polo made a return voyage difficult, ships rarely sailed there. One would land there only by accident or be sent there only to be soon forgotten. These settlements were located beyond the regular shipping zone of the western Indian Ocean.

Between Mogadishu and Madagascar, an entire world sprawled across the length of the coasts of southern Somalia, Kenya, Tanzania, and the northern half of Mozambique, while also encompassing the islands within reach of the coastline, such as Zanzibar, and more remote archipelagos like the Comoros. A world, a civilization both African and Muslim, rooted to land yet open to the sea, agropastoral and urban (↦21). It was the Swahili civilization, of which Marco Polo would have known nothing, or rather which he would have glossed over by speaking only of what suspicious merchants and sailors duped by legends were able to say about it. But what Marco Polo's confusion embodies—the yoking together of the two extreme points of this East African universe facing the Indian Ocean, a Mogadishu as distant as Madagascar and a Madagascar at the gates of Mogadishu—is precisely, in a nutshell, the depth and unity of this world.

BIBLIOGRAPHICAL NOTE

All citations from Marco Polo's *Description of the World* are taken from the translation and annotation by Henry Yule and Henri Cordier, which has been reissued in a beautiful illustrated edition: *The Travels of Marco Polo* (New York: Sterling Signature, 1993), pp. 312–314. When inadequate, the text of this edition was corrected after the edition in modern French by Louis Hambis, *La Description du monde* (Paris: Klincksieck, 1955). The up-to-date critical edition of the original Old French version is that of Philippe Ménard (ed.), *Le Devisement du monde*, 6 vols. (Geneva: Droz, 2001–2009). On the peopling of Madagascar, see Alexander Adelaar, "The Indonesian Migrations to Madagascar: Making Sense of the Multidisciplinary Evidence," in Alexander Adelaar, T. Simanjuntak, I.H.E. Pojoh, and M. Hisyam (eds.), *Austronesian Diaspora and the Ethnogenesis of People in Indonesian Archipelago* (Jakarta: Indonesian Institute of Science, 2006), pp. 1–23; Roger Blench, "New Palaeozoogeographical Evidence for the Settlement of Madagascar," *Azania* 42 (2007): 69–82; and Philippe Beaujard, "L'Afrique de l'Est, les Comores et Madagascar dans le système-monde eurasiatique et africain avant le 16e siècle," in Didier Nativel and Faranirina Rajaonah (eds.), *L'Afrique et Madagascar* (Paris: Karthala, 2007), pp. 29–102. Regarding Mogadishu, see the useful entry "Makdishū," by E. Cerulli and G.S.P. Freeman-Grenville, in *Encyclopedia of Islam*, 2nd ed. The extracts from Ibn Battûta are taken from H.A.R. Gibb, *The Travels of Ibn Battûta, A.D. 1234–1354* (Cambridge: Hakluyt Society, 1962), pp. 373–375.

CHAPTER 23

The Work of Angels

*Lalibela, Ethiopian Highlands, around the
Thirteenth Century*

Viewed from above, the monument is cruciform in plan, standing in the middle of a square pit such that its flat roof is not much higher than the surface. Parallel to the edges of the roof, the arms of a Greek cross are carved in relief, a smaller cross in the center. Stone stringcourses run the length of the monument's facades, with no ornamentation save for the parallel lines cut into them. Along the top register, arcaded bays are framed by uprights and surmounted by an arabesque molding and a cross. Along the lower register, at about the height of a person standing on tiptoe in the courtyard, are false windows with no openings that mimic wooden window frames. One would think that the two levels date from different periods and yet it's impossible: the monument is a single block, literally sculpted from the rock. Passing through the doors, one notices that the hollowed-out interior has pillars, arches, and vaults. It's a Christian church; in its eastern section is a room called the *maqdas*, the curtain-veiled sanctuary only priests can enter. It is there that the stone or wooden altar, the *tabot*, a replica of the Ark of the Covenant from the Old Testament, is found. This one is dedicated to Saint George (Giyorgis in Ge'ez).

The church of Giyorgis is not, strictly speaking, a "building," since it was not constructed from pieces of stone or wood placed on top of one another. It has been hewn both inside and out, carved and hollowed out from the living rock. It displays no more joints than the tunic of Christ does seams. Great effort was expended to make the work of man invisible to better celebrate the work of God.

The architectural complex of Lalibela includes other monolithic churches of this type, dedicated to Mary, Christ the Savior, and Christ Emmanuel. Some, called "semimonolithic," remain attached to rock on one side. Others are underground. There are a dozen churches in total, grouped together by ditches similar to moats, and linked to one another by corridors. The priests and the faithful say that they were built in several days with the help of angels at the time of King Lalibela, a Christian sovereign of the first third of the thirteenth century whose name was later given to the site. Scholars not given to the belief that angels helped the sculptors complete the churches often see the hand of foreign architects in this magnificent complex: men who either came down from the kingdom of Aksum in the north of Ethiopia, or were strangers entirely, from Egypt, in Lalibela's day. Romantics and best-selling novelists see the influence of the Knights Templar.

All these theories are, to say the least, poorly supported; they are mostly useless, because, however seductive to our imagination are the explanations they give, they explain only what is not proven, and what everyone seems to agree on: that the architectural complex of Lalibela was the culmination of a single architectural program. What could better explain this architectural jewel that appeared suddenly and ready-made from the matrix of the earth than an outside power, whether celestial or terrestrial?

If it's easy to trust in this single chronological attribution, it's because the evidence that would allow us to think differently is missing. Studying an archaeological site most often consists of examining the sequence of successive layers generated by human activity. It is done by digging in the ground. But when human activity in the past consisted of repeated diggings, we can't expect to discover the strata corresponding to the different phases of the site's history. The problem seems all the more intractable in the case of "hollow" monuments, where each new transformation required the removal of more rock and, in this way, gradually effaced previous features. A sculpture—and these churches are indeed sculptures—retains only the marks of the last chisel to have cut it.

The history of this place thus escapes us. Really? When closely considered, nature has certainly undermined the desired miracle of a building that had not been "built": beneath an open sky, the structures have accumulated sediment that over the centuries amassed in occupation or circulation levels. The oldest photographs show that courtyards in front of or around the churches, the large trenches that surround them, were then blocked, sometimes filled with sediment. No doubt here there was evidence of the many-layered phases of occupation since the Middle Ages. Unfortunately, most of the potential evidence for a stratigraphy was removed, with the best of intentions, during the last decades of the twentieth century by national and international heritage agencies in their attempts to improve the site. Contemplating this missing rubble leads us to wonder where those who worked on the churches deposited the resultant debris: perhaps it could provide evidence of the works' successive phases; perhaps it might preserve the remains of tools; perhaps it might conceal earlier occupations. Here the combined use of satellite imagery and ground surveys has allowed us to locate the debris; it is, quite simply, at each of the four corners of every church. We have been walking on it without seeing it for centuries. The task before us is to excavate this thankless rubble, made up of dust and stone chippings.

If we look closely at the monuments, we can see traces of the interventions men have made on the stone; the marks of changes in style and fashion; the changing function of the buildings. Let's take a look at the face of the church dedicated to the archangels Gabriel and Raphael. The entrance is on the left; a walkway recently built over the trench provides access to it. Before the door, there is a small flight of stairs. But the stairs don't lead anywhere; eight meters below there is a courtyard where a cistern has been dug, but which we can't access. On the right side of the facade, a second door leads to a hanging terrace. These are relics of structures long since disappeared: there must have been a large open-air terrace granting double access to a monument decorated with windows pierced in blind bays. The terrace was then truncated by the sinking of the courtyard to the reservoirs. Prior to that there was certainly an underground chamber in the rock, with a simple courtyard set out before a rectangular door decorated with a square frame. The original courtyard disappeared when the facade was opened. And prior to that there was just the rock.

There is certainly no longer much horizontal stratigraphy on the ground at Lalibela, but we can undoubtedly still interpret a succession of gestures and intentions vertically along the walls. They reveal that there were several architectural programs on the site, which one after another modified the previous designs: disavowing the earlier function of this monument, which was not originally a church; forgetting the initial purpose of that trench, which was not originally a protective moat; neglecting the ancient usage of this passage, which was a door before it became a high, overhanging window. These successive transformations have left time for people to forget what previous states of the site looked like; they have left room to reinvent the history and the purpose of the site. It goes without saying, then, that it is improbable, even setting aside the angels, that the Lalibela complex as we know it today was the work of one hand and one period.

At the top of some of the sculpted walls, hanging above the space hollowed out over subsequent centuries, we find little dome-shaped chambers and narrow tunnels running under the surface of the rock. These are the remains of small, troglodytic dwellings that belonged to the site's original inhabitants before the first church was cut from the rock. Here or there we notice Aksumite, Coptic, Islamic, or other influences on the churches' decoration and architectural elements. But for knowledge of the site's geology and the mechanical properties of the bedrock, the techniques of architects well versed in three-dimensional representations of the underground spaces, and the experience of stone carvers, we need look no further than local know-how. Furthermore, throughout Ethiopia rock-hewn churches are often connected with the presence of ancient troglodytic dwellings. To better understand the men and women who made the rock-hewn churches of Lalibela, we must lose the habit of seeing in their actions only techniques learned from others.

BIBLIOGRAPHICAL NOTE

David Phillipson's lavishly illustrated *Ancient Churches of Ethiopia* (New Haven, CT: Yale University Press, 2009) is largely dedicated to the site of Lalibela. For an introduction to the latest research conducted at Lalibela, see François-Xavier Fauvelle-Aymar, Laurent Bruxelles, Romain Mensan, Claire Bosc-Tiessé, Marie-Laure Derat, and Emmanuel Fritsch, "Rock-Cut Stratigraphy: Sequencing the Lalibela Churches," *Antiquity* 84 (2010): 1135–1150, and Claire Bosc-Tiessé, M.-L. Derat, Laurent Bruxelles, François-Xavier Fauvelle, Yves Gleize, and Romain Mensan, "The Lalibela Rock Hewn Site and Its Landscape (Ethiopia): An Archaeological Analysis," *Journal of African Archaeology* 12 (2014): 141–164. The idea of an Egyptian origin of the Lalibela complex and the architectural know-how on display there is defended by Claude Lepage, "Un métropolite égyptien bâtisseur à Lalibäla (Éthiopie) entre 1205 et 1210," *Comptes-Rendus des séances de l'Académie des Inscriptions et Belles-Lettres* 146 (2002): 141–174. The association between the rock-hewn churches and troglodytic dwellings was suggested by F. Anfray, "Des églises et des grottes rupestres," *Annales d'Éthiopie* 13 (1985): 7–34.

CHAPTER 24

The Sultan and the Sea

Coast of Present-Day Senegal or Gambia, around 1312

The titles alone of books and articles devoted to a supposed African settlement of pre-Columbian America could fill a whole book. This bibliography can be divided into two sections. The first, largely produced by Europeans, especially in the nineteenth and early twentieth centuries, sought to demonstrate that Mesoamerican civilizations owed their rise to an original seed transmitted by migration from pharaonic Egypt, mother of civilizations, and were therefore linked to what contemporaries considered the glorious civilizations of the ancient Mediterranean. The second, produced mostly by African Americans and Africans in the second half of the twentieth century, desired to believe roughly the same thing, but with the premise that Egypt was a black civilization, and the implication that credit for having been the cradle of all civilization redounded to Africa. "Eurocentrism" against "Afrocentrism": a battle of ideologies that conceals a war over memory. It is summed up well by the question "Who owns ancient Egypt?"

There is not the slightest bit of evidence to support the idea of an extra-American origin for the Olmec, Mayan, Toltec, or Aztec civilizations. Pairs of similar phenomena will always be compared; it's the strategy of a number of authors who find things that resemble each other and see in them something more than mere "coincidence": the pyramids of Egypt and the pyramids of Mexico, a Mayan glyph and a Saharan rock engraving, a monumental Olmec statue and an African face. Attention is especially given to the slightest trace of direct contact between the two continents before the fateful date of 1492. If there had been Vikings in the "Vinland" of the ancient Icelandic sagas, that is to say Newfoundland, before Christopher Columbus, and they settled there for at least several decades during the eleventh century, why couldn't African adventurers have also reached the New World, preferably its central and southern part (since it was here that cultural forms best perceived as civilizations developed)? Such an episode, if it really happened, does not a "civilizing hero" make, no more than in the case of the Vikings (the voyage needed to have unleashed a continuous and irreversible movement of settlers); but why not discoverers?

Yet there is indeed a story that seems to substantiate this hypothesis. It is related by Ibn Fadl Allâh al-Umarî, who was for a time, before he fell out of favor with the sultan, secretary of the Mamluk chancery in Egypt, and later, more famously, an encyclopedist very curious about the lands of sub-Saharan Africa. Al-Umarî, who wrote in the 1340s, took this story from the emir Abû l-Hasan Alî, who was governor of Cairo when Sultan Mûsâ of Mâli passed through the Egyptian capital on his pilgrimage to Mecca in the year 724 of the Hijra, that is, 1324 CE. The emir was full of anecdotes about the sultan. Once he asked him how he came to power. Al-Umarî, who heard the tale, preserved the monarch's response.

"We belong," said Mûsâ, "to a house which hands on the kingship by inheritance. The king who was my predecessor did not believe that it was impossible to discover the furthest limit of the Atlantic Ocean and wished vehemently to do so. He equipped 200 ships filled with men and the same number equipped with gold, water, and provisions enough to last them for years, and said to the man deputed to lead them: 'Do not return until you reach the end of it or your provisions and water give out.' They departed and a long time passed before anyone came back. Then one ship returned and we asked the captain what news they brought. He said, 'Yes, O Sultan, we travelled for a long time until there appeared in the open sea [as it were] a river with a powerful current. Mine was the last of those ships. The [other] ships went on ahead but when they reached that place they did not return and no more was seen of them and we do not know what became of them. As for me, I went about at once and did not enter that river.' But the sultan disbelieved him.

"Then that sultan got ready 2,000 ships, 1,000 for himself and the men whom he took with him and 1,000 for water and provisions. He left me to deputize for him and embarked on the Atlantic Ocean with his men. That was the last we saw of him and all those who were with him, and so I became king in my own right."

The story speaks to us of a maritime expedition, a fleet of small boats that never returned—perhaps because, one can imagine, one may want to believe, it had reached the opposite shore. Are these the real discoverers? And since they were surely not just a handful of people at landfall, must they have transmitted some aspects of African civilizations across the Atlantic? And since they were capable of doing it once, had they not been able to do it before? But note that the story doesn't tell us about a continent at the end of the ocean. No one in the chain of informants who participated in the elaboration and transmission of this account evoked a land located on the other coast of the Atlantic. Given that the sultan seemed so intent on proving that the crossing was possible, it is therefore quite clear that the idea that there was something at the other "end" of the ocean rather than nothing at all (a chasm, the edge of the world, darkness) was a theory that had not yet been validated by experience: no one had returned to vouch for it. Yet if they really had taken place, the expeditions of four hundred and two thousand small boats did not return, and if any discovery was made, it wasn't known. To discover something, one has to reach somewhere; to have discovered something, one has to come back to where one started.

Never mind that Raymond Mauny, a famous French historian of Africa, believed he had shown definitively that such an expedition was impossible given the practical conditions of the time. The expedition of Mûsâ's predecessor is to be situated, to paraphrase Mauny, in a world of paddled canoes: a world with no tradition of maritime sailing, either along the coast or on the high seas, which had never settled the Atlantic archipelagos (Cape Verde was not inhabited when the Portuguese arrived), and which was ignorant of wind patterns and currents. To use Mauny's expression, it was only a failed attempt that falls into the "martyrology of maritime discovery." But if his demonstration has convinced only those who wanted to be convinced, it is because it's an almost impossible task to prove that something did *not* happen.

Fourteenth-century Mâli (↦26, 28, 29) was a vast kingdom—it is sometimes called an empire since its Muslim monarch had several kings as vassals, kings whom he had either conquered or forced to pay him homage by some other means. Among them was a monarch whose realm bordered the Atlantic coast between the Senegal and Gambia Rivers. It was the empire's maritime window, certainly very far from the centers of power in the Malian savanna. But the country's merchant and itinerant elites surely knew this littoral province, and so the western sea was not unknown to people from the heartland of Mâli. Whether the expedition took place or not, we are definitely talking about what is called the Atlantic Ocean today, and not about other bodies of water, allegorical or real ("sea" is a word used in many languages, including Arabic, to designate lakes). Maybe this story was an allusion to Arab maritime voyages of the time transmitted by foreign ulamas* who traversed the land in order to convert people to Islam? But there were scarcely any. Contemporaneous geographers reveal their ignorance about all things oceanic, and those who were really knowledgeable (i.e., sailors) were too few to venture along the Atlantic coasts south of Morocco; as for setting sail on the open sea, they probably did not do so, and consequently were unaware of the Canary Islands and Madeira. There was also the legend associated with Uqba ibn Nâfi, the conqueror of North Africa who was credited in many places with all sorts of miracles (↦5); the narrative of his conquests may have circulated in Sahelian countries. It says that, having entered Africa by way of Egypt, he reached Sous on Morocco's Atlantic coast. There he rode his horse into the sea, calling God to witness that he would have continued his path if the continent had extended to the west. Would the sultan of Mâli have remembered this scene, would he have tried to reenact it, as if to showcase both his historical accomplishment as a Muslim monarch and the political and religious project his ships carried with them? Calmly recounted by Mûsâ, his immediate successor, to a high-ranking official of Mamluk Egypt, the anecdote was infused with a valuable diplomatic message: I spring from a dynasty so devout that it claims to carry Islam beyond the ocean and to die a martyr's death while doing so.

But, truth be told, there are reasons to doubt that this is really what the text is talking about, and when we reconsider its tenor, it certainly looks as though the anecdote must have inspired envy in those who heard about an enterprise so obviously devoid of interest and perhaps even marked by excessive vanity. However, the hypothesis has the merit of bringing us back to the literal meaning of the text. The sultan responded roughly as follows: "We belong to a house which hands on the kingship by inheritance. The king who was my predecessor did not believe that it was impossible to discover the furthest limit of the Atlantic Ocean. He wished to do so and *failed*. And so I became king in my own right." In this story, which is first of all the story of a royal succession, there is perhaps something more profound and interesting than a catalyst for quarrels over precedence when it comes to crossing the Atlantic.

We often read that Mûsâ's unfortunate predecessor was called Abû Bakr or Abu-Bakari. This was absolutely false, even though author after author diligently repeated it. This erroneous idea originated with a misunderstanding of the text of the famous historian Ibn Khaldûn that recounted the genealogy of the sultans of Mâli. The correct reading is that Abû Bakr was Mûsâ's father, but not that he preceded his son on the throne. Mûsâ's predecessor as sultan of Mâli was named Muhammad; he belonged to another branch of the dynasty, which had passed on the title from father to son since the time of the line's progenitor, Mâri-Djâta, in the mid-thirteenth century. It was Muhammad whom Mûsâ succeeded around 1312. These details are important, for they signify that Mûsâ's accession had brought another branch of the ruling dynasty to power. The story of the maritime expedition has perhaps something to do with the succession, which was certainly not peaceful inasmuch as Mûsâ issued from a collateral branch, and which couldn't help but raise grave problems of legitimacy. The account Mûsâ gave of his accession to power is perhaps not to be understood as the seemingly off-topic narration of a maritime expedition, but as the reasoning behind his legitimate rule. He began his story with the words "We belong to a house which hands on the kingship by inheritance." Thus we should take him at his word and listen to *how* the kingship was inherited.

There is always a risk, as mentioned above, when making comparisons. But let's do it anyway, while remaining cognizant of its limitations, by bringing together several pieces of a puzzle, which will make it possible to illuminate a practice encountered in several African societies.

There are several myths about the origin of the kingdom of Loango, which flourished in central Africa, in what is today the western part of the Republic of Congo and the Angolese enclave of Cabinda, from the sixteenth century on. One of these myths evoked the civilizing hero, who is credited with teaching humanity how to make fire and increase fertility. He also introduced the institution of monarchy. Having reached the mouth of the river he was sailing on, he appeared to the inhabitants to be coming from the sea. They acknowledged him as king. Another recounted the origins of the kingdom's second dynasty. The people could no longer tolerate their monarchs' misrule and overthrew them; they sought a foundress for a new royal line. She was discovered in the forest, a young Pygmy girl, a member of a population endowed with strange, sacral attributes. She was accompanied to the seashore, then made to sail a bit farther to the kingdom promised to her descendants. She married and her son became the first king. In these two cases, the detour to the sea is synonymous with recognition or perhaps the ordeal par excellence; carried out under the beneficent aegis of a rain deity, it legitimated the new king, especially in the precise case of a dynastic void.

Let's turn now to what was perhaps southern Somalia or northern Kenya a few centuries earlier. In 922, a storm tossed ashore a ship full of Omani merchants bound for Kanbalu on the coast of Zanj. Nowhere near a familiar port, the men were almost certain, they believed, to be eaten. But the

African population was welcoming and its young king favorable to trade. As they were leaving, the ungrateful Arabs kidnapped the king and took him as a slave (at the same time, moreover, some two hundred other individuals were purchased locally). The king would be sold at Oman in the southeastern corner of the Arabian Peninsula. A few years later, the same merchants suffered another storm in the same vicinity, which, to add insult to injury, tossed their boat onto the same stretch of coast. To their great surprise, they met the king, who recognized them and gave them a cold reception. Ultimately magnanimous, he pardoned them and told his story. Taken to Baghdad after he had been sold at Oman, the young man had learned Arabic and became a Muslim. He then escaped, going first to Mecca, then to Cairo, and eventually managed to find the beach where he had been seized. He was afraid to disembark, for he believed that the new king of the country would quickly have him killed. But the seers had warned against taking a new king until there was news of the missing one. He thus arrived at the palace, where he was recognized and warmly welcomed. This tale is certainly full of the folklore of Arab and Persian sailors, but a story is embedded here that we can think of as African. It matters little whether the adventure really happened or was just a myth; what catches our attention is that a long journey across the sea was necessary to see our young man confirmed twice over: as king, by his people, and as Muslim, by the traveling merchants.

There are certainly elements missing here—historical, ethnological, mythological—that need to be found. But those we have are already enough to enable us to formulate a hypothesis: that a common mythology of the origin of royalty existed in several regions of Africa, perhaps a common ritual for the investiture of a new king during times of crisis. Whether this served to describe how authority emerged from a power vacuum, or prescribes a ritual the king must undertake to be acknowledged as ruler, it was the detour by the ocean, father of all waters, that made the monarch.

Did the expeditions of Muhammad take place? Perhaps not, if we take Mûsâ's account of them to be only the story of a dynastic crisis expressed in the political language of the kingdom of Mâli. But if it did, it's a safe bet that his political act—whose precise religious frame we struggle to recognize: royal initiation, purification ritual, trial by ordeal?—was designed to challenge the ocean and return from it with a reinforced claim to the throne. It was a failure. But there was a winner: the storyteller himself, King Mûsâ.

BIBLIOGRAPHICAL NOTE

The sultan's story as recounted by al-Umarî is taken from Nehemia Levtzion and J.F.P. Hopkins (eds.), *Corpus of Early Arabic Sources for West African History* (Princeton, NJ: Markus Wiener, 2000), pp. 268–269. Regarding the Afrocentric theory of a civilizing settlement of America by Africans, see, among a huge literature, Ivan Van Sertima, *They Came before Columbus* (New York: Random House, 1976). The question "Who owns ancient Egypt?" is borrowed from the title of the excellent review article by Wyatt MacGaffey, "Who Owns Ancient Egypt?" *Journal of African History* 32 (1991): 515–519. Raymond Mauny's reflections on the supposed maritime expedition of Mûsâ's predecessor are laid out in *Navigations médiévales sur les côtes sahariennes antérieures à la découverte portugaise (1434)* (Lisbon: Centro de Estudos históricos ultramarinos, 1960). The most up-to-date study on the genealogy of the sultans of Mâli remains that of Nehemia Levtzion, "The Thirteenth and Fourteenth-Century Kings of Mali," *Journal of African History* 4 (1963): 341–353. The Loango myths come from Luc de Heusch, *Le Roi de Kongo et les monstres sacrés* (Paris: Gallimard, 2000), pp. 44–48. The story of the Omani sailors, which appears in a ninth-century work by a Persian navigator, Buzurg ibn Shahriyâr, has been translated into English by G.S.P. Freeman-Grenville, *The East African Coast* (Oxford: Clarendon Press, 1962), pp. 9–13.

CHAPTER 25

Ruins of Salt

Taghâza, Extreme North of Present-Day Mali,
from the Eleventh to the Sixteenth Century

In 1934, Théodore Monod—who had wanted to be an oceanographer and instead became a desert explorer—although he had not yet acquired the renown as an expert of the Sahara that he would later have, followed the *azalaï*, the great biennial caravan departing from Timbuktu. Three thousand camels driven by Tuareg traders left for Taoudenni in the far north of the Malian Sahara to return to Timbuktu loaded with bars of salt from the mine at Agorgot. The route was 800 kilometers long. Having arrived at its end, Monod wanted to visit Taghâza, still 150 kilometers to the northwest. He would not be disappointed: "Two ruined villages are still visible," he wrote, "where we find the remains of buildings. . . . And it's not only the bases of leveled walls, but sometimes even real architectural fragments, semicircular arches, for instance. In sodium chloride. . . . On the ground, there is a lot of rubble, shards of painted and glazed Moroccan pottery, copper objects, beads, innumerable fragments of broken bracelets made of multicolored glass threads. At the heart of a very arid region, Teghazza [Taghâza] is devoid of pasturage; it is not a place where one can loiter. I spent only a few hours there."

Monod knew his classics. He knew that before him the French traveler René Caillié, who made the same journey disguised as an Arab in 1828 when returning from Timbuktu, had halted at Telig, the mine situated a short distance (a half day's journey) from Taoudenni; there, Caillié learned that black slaves produced blocks of salt under the supervision of "Moors," that is to say, Muslim Berbers. A few days later, having resumed travel on the road to Tafilalet, he arrived at Taghâza. There, he says, one encounters "big blocks of salt, and, a short distance from where the animals were watered, several houses made from bricks of salt." Long before him, Ibn Battûta had stayed at Taghâza. It was March 1352: "We stayed there for ten days, under strain because the water there is brackish. It is the most fly-ridden of places." He noted the curious architecture: the houses and the mosque were built from blocks of salt, the roofs from camel skins. Rock salt was mined there, the salt deposits being only three to four meters below the surface. The work of cutting the salt was done by the Berbers' slaves, who lived on dates brought from Morocco and pearl millet imported from the Sahel. This is indicative of the importance of trade at Taghâza in the Middle Ages. Centuries later, a contemporary of Monod made the same assessment of Taoudenni. The living conditions in the two neighboring mines must not have been very different: "Taoudenni is uninhabitable; its brackish water kills within a few years the black workers they bring there and force to work. There must be no industrial hell on earth that could compare to this one."

Taghâza is located in a vast *sebkha*, a natural flat pan that, millions of years ago, was on the seashore. Equidistant from the northern steppe and the Sahel to the south, the salt slabs cut there were transported to the "Land of the Blacks" for centuries. It was perhaps already the locality called Tâtantâl (in the Arabic sources) in the eleventh century, where there apparently stood "a castle built from rock-salt. The houses, battlements, and rooms are all of this salt." Salt production at Taghâza was so important to the economy of trans-Saharan trade that it excited envy. Caravans from Mali and Morocco stocked up on supplies of salt there when it was under the control of the Massûfa Berbers. The Songhai kingdom administered it for a time from Timbuktu. The sultans of Morocco captured it in the middle of the sixteenth century, with no other effect than shifting mining toward Taoudenni, a less easily exploitable site, but one slightly closer to Timbuktu. Taghâza, however, was not abandoned: people settled there again in the seventeenth century. Monod collected pottery shards from this period at the site, and the few archaeological surveys that have been carried out there have mostly uncovered evidence from these later occupations.

Hasan al-Wazzân, better known as Leo Africanus, who spent several days in Taghâza around 1510, tells us that it was from there that salt was transported to Timbuktu "where there would otherwise be extreme scarcity of salt." Ibn Battûta tells us about the price of salt: "One load of it is sold . . . at the city of Mali for 30 or twenty mithqals. It has sometimes fetched 40 mithqals." But already at the time when the mine was called Tâtantâl and the city of Ghâna (↦7, 8) held sway over the western Sahel, "the king took a gold dinar for every load of salt that entered his kingdom, and two for every load that left." This means that the salt was imported, evidently from the desert, only to be reexported to the savanna regions. "They stand in pressing need of the [goodwill] of the kings of Awdaghust [Aoudaghost, a vassal state of Ghâna]," we read, "because of the salt which comes to them from the lands of Islam." Between the open-air mine, administered by nomads who worked it with their slaves, and the sedentary populations of farmers to the south stretched an ancient route, which varied only in its southern terminus—Ghâna, Mâli, Timbuktu—over the centuries. The existence of this salt road illustrates the demand that it satisfied for a product as precious in the south of the Sahara as gold was in the north. For the African soils, while rich in ores, are lacking in mineral salts and transmit this insufficiency to plants and animals. Camels and cows overcome this deficiency by the practice of the "salt cure," an annual pasturage that consists of leading the herds to grazing areas rich in minerals where the livestock are left to graze or lick salt crystals. For humans, the consumption of salt (sodium chloride and micronutrients) remedies the salt deficiency that engenders mineral malnutrition (the cause of such disorders as anemia and goiter) and increases the metabolic resistance to heat.

Raymond Mauny has highlighted the diverse ways salt is produced in West Africa. The complex techniques that he identified have distributions closely correlated with ecologic zones. Along the coast in southern Mauritania and northern Senegal, salt is produced by the evaporation of seawater in natural or artificial basins. But to the north and south of this littoral portion, the elevated rate of nocturnal humidity precludes this method. To the south, along the littoral regions of the Gulf of Guinea, the boiling of seawater is practiced, and the resultant salt loaves are resold throughout the forest zone. The vast savanna zone corresponds to the distribution of diverse techniques for obtaining plant salts: halophytes are burned in fireplaces; the ashes are washed and then put through a process of decantation to produce salty brine. The brine is evaporated from clay molds placed above kilns. In the area bounded by the Niger River, Lake Chad, and the Aïr Massif, a similar process is used: there salty earth is collected and washed. The brine is brought to a boil to form salt loaves at the bottom of clay basins. The whole western Sahelian zone is dependent on a more practical saline resource, though one that is more difficult to exploit. More practical, for here salt, which appears as fossilized pure sodium chloride, rock salt, lies in regular deposits interspersed with thin beds of clay. The Arab sources were familiar with the mines of the Sahara. Taghâza is one of them. They also mentioned Awlîl, which must have been located on the coast of southern Mauritania, and even Tawtok or Toutek, a subterranean mine whose exact location remains a mystery, but which might have been situated in the extreme east of Mali or near the southeast Algerian border; the people of Gao imported their salt from this mine and used it for currency. And that's basically all we know. To the problem of rarity one might add other difficulties: the labor-intensive exploitation cannot depend on family relationships, nor can it emerge from a domestic or local economy. In other words, the supply of salt depends on an activity that can only be "externalized" and submitted to the laws—to the risks—of long-distance trade. A staple of life, salt was endowed with an importance in sub-Saharan Africa that explains the attraction a place as miserable as Taghâza exercised for centuries over the powers bordering the Sahara.

BIBLIOGRAPHICAL NOTE

Nicole Vray has written a biography of Théodore Monod: *Monsieur Monod, scientifique, voyageur, protestant* (Arles: Actes Sud, 1994). The excerpt about Monod's visit to Taghâza is from his work *Méharées* (Arles: Actes Sud, 1989, 1st ed. 1937), p. 266. The one about René Caillié comes from his *Voyage à Tombouctou* (Paris: La Découverte, 1996), 2:294; regarding Taoudenni, see pp. 284–285 of the same work. For the working conditions at this mine, see Dominique Meunier, "Le commerce du sel de Taoudeni," *Journal des africanistes* 50 (1980): 133–144, and the abundant bibliography provided by the author. Ibn Battûta's account of Taghâza, al-Bakrî's description of Tâtantâl, and Ibn Hawqal's comments on salt and the kings of Aoudaghost may be found in Nehemia Levtzion and J.F.P. Hopkins (eds.), *Corpus of Early Arabic Sources for West African History* (Princeton, NJ: Markus Wiener, 2000), p. 282, p. 76, and p. 49, respectively. For Ibn Hawqal's comments on the dues levied on salt by the kings of Ghâna, see Joseph Cuoq, *Recueil des sources arabes* (Paris: Éditions du CNRS, 1985), p. 74. For a synthesis of the meager archaeological data relative to Taghâza, for the most part unpublished, see Raymond Mauny, *Tableau géographique de l'Ouest africain au Moyen Âge* (Dakar: Institut français d'Afrique noire, 1961), pp. 116–117, 328–332. Pages 321–334 are devoted to the techniques of salt production in West Africa and the Sahara (the invaluable map deserves careful attention). In the same vein, but lacking the archaeological documentation, see E. Ann McDougall, "Salts of the Western Sahara: Myths, Mysteries, and Historical Significance," *International Journal of African Historical Studies* 23 (1990): 231–257. The complete text of John Pory's translation of Leo Africanus's *History and Description of Africa* (1600) has been published by the Hakluyt Society: John Pory (ed.), Leo Africanus, *History and Description of Africa*, 3 vols. (London: Hakluyt Society, 1896). Leo's description of Taghâza is found on 3:800–801. (The spelling has been modernized.) A remarkable document preserving for us an account of the caravan journey between Taghâza and Sijilmâsa in 1685 may be found in Larbi Mezzine, "Relation d'un voyage de Taġāzā à Siġilmāsa en 1096 H./1685 J.-C.," *Arabica* 43 (1996): 211–233. Monod's contemporary cited in the text is Émile-Félix Gautier; for the citation see his *Le Sahara* (Paris: Payot, 1923), p. 163. On the history and health impact of iodine (the nutrient contained in salt) deficiency, see B. S. Hetzel, *The Story of Iodine Deficiency: An International Challenge in Nutrition* (Oxford: Oxford University Press, 1989). On salt deficiency in animals, see T. W. Schillhorn van Veen and I. K. Loeffler, "Mineral Deficiency in Ruminants in Subsaharan Africa: A Review," *Tropical Animal Health and Production* 22, no. 3 (1990): 197–205.

CHAPTER 26

The Customs of Mâli

Oualata, Present-Day Mauritania, around 17 April 1352

First of all, you will have to deal with a desert mafia. For if they are not your guides and your guards, they will rob you. In the past, the severed heads of these Berber bandits covered the ground of the palace at Sijilmâsa (↦16); there were highwaymen, then, who stopped you across the Sahara en route to the Land of the Blacks. It was the end of the thirteenth century. Authority in North Africa belonged to the Almohads. Though very much concerned with moral and legal precepts, they were not much concerned with protecting their neighbors' lives. In other periods, robbers were converted into protectors—for a price, of course. Between mid-February and mid-April 1352, Ibn Battûta, the Moroccan traveler who delighted in exploring the whole of the Islamic world (↦29), crossed the Sahara. The Masûfa, a tribe of the Sanhâja confederation, controlled the caravan. Let's be clear: the leader of the caravan, the scouts, the camel drivers, the guards were all from this tribe. It was better to *put* one's fate into their hands than to *fall* into their hands. Anyway, one was forced to trust them: the guide of Ibn Battûta's caravan was blind in one eye, or at least that's what the caravan members were led to believe, but he remained the authority on a route that was not easily visible, as a Roman commercial road would be, a route that wound through loose, stony ground and was always susceptible, as they were also led to believe, to being hidden beneath "mountains of sand."

Then there was the problem of water. It would be even better to say the problem of thirst, your constant companion during the crossing. All travelers, all geographers say the same thing: the water is sometimes "fetid and lethal" and, Yâqût humorously reckons, "has none of the qualities of water other than being liquid." Such a beverage inevitably generates intestinal pains that make life difficult and sour the memory of the trans-Saharan experience. In good years, when there had been plenty of rain, water filled the rocky gullies, and people could drink and do laundry. In bad years, the burning wind dried out the water in the goatskins; consequently, a camel's throat had to be cut and its stomach removed. The water it contained was drawn off into a sump and drunk with a straw. In the worst-case scenario, one could kill an addax antelope and follow a similar procedure to extract greenish water from its entrails. Some authors remembered that the Maqqarî had formerly "established the desert route by digging wells and seeing to the security of merchants." But it was during the period when the big merchants of North Africa purported to deal with the material organization of the caravan and the route themselves; it was a time when captured bandits had their heads cut off. At that time, the caravan's departure was announced by the beating of a drum, while a standard, probably that of the ruler of Sijilmâsa, fluttered in the wind in front of the caravan. Since then, the merchants resigned themselves to outsourcing the organization of the crossing to the desert nomads, and, whether the maintenance lapsed under the reformed bandits or whether the new caravan masters thought it right to justify their services' high prices, the wells disappeared. Thirst would kill you, but death is less painful than what brings it about: first you experience a sort of sluggishness before losing consciousness; had you been lost alone, you would either be found or not. "It's the leading cause of death in the Sahara," a twentieth-century French colonial officers' manual warned its readers.

A shopkeeper's mind-set was needed in the caravan. You would buy your camels at Sijilmâsa, then let them fatten for four months, as Ibn Battûta did, so that they could handle the crossing. Some big merchants had hundreds of the beasts, others only a few. One could never depart with only one camel; at least two were needed: one for you, one for the baggage. If you rode a horse, you had to bring water for it to drink. Before departure, each merchant made arrangements for his merchandise as well as for his saddlery and supplies. At the last moment, the members of the caravan filled their *guerba*, water containers made of goatskins. It was also necessary to get recommendations about where to stay when one reached one's destination—someone needed to book a house or room. En route, everything has its price; nothing is held in common. The nomads provided only their knowledge of the route and the security of the column. At the hottest time of the day, all pitch their tents. The travelers needed to be able to count on their servants for the menial tasks. The guards had to be bribed to watch your goods or to refrain from stealing them themselves. On the return trip, you'd be well advised to keep an eye on your gold and slaves. But even if you kept a watchful eye, this business still came with troubles. The following anecdote, which dates from the early thirteenth century, has the value of a parable: "My maternal uncle," a merchant says, "undertook a voyage to the south to trade gold. He bought a camel to get there. While traveling, he found himself in the company of a city-dweller. . . . The city-dweller had started his slave business. Both of them took the caravan back home. My uncle felt comfortable and free from worry: if the caravan left, he mounted his camel; if the caravan halted, he pitched his tent and rested. But our city-dweller was exhausted and overwhelmed with worries about his slaves: one was wasting away, another was hungry, this one escaped, that one got lost in the erg.* When the caravan stopped, each attended to his own affairs. Our city-dweller was entirely worn out. During this time, he looked at [my uncle], who was seated peacefully in the shade with his fortune." How many stories circulated about old seasoned travelers taking advantage of city-dwellers as ambitious as they were inexperienced?

And then there were the small, but numerous and in the end obnoxious, daily inconveniences: the omnipresent fleas, which you would try to drive away by wearing cords soaked in mercury around your neck; the numerous flies everywhere there was a rotting carcass (i.e., precisely around the wells and the camps); the snakes. In the caravan of February 1352—Ibn Battûta's caravan—a certain al-Hâjj Zayyân, a merchant of Tlemcen in present-day Algeria who loved to catch snakes and play with them, was bitten on his index finger. The injury was cauterized with a red-hot iron; then, as a remedy, he cut the throat of a camel and put his hand into the animal's stomach and left it there the whole night. Was it really useful?

He thought so. In any case, it wasn't enough: he had to cut it off at the joint. The Masûfa must have laughed a lot at these city-dweller pastimes. Either pretending to be experts or eager to paint a bleak picture of the risks, they said that the bite would have been fatal if the serpent hadn't drunk water before biting him. Finally, there are the demons, which Ibn Battûta says are numerous in the desert. These imperceptible deities like to toy with isolated travelers. Mischievous, they seduce you so that you end up losing your way.

The caravan tempers these harsh conditions with strict discipline; it diminishes them through distractions. You will put distance between your-self and the column only at your own risk, the Berber leader must have said. The camels, indeed, walk as if to the beat of a metronome. They will stop when they receive the order to do so, that is to say, at the planned halt on a beeline route. And while the camels carrying the loads were under way at a regular pace, under the guidance of the impassive Masûfa, those who paid for the crossing would amuse themselves hunting addax, letting their dogs run free, and riding a bit ahead of the caravan to let their horses graze and to enjoy the invigorating wait. But the games, the intemperance of the city-dwellers, could cost them dearly. Even though caravans could be made up of hundreds, sometimes even thousands, of camels, one could quickly lose sight of them behind a curtain of dunes. Two cousins, Ibn Zîrî and Ibn Adî, were members of our Moroccan traveler's caravan. The two argued, and Ibn Zîrî let himself pull back from the rest of the caravan to show his annoyance. That was the first mistake! "[W]hen the people encamped there was no news of him," writes Ibn Battûta. "I advised his cousin to hire one of the Masûfa to follow his track in the hope of finding him, but he refused." Second mistake! "Next day one of the Masûfa under-took, without pay, to look for him. He found his trace, which sometimes followed the beaten track and sometimes left it, but could get no news of him." Should he have sent this guard unpaid? This was perhaps the third mistake. We will never know which one of these mistakes was fatal. A few centuries later, on the same stretch of desert, but from the opposite direction, a caravan of pilgrims lost two of its members in a row and yet noticed only a day and a night after they disappeared. The author of the story concludes philosophically: "But our conscience was clear because we had warned them of the risks they were running by not abiding by the rules of the caravan."

After a two-month journey, you will arrive at the end of the crossing. In the fourteenth century, the point of arrival was Oualata, in what is now southeast Mauritania. You are already in another world. A few days earlier, a messenger hurried ahead to announce the caravan's arrival. He carried letters from the travelers to the city's merchants. At the news, the people of Oualata sent loads of water, which of course were sold to the travelers, but which would help the men and horses to cross the final segment of the route, through a sweltering, sterile desert—so sweltering, in fact, that the caravan could travel only at night.

Ibn Battûta arrived in Oualata at the beginning of the first month of Rabî in the year 753 of the Muslim calendar (i.e., in the days following 17 April 1352). The heat there was torrid. "There are," he writes, "a few little palm trees there in the shade of which they sow water melons. Their water comes from *ahsâ'* [water holes] there. Mutton is abundant there and the people's clothes are of Egyptian cloth, of good quality. . . . [The] women are of surpassing beauty and have a higher status than the men." These are the impressions of a tourist, a bit short on detail for someone who stayed in the city for fifty days. The population was Masûfa Berber. North African merchants had established a residence there; it was through a man from Salé, another Moroccan, that our traveler found a house to rent. But the order that reigned there emanated from Mâli, the powerful black kingdom that had already made Oualata one of its possessions, the "first district of the Sûdân," at a distance of twenty-four days from the capital to the south. You see the governor of the city, the *farbâ*, a Manding title. "He was sitting on a carpet . . . with his assistants in front of him with lances and bows in their hands and the chief men of the Masûfa behind him. The merchants stood before him while he addressed them, in spite of their proximity to him, through an interpreter, out of contempt for them." The arrangement was as precise as the rules of the protocol: the armed guards stood before the governor, the local dignitaries behind him.

The camels had barely set foot in the city, Ibn Battûta tells us, when "the merchants placed their belongings in an open space, where the Sûdân took over the guard of them" while the merchants went to pay tribute to the governor. This haste and the marks of respect that the merchants made to the *farbâ* shocked our author: "At this I repented at having come to their country because of their ill manners and their contempt for white men." Invited later by the *mushrif*, an Arabic term for tax collector, to a light meal to welcome the caravan, he stiffened again; it was as if he barely glanced at the dish of crushed millet mixed with honey and yogurt served to the guests in a gourd. "Was it to this that the black man invited us?" he asked his companions with, one guesses, an affected frown. "They said: 'Yes, for them this is a great banquet.'"

Such haughtiness prevented Ibn Battûta from seeing what was at stake around him. The rules of etiquette, the discipline, the assaults of politeness to which each yielded with diligence are testament to a world of subtler codes than the severity of the caravan drivers. The merchants, who had dearly longed for the moment they could at last escape from the control of the caravanners, entered this new world right away, but not the tourist, who traveled bringing his own world with him. At Oualata, the merchant entered Mâli. It was a frontier post, then a customs post. If the merchants immediately unloaded the camels on the open space and left everything under guard, it was because this was necessary for calculating the appropriate tax to be paid based on the weight of the merchandise. When the scouts were sent ahead of the caravan, it was perhaps also to avoid venturing onto a smuggler's route. You have left the mafia; you have entered the state.

The extracts cited either directly or indirectly from the work of Ibn Battûta may be found in Nehemia Levtzion and J.F.P. Hopkins (eds.), *Corpus of Early Arabic Sources for West African History* (Princeton, NJ: Markus Wiener, 2000), pp. 282–285. The excerpts from Yâqût (the cesspool technique) and Ibn al-Khatîb (the Maqqarî brothers) are found on pp. 169 and 307, respectively. The story of the gold merchant and the city-dweller may be found in Joseph Cuoq, *Recueil des sources arabes* (Paris: Éditions du CNRS, 1985), p. 168. Raymond Mauny, *Tableau géographique de l'Ouest africain au Moyen Âge* (Dakar: Institut français d'Afrique noire, 1961), devotes several excellent pages to the practical conditions of the caravan trade (pp. 397–403). The excerpt concerning the author who kept a clear conscience about the two travelers left behind is taken from Larbi Mezzine, "Relation d'un voyage de Taġāzā à Siġilmāsa en 1096 H./1685 J.-C.," *Arabica* 43 (1996): 211–233 (here p. 216). The guide to the Sahara cited in the text is the manual by Émile-Félix Gautier, *Le Sahara* (Paris: Payot, 1923), p. 94 (there are multiple editions).

CHAPTER 27

A Wreck in the Sahara

Central Mauritania, the Eleventh, Twelfth, and Thirteenth Centuries

The small team consisted of Théodore Monod, an antelope hunter named Salek ould Guejmoul, and two Mauritanian soldiers. It made its way with six camels, two of which carried heavy metal kegs filled with water. It left Ouadane on 2 December 1964; on 7 December, it stopped at a watering point, the last, where it took on reserves. Starting from there it would travel straight to the southeast, without changing course, for ten days. In his notebooks, Monod scrupulously recorded the daily walking times and the reasons for slowing down: thirty-six hours of rain and hail around 9 December, for example, which put the brakes on the team's progress. The notebooks alone give reliable approximations of the distance traveled in kilometers, in an environment where nothing, absolutely nothing, could serve as a landmark. At the end of the journey, he estimated that they had traversed two hundred and fifty kilometers since leaving the watering point. In order to allow for cross-checking, Monod also tallied the dune ridges. He counted 130 of them. On 17 December, the team turned northeast for two hours, then north; it then recrossed the last four ridges. A pause gave Salek the time to find the site again. Then they set off to the southeast for half an hour. The mission's objective was there, on the northwest flank of the 127th dune ridge from the last water point. The team had to leave the next day, setting out in the middle of the afternoon, to walk again for ten days with no water save what was left in the kegs. The observations would thus have to be made in the narrow window of time (a few hours) between the outbound leg and the return.

Given these research conditions, it was immediately apparent that Monod or someone else would need to return one day to continue the work. Because of this, his field notes had to both bring together his field observations and provide the necessary details to enable finding the site again. In the absence of geographical coordinates provided by satellites (nowadays GPS allows us to record and recover any point on earth within just a few meters), we can rely only on the record of the itinerary; the official memory rigorously recorded by Monod in his notebooks, but which he was sure would be insufficient; and the living memory of his companions and a few others who were reputed to have recently seen the site, addax hunters or military auxiliaries whose names and tribal affiliation are given to us.

Since then, this site has been designated by the fine expression "caravan wreck." Centuries ago, men abandoned their cargo, or rather carefully deposited it in the sand, probably intending to return for it later. Who were these men? Had they lost their way? Was it their goods or their plunder that they stashed in this manner? Why did no one come back for them? These are questions that are insoluble today. In order to discover the diminutive hillock, some tens of centimeters tall, that marks out the site in an ocean of sand, one has to pass its immediate vicinity by chance, on the edge of a sand dune that resembles a hundred thousand others. That didn't happen until February 1962, when Mauritanian nomads hunting in the environs discovered the place and brought back some brass bars from the wreck. It was quickly called Maaden Ijâfen, the "mine" of Ijâfen, the name of the region. The rumor reached Ouadane, and as the Sahara is an echo chamber, it reached Monod, who was then at Dakar. His first attempt at finding the place failed in January 1964; his second succeeded.

We thus have to rely on half a day's work (i.e., six to eight hours) on-site. First on the agenda, the visual survey. A measuring rod exactly a meter high was planted in the ground on the edge of the site. In all four perspectives facing the cardinal directions, Monod prominently featured this rod that simultaneously furnished a spatial reference point and the scale for his sketches. Some pencil strokes lead us around a slight butte peppered with metal bars. Some were planted straight into the top centuries ago, perhaps as a sort of beacon. The sand is represented by dots; the dune in the background by fine, closely spaced lines. The spread of cowries* is left white. Then it was necessary to take pictures. At this time they were analogue; Monod had to be parsimonious: two general views of the site, where the measuring rod, still at the same place, would allow the sketches to be transformed into a layout; two close-up shots of the metallic bars in place and the cowries. Then came the excavation. The survey would inevitably be hasty: a meter-wide trench was dug outward starting from the middle of the hillock. The trench was dug to sixty centimeters in depth, but the lower thirty centimeters was already sterile sand. Six bundles of metal bars had been placed on top, each approximately a meter in length for a diameter of some twenty centimeters. They were intact, although some were a bit welded together by corrosion. The bars scattered on the surface came from similar bundles. The sacks of shells (which probably burst open very quickly) had been placed above them. There wasn't time to make a plan of the site; two photos with the rod would have to suffice. But at least Monod drew what he understood of the site's initial state. Of course, he also reported all his observations: the granulometry of the sand under the wreck, the total of bars from two whole bundles: 108 and 111, respectively. Since bits of cloth were observed during the excavation, most likely the remains of the bundles wrapped around the metal and the cowries,* it was necessary to examine them more closely and draw their fabric; since there were fragments of cord, and of different types, most likely the remains of the ties that held the bundles, it was necessary to draw them and enumerate them: types A, B, C, D. Then, one had to choose what to take, keeping in mind that the expedition had to travel light. Twenty-five metal bars. When weighed in the laboratory, they made it possible to calculate the freight loads; when observed and measured, they made it possible to formulate hypotheses on the production methods; when analyzed, they made it possible to make comparisons with the chemical composition of known ore deposits. A bucket of cowries* weighing nearly four kilos comprised 3,220 specimens in total. When classified, they revealed one variety, *Cypraea moneta*, to predominate. Fragments of vegetable fibers from the exceptionally preserved packing fabrics: once observed up close, they would be compared to other known fabrics. And since it was an organic material, it could be dated.

The archaeological wreck of Maaden Ijâfen is equivalent to the load of five to six camels. They were heading south. They were taking a little more than two thousand brass bars, roughly a ton, certainly produced in Morocco. The *moneta* themselves were collected around the beaches along the rim of the Indian Ocean, but it was only in the Maldives archipelago, off the coast of southwest India, that they were harvested and exported en masse throughout the Middle Ages. Here, then, were two commodities exported from Islamic lands that were in high demand in the Sahel. The metal bars were ingots destined to be melted down and made into jewelry, weaponry, and copperware. We know of several sites in West Africa where metallurgy of this type was practiced: Aoudaghost (↦6) in Mauritania, Sintiou Bara in Senegal, Marandet in Niger, Durbi Takusheyi in Nigeria. Cowries* have served as currency throughout the Sahelian zone since the Middle Ages; they thus had a considerable exchange value between the hands of North African merchants. As for the site's location, far from all known routes, Monod felt he could demonstrate that the abandonment of this wreck was compatible with a caravan leaving southern Morocco, perhaps from the Draa or Noun river valleys, headed toward Oualata. He ventured a hypothesis on the circumstances of the wreck: "The caravan had camped for the night; . . . the camels had been released from their restraints; at dawn, the camel drivers must have realized that they were missing a dozen animals: a party of marauders, who followed the caravan, snatched these beasts by moonlight, or else it attacked the camp and, repulsed, couldn't take any more. Regardless, our merchants were in trouble here. . . . A sole solution presented itself: to abandon, at least for the time being, a part of the cargo on site." Another theory, purely hypothetical: the camels and their loads fell into the hands of the same party of marauders, who led them off the beaten track, precisely where prudent city-dwellers refused to venture, the domain of addax hunters. In any case, the event, as hypothetical as it may be, took place between the eleventh and the thirteenth century; the fibers that wrapped the merchandise date from these centuries.

Today we would need to excavate the site completely, collect and study the whole wreck, submit some of the remains to the most recent methods of analysis, and widen the surveying in the immediate vicinity. But all that we know about this site comes from Monod's report. It has never been rediscovered.

BIBLIOGRAPHICAL NOTE

Monod's original report has been published as "Le 'Ma'aden Ijâfen': une épave caravanière ancienne dans la Majâbat al-Koubrâ," in *Actes du premier colloque international d'archéologie africaine* (Fort-Lamy: Institut national tchadien pour les sciences humaines, 1969), pp. 286–320. The account of his previous expedition, in January–February 1964, the one that failed, appears in "Majâbat al-Koubrâ (2e supplément)," *Bulletin de l'Institut français d'Afrique noire*, ser. A, 26 (1964): 1393–1402; we see that Monod put the expedition to good use and significantly increased observations on the area's soil, flora and fauna, and Neolithic archaeological sites. At the time, Théodore Monod was director of the IFAN at Dakar, an institute that carried out archaeological and scientific research throughout West Africa and the Sahara. The objects brought back from Ma'aden Ijâfen were thus stored at IFAN, where they still are to be found. The metal bars were later studied by R. Castro, "Examen métallographique d'un fragment de baguette de laiton coulé provenant d'une épave caravanière 'Ma'aden Ijâfen,'" *Bulletin de l'Institut français d'Afrique noire*, ser. B, 36 (1974): 497–410. The chronological estimate given above (from the eleventh to the thirteenth century) for the archaeological site is not that of Monod, who attributed the wreck to the beginning of the twelfth century based on two converging datings of pieces of packing cloth. The difference between these two estimates derives from a recalibration I carried out in 2011 with the help of computer software, oxCal v.4.1.7, which gives a more accurate, although less precise, result than Monod's. Only a few archaeological equivalents to Ma'aden Ijâfen's metal bars have been found in sub-Saharan Africa; nevertheless, compare with the brass bars from the tumuli of Takusheyi in Detlef Gronenborn (ed.), *Gold, Sklaven & Elfenbein. Mittelalterliche Reiche im Norden Nigerias / Gold, Slaves & Ivory. Medieval Empires in Northern Nigeria* (Mainz: Verlag des Römisch-Germanischen Zentralmuseums, 2011), pp. 76–79, 104–105. For an overview of copper metalurgy in precolonial sub-Saharan Africa, see Michael S. Bisson's chapter titled "Precolonial Copper Metallurgy: Sociopolitical Context," in M. S. Bisson, S. T. Childs, Ph. De Barros, and A.F.C. Holl (eds.), *Ancient African Metallurgy: The Socio-cultural Context* (Walnut Creek, CA: Altamira Press, 2000), pp. 83–145. Cowries,* introduced in the Sahel around the eleventh century by Maghrebian merchants, became the cornerstone of the monetary system in the region of Mali in the fourteenth century. Starting from the sixteenth century, this shell became the principal currency throughout the Gulf of Guinea. On cowrie* production in the Maldives and the history of these shells in international commerce during the medieval period, see Jan Hogendorn and Marion Johnson (eds.), *The Shell Money of the Slave Trade* (Cambridge: Cambridge University Press, 1986). For the Asian side of the cowrie* trade, see Bin Yang, "The Rise and Fall of Cowrie Shells: The Asian Story," *Journal of World History* 22 (2011): 1–25; M. Johnson, "The Cowrie Currency of West Africa," *Journal of African History* 11, no. 1 (1970): 17–49 (pt. 1) and 11, no. 3: 331–353 (pt. 2), for its part, presents a substantial amount of the available information pertaining to the place of cowries* in West Africa. Serge Robert, the French archaeologist who excavated Kumbi Saleh, told me that he and his wife, Denise Robert, tried to find the site by helicopter in 1976 but were unsuccessful. Monod died in 2000. The three men who worked on his team at Maʿaden Ijâfen have all passed away.

CHAPTER 28

The Golden Orb

Kingdom of Mâli, Fourteenth Century

In the opinion of specialists, it is the most beautiful cartographic work produced in the Middle Ages and one of the most important for the history of cartography. This unique work, drawn on vellum, lavishly illustrated, was listed in the inventory of the manuscripts of Charles V, king of France, in 1380: it was perhaps a gift from another sovereign, in this case Iberian. It bears a date: 1375. It is called the "Catalan Atlas." It is in fact, in the modern sense, an atlas, which is composed of two astronomical and astrological plates and four maps containing nautical and geographical information. One of them covers what we will call the western Mediterranean and the continental regions from the shores of the North Sea to the banks of the Niger. It was a world radiating around Majorca, the largest of the Balearic Islands, where it was produced, but which spread afar. A second map was joined to the first to complete the peri-Mediterranean world.

The eye falls on the most colorful part of the map, the bottom. We are in Africa. To the west, a white man in a green tunic wears a veil across the bottom of his face, riding an animal that can only be a camel—although painted by an artist who had certainly never seen one; the camel driver is a Berber nomad. To the east, another white man dressed in indigo wears a turban; he holds a scimitar. It's the king of Organa, perhaps Ouargla, in modern Algeria. The glances of the two men converge on a third figure in between them. He is seated on a throne, his chest facing the viewer, his face in profile. His skin is black. He has a trimmed beard and mustache. His feet and his forearms are bare; his loose clothing is gold in color. A gold crown is on his head; a scepter adorned with fleurs-de-lys is in his hand, a gold orb in the other, as if he is offering it for the world to see.

The region over which our king reigned bore the name Ginyia. The cartographer surrounded the sovereign with four localities: Tagaza (Taghâza; ↦25), Tonbuch (Timbuktu), Gougou (Gao), and Buda (Bûda, in the Algerian oasis of Tuat, ↦32). Two other toponyms, a little to the left, also designated regions under his rule, though at different scales: Sudam (from Sûdân, the Arabic word for "Blacks") and Ciutat de Melly (Catalan for

City of Mâli or Mâli City). A caption accompanies the image; it reads (still in Catalan): "This Black lord is called Musse Melly, lord of the Blacks of Geneua. This king is the richest and most noble lord of the whole region because of the abundance of gold that is collected in his land."

One shouldn't rely on all the map's details. The crown and the scepter belong to the symbolic repertoire of European royalty; they are painted here to help the reader identify a powerful sovereign. The origins of the name Ginyia (or Gineua) are obscure; Ginyia would give us Guinea when the Portuguese discovered the Atlantic route to West Africa. The sovereign's posture and the shape of his throne irresistibly bring to mind an older map, that of Angelino Dulcert, also produced at Majorca, but a few decades earlier, in 1339. The latter already mentions the king of Mâli, "rex Melly" (in Latin), for the first time, but shows him with a turban wrapped around his head, his index finger pointed as if teaching. It calls him a "Muslim king," and already claims that he had gold mines in abundance. On the second map, ours, very similar to the first when it comes to the Sahelian regions, the name of the sovereign, Mûsâ, made its appearance, although a little late since Sultan Mûsâ died in 1337. From this simple fact, we can infer that the African part of the Catalan Atlas both derived from that of 1339 and updated it with information such as the name of the king and the cities of his kingdom, information whose precise origin is unknown.

Though technically anonymous in the sense that it bears no signature, the Catalan Atlas is often attributed to two Jewish cartographers from Majorca, Cresques, son of Abraham, and Jafuda or Yehuda, son of Cresques. Indeed, we know that the two men did produce maps at this date, though the argument is of course insufficient. Whatever the case, irrespective of the mapmakers, there are still legitimate reasons to think that the map was produced in Majorca and based on information collected by Jews. In the mid-fourteenth century, Majorca was the principal center of cartographic production in western Europe. The main reason for this centrality was that since 1229, the year the Balearics were captured by the Christians from the Muslims, the island became an important commercial crossroads in the western Mediterranean. The island's numerous and influential Jewish merchants were settled there at the request of the Aragonese monarchs, who did not hesitate to give them privileges to bring this about. These incentives were especially targeted at the Jews of the Maghreb. In 1247, King James I, the Conqueror, invited Solomon ben Ammar, a Jew of Sijilmâsa (↦16), along with all his coreligionists to come settle in Majorca and Catalonia. The offer of religious asylum could not fail to tempt the Maghrebian Jews after decades of persecution under the Almohads. But there was an ulterior motive to the offer: the sovereigns of Aragon wanted nothing more than to attract the Jews' centuries-old commercial networks to the detriment of the Maghrebian commercial outlets. The fact that the king's invitation was specifically addressed to the Sijilmâsa community indicates quite clearly that the objective, whether admitted or not, was to divert the trans-Saharan trade. A century later the Majorcan maps, the first in the Western world to do so, depicted the commercial stopovers running from the big North African cities to Sijilmâsa, then from Sijilmâsa, via Taghâza, to the kingdom of Mâli, where a king sat holding aloft a golden orb, illustrative of his success.

If some of the information relating to the Mâli of King Mûsâ came down to us thanks to the Jewish communities established along the commercial routes of the Maghreb and western Mediterranean, it is probable that it was captured at the source—that is, from the North African merchants who made the crossing of the Sahara. Such seems to be the case with the miniature building representing Timbuktu on the map in the Catalan Atlas. Unlike the other localities of this part of Africa, which are all represented on the map by stereotypical towers topped with circular disks, the vignette for Timbuktu depicts a unique monument, a rectangular building surmounted by rows of cupolas. There is an anomaly here that attracts our attention and suggests that the tiny building evokes the traditional architecture of the city as reported by eyewitnesses. Could it perhaps be the great banco* mosque of Djinguereber at Timbuktu, a monument that a Malian tradition attributes to the Andalusian architect and poet Abû Ishâq al-Sâhilî, called the Granadian, and which dates precisely to the reign of Mûsâ? But besides the fact that we know basically nothing about this first mosque, the tradition has perhaps nothing genuine about it; it derived, possibly, from Arabic sources. Perhaps from the account of Ibn Battûta, who reported having visited the architect's tomb in Timbuktu; this was in 1353. Or from the account of Ibn Khaldûn, who in 1387 met Abû Ishâq's grandson somewhere on the shores of the Red Sea and learned from him that his ancestor, who died in 1346, had met the king of Mâli in Mecca in 1324. He then accompanied the monarch to his kingdom, where he built "a square building with a dome. He had a good knowledge of handicrafts and lavished all his skill on it. He plastered it over and covered it with coloured patterns." In a country that, the author tells us somewhat dismissively, had never before known a building tradition, the monument was a veritable marvel. Abû Ishâq was paid ten thousand mithqâls* of gold, a colossal sum. We cannot say whether the monument representing Timbuktu in the Catalan Atlas is a mosque. But we can note the coincidence of several fourteenth-century Arabic sources pointing out the rise of what was possibly a distinctive architectural tradition associated with Timbuktu.

Should we be surprised that such precise information on a monument built in the Land of the Blacks had been able to make its way into the atelier of a cartographer from the Balearic Islands, or that it took several decades to do so? Neither. King Mûsâ's fame filtered through slowly toward the Islamic and Latin worlds, but it did so irresistibly and inundated the fourteenth century. Mûsâ and his entourage's sojourn in Cairo, while on pilgrimage to Islam's holy places in Arabia, left a deep impression. People were still talking about it half a century later. An Egyptian author contemporary with the Catalan Atlas recounts: "[In 1324] the king Mûsâ ibn Abû Bakr arrived on Egyptian territory with the goal of making a pilgrimage to the venerable house of God and of visiting the tomb of his Prophet [Muhammad], most glorified and honored. He was a young man, brown-skinned, and good looking, with a handsome face. . . . He was seen in the midst of his soldiers, magnificently dressed and riding his horse. His entourage was composed of more than ten thousand of his subjects. [He brought] presents and gifts remarkable for their beauty and splendor. It said that it would take someone three years to walk across his kingdom and that he has fourteen subordinates on hand, kings as well as governors."

Wisdom, piety, wealth. That is perhaps how to best describe the impression the sultan of Mâli left on the people of Cairo. Twenty-five years after his stay in the city, numerous stories about it continued to circulate: "From the beginning of my coming to stay in Egypt," wrote al-Umarî, "I heard talk of the arrival of the sultan on his Pilgrimage and found the Cairenes eager to recount what they had seen of the African's prodigal spending." Ever the biographer, he collected some of their reminiscences. Here is the *mihmandâr* of the time, the Mamluk official charged with accompanying foreign delegations to the sultan's court, who painted this portrait of the sovereign of Mâli: "opulence, manly virtues, and piety of this sultan." "When I went out to meet him (he said), that is, on behalf of the mighty sultan al-Malik al-Nâsir, he did me extreme honor and treated me with the greatest courtesy. . . . Then he forwarded to the royal treasury many loads of unworked native gold." Here is the son of the emir *hâjib*, the chamberlain: "He was noble and generous and performed many acts of charity and kindness. He had left his country with 100 loads of gold which he spent during his Pilgrimage on the tribes who lay along his route from his country to Egypt, while he was in Egypt, and again from Egypt to the Noble Hijâz [region in the west of the Arabian Peninsula that shelters Islam's holy sites] and back. As a consequence he needed to borrow money in Egypt and pledged his credit with the merchants at a very high rate of gain." Sumptuous spending, presents, liberality in gifts and borrowing: Mûsâ combined a seemingly virtuous detachment, even if some suspected a naïveté that was abused, with generosity. But what people really remembered was the gold that flowed through Cairo: the gold exchanged between the sultans during a finely tuned ceremonial; the damascened arms and embroidered clothing of Mûsâ's entourage; the gold that passed through the hands of Mamluk officials. Let's let the *mihmandâr* speak again: "This man flooded Cairo with his benefactions. He left no court emir nor holder of a royal office without the gift of a load of gold. The Cairenes made incalculable profits out of him and his entourage in buying and selling and giving and taking. They exchanged gold until they depressed its value in Egypt and caused its price to fall." Twelve years after the events in question, al-Umarî expressed himself more precisely on the matter: "Gold was at a high price in Egypt until they [the sultan Mûsâ and his entourage] came in that year. The mithqal [*i.e.* the dinar] did not go below 25 *dirhams** and was generally above, but from that time its value fell and it cheapened in price and has remained cheap till now. The mithqal does not exceed 22 *dirhams* or less. This has been the state of affairs for about twelve years until this day by reason of the large amount of gold which they brought into Egypt and spent there." In modern terms, we are dealing here with one of the classic phenomena in a bimetallic monetary system. Both units having a variable parity, gold currency sees its value drop precipitously and long-lastingly (by more than 10 percent) in comparison to silver owing to the sudden abundance of the yellow metal on the market. The golden orb, a sort of enormous gold nugget, raised by the black king of the Catalan Atlas, may well reflect the brilliance of the memory left by the passage of Mûsâ and his entourage.

It has often been said that the golden orb Sultan Mûsâ held in his hand is the representation of a gold nugget. But it's not asked why it should be so. We find it normal to hold a gold nugget to depict the economic power of a kingdom possessing gold mines capable of exercising so powerful a fascination over the wide expanse of the Mediterranean region, Islamic lands as well as Christian. But was the nugget held aloft in the monarch's hand and thus displayed to the world, only a symbol of wealth, or was there more to it? The historian Ibn Khaldûn, who wrote his *Book of Lessons* over a thirty-year period beginning in 1375—his account is thus contemporaneous with the Catalan Atlas or slightly later—perhaps gives us an answer: in 1373 Mârî Djâta II, king of Mâli, died. This sovereign did not have a good reputation: "[H]e ruined their empire, squandered their treasure, and all but demolished the edifice of their rule." "His extravagance and profligacy reached such a point that he sold the boulder of gold which was a prized possession of their treasury. It was a boulder weighing twenty *qintâr* [Arabic term that has given us "quintal," and which was roughly equivalent to fifty kilos] which had been transported from the mine without being worked or purified by fire. They regarded it as the rarest and most precious of treasures because its like is so scarce in the mines. [Mârî Djâta,] this profligate king, offered it to the Egyptian traders who travel back and forth to his country, and they bought it at a derisory price. This in addition to the other royal treasures which he squandered in loose living."

Was this the same nugget—if we can still call it that in spite of its size—that previously belonged, according to several earlier authors, to the sovereign of Ghâna (↦8)? It's not clear; but perhaps when Ghâna became a province of the kingdom of Mâli, this royal symbol was translated to the latter's treasury. The nugget, in any case, could already be found in the treasury of the sultan of Mâli in the reign of Mâghâ I, the father of Mârî Djâta II, who reigned immediately after Mûsâ, and whose time in power, incidentally, was very short. It's not unreasonable to assume that Mûsâ already had it in his possession.

BIBLIOGRAPHICAL NOTE

The Catalan Atlas is kept in the Bibliothèque nationale de France in Paris, shelf number Ms Esp. 30. It has been the object of numerous editions, of which two, in facsimile, deserve special mention: one (in French) is in the luxurious book collection of Prince Youssouf Kamal, *Monumenta cartographica Africae et Aegypti*, 5 vols. (Leiden: printed for the author, 1926–1951), here vol. 4—*Époque des portulans, suivie par l'époque des découvertes*, fols. 1301–1303; another (in English) by Georges Grosjean, *Mapamundi, the Catalan Atlas of the Year 1375* (Zurich: Urs Graf Verlag, 1978). The judgment issued in the introduction to this chapter was outlined, for example, by Tony Campbell at the beginning of his review of G. Grosjean's *Mapamundi* in *Imago Mundi* 33 (1981): 115–116. Likewise, I subscribe to the review's reservations regarding the atlas's attribution. The text and place-names mentioned in this chapter follow the edition of the atlas's text given by J.A.C. Buchon and J. Tastu, *Notice d'un atlas en langue catalane, manuscrit de l'an 1375 conservé parmi les manuscrits de la Bibliothèque royale . . .* (Paris: Imprimerie royale, 1839), occasionally corrected based on photographs. For the prominent role Majorca played in the development of cartography at the time, see Gonzalo de Reparaz Ruiz, "L'activité maritime et commerciale du royaume d'Aragon au XIIIe siècle et son influence sur le développement de l'école cartographique de Majorque," *Bulletin hispanique* 49 (1947): 422–451. Michel Abitbol's article, "Juifs maghrébins et commerce transsaharien du VIIIe au XVe siècle," in *Le Sol, la parole et l'écrit. Mélanges en hommage à Raymond Mauny*, 2 vols. (Paris: Société française d'histoire d'outre-mer, 1981), 2:561–577, traces the history of the Maghreb's Jewish communities and their relation to the gold trade. Abitbol proposes that there were Jewish communities to the south of the Sahara, but Nehemia Levtzion, "The Jews of Sijilmasa and the Saharan trade," in M. Abitbol (ed.), *Communautés juives des marges sahariennes du Maghreb* (Jerusalem: Institut Ben Zvi, 1982), pp. 253–264, for his part, argues that the sources at our disposal suggest otherwise. Both authors mention the links between Sijilmâsa and Majorca. The excerpts from Ibn Khaldûn and al-Umarî cited in the text, along with Ibn Battûta's comment about visiting the tomb of Abû Ishâq al-Sâhilî in Timbuktu, are found in Nehemia Levtzion and J.F.P. Hopkins (eds.), *Corpus of Early Arabic Sources for West African History* (Princeton, NJ: Markus Wiener, 2000), pp. 335–336, pp. 269–271, and p. 299, respectively. The citation from the Egyptian author, Badr al-Dîn al-Halabî, writing just before 1376–1377, is found in Joseph Cuoq, *Recueil des sources arabes* (Paris: Éditions du CNRS, 1985), pp. 327–328. Recent archaeological surveys (not yet published) carried out by Bertrand Poissonnier in the Djinguereber Mosque in Timbuktu have identified the archaeological levels corresponding to the early fourteenth-century mosque. It is worth pointing out that earthen architecture (in this case in banco*) is vulnerable to significant damage caused by heavy rains, and is therefore subject both to constant repair and to occasional complete restoration. Hence the judicious observation by Raymond Mauny that "the monuments we are going to discuss are often the third or fourth 'edition' of the 'original.' We have no idea the degree to which they resemble the earliest building"; see his "Notes d'archéologie sur Tombouctou," *Bulletin de l'Institut français d'Afrique noire* 14 (1952): 899–918. John O. Hunwick, "An Andalusian in Mali: A Contribution to the Biography of Abū Ishāq al-Sāhilī, c. 1290–1346," *Paideuma* 36 (1990): 59–66, gives a first biographical sketch of the architect; but it is good to keep in mind the critical view of Suzan B. Aradeon, "Al-Sahili: The Historian's Myth of Architectural Technology Transfer from North Africa," *Journal des africanistes* 59 (1989): 99–131, which rightly dismisses the idea that the Andalusian poet had imported "architecture" into the Sahelian regions, which were supposedly ignorant of its techniques and use until then. For the interesting suggestion that the words "Guinea" and "Gnawa" (which in Berber and Arabic designates diasporic black communities in Maghreb) may be related, see Chouki El Hamel, *Black Morocco: A History of Slavery, Race and Islam* (Cambridge: Cambridge University Press, 2013), pp. 273–274.

CHAPTER 29

The King's Speech

In Mâli City, Capital of the Kingdom of Mâli,
from June 1352 to February 1353

"He is the sultan *mansâ* Sulaymân. *Mansâ* means 'sultan' and Sulaymân is his name. He is a miserly king from whom no great donation is to be expected." With these words, Ibn Battûta conjured up the reigning sultan at the time of his journey. One day he was told that the sultan had just sent him the welcome gift, what he hoped were clothes and a present. He went with the message-bearer: "I got up, thinking that it would be robes of honor and money, but behold! It was three loaves of bread and a piece of beef fried in *ghartî* [shea* butter] and a gourd containing curdled milk. When I saw it I laughed, and was long astonished at their feeble intellect and their respect for mean things."

Throughout his life, say, after he reached the age of twenty, Ibn Battûta was an insatiable freeloader, living off the largesse of the sultans and religious leaders of the Islamic world. Born in 1304 at Tangier on the Strait of Gibraltar, he crossed large parts of the Islamic world: he made the pilgrimage to Mecca several times; spent a few years in India, where he resided at the court of the sultan of Delhi; and even ventured as far as the Maldives archipelago, where he served as a judge. If visiting the entire Islamic world was not the goal of his travels, describing the totality of that world was, in any event, the ambition of his written work. This encyclopedic project, which painted landscapes of the Islamic world's important places as well as portraits of its elites, was so important that he had to take certain liberties with the truth. Thus the reality of his "travels" to China, the Volga River valley, or East Africa can be doubted. We can even be suspicious about Mâli: the description seems thin for an eight-month sojourn. Judging from what Ibn Battûta experiences, enjoys, and describes in the rest of his book, his description of Mâli is missing everything that shouldn't be missing: daily life, the climate, entertainment, the surrounding countryside, women. We find there only what we were sure to find there: the moral portrait of the sultan, the list of the distinguished persons, the protocol, descriptions of the audiences and grand ceremonies. But let's not conclude from the story's uncertainties that the trip was impossible, nor from the trip's impossibility that the story was entirely false. The testimony's inadequacy can result from other factors beyond feigned firsthand experience; and in any case the lack of firsthand experience can be mitigated by good sources. Let's proceed as if everything related by Ibn Battûta had been seen by him.

Ibn Battûta didn't bother to describe for us the exact route leading from Oualata (↦26) in southern Mauritania to the capital of Mâli. We know only that one had to go south. "The road has many trees. Its trees are of great age and vast size, so that a whole caravan may get shelter in the shade of one of them." He is certainly describing baobabs here, whose giant silhouettes are characteristic of the arboreal savanna. From his description of local products we can equally recognize the shea tree,* whose ground-up kernel produced a butter that could be used for frying, ointments, and, as Ibn Battûta informs us, coating dwellings. His caravan passed through many well-supplied villages. Ten days after leaving Oualata, they arrived at Zâghari, a large village home to black merchants, the Wangâra (↦17), and some whites, also Muslims, but schismatics, the Kharijites (↦5). Next came Kârsakhu, a city near a "great river," which, he says, flowed in the direction of Timbuktu. Finally they crossed another river, the Sansara. Ibn Battûta and his companions entered the city of Mâli, "capital of the king of the Land of the Blacks." The fast-paced journey had lasted twenty-four days. The problem is that with the exception of the starting point, Oualata, no name is recognizable to us.

Starting with what is known from the text, scholars have played around a lot with maps and compasses. Twenty-four days from Oualata, depending on whether one goes southeast rather than southwest, on what rivers one crosses, on how fast one travels, certainly on one's opinion about the capital's conceivable locations, and finally on the degree of trust one has in toponymic approximations, one determines that the capital of medieval Mâli has been found in the small village of Niani located in the east of present-day Guinea-Conakry; or in a village named Mali on the banks of the upper Gambia in modern Senegal; or else somewhere halfway between

Bamako and Niamina on the left bank of the Niger, in present-day Mali. Three hypothetical locations in three different modern countries. One might think the enigma can be resolved by positing that the empire of Mali had several successive or simultaneous capitals, a credible hypothesis but one irrelevant in accounting for what Ibn Battûta spoke about. It is instructive that the zone swept up in these hypotheses covers a region approximately eight hundred kilometers in length by four hundred kilometers in width. We would be in a similar quandary with Europe if we had only the text of a tenth-century Andalusian traveler to help us decide whether the capital of the Carolingian Empire was located at Aix-la-Chapelle, Aix-les-Bains, or Aix-en-Provence.

But if the search for the city's location has so far been unsuccessful, that is not at all the case when it comes to visualizing its spatial organization. One can at least attempt a description of Mâli City's most significant features based on Ibn Battûta's narrative of the different ceremonies and festivities he attended there—ceremonies that furnished yet more material for him to compare with the various displays of royal pomp he had seen on his travels.

First of all we discover a palace; or, rather, we catch a glimpse of it. Only the royal family and the slaves who attended them could enter it, and we thus have no description of its appearance. It is thought that it was a complex made up of several enclosed spaces; it must have had clusters of dwellings forming living quarters for the king, his family, and dependents, and spaces for royal offices and regalian functions. It was certainly a vast architectural ensemble in banco.* In a corner of this complex lay a domed room. Perhaps it was this room that had been built a quarter century earlier by *mansâ* Mûsâ (↦28), Sulaymân's brother. Ibn Battûta simply says that it was a domed, one-room building. It seems there was only one door, which opened onto the interior of the palace. The exterior side, overlooking the esplanade called a *mashwâr*, an Arabic term that in North Africa designated a place for public ceremonies, was pierced only by windows. This facade was remarkable; it was decorated with two registers, each made up of three wooden windows. The windows of the upper register were covered with sheets of silver, those of the lower register with sheets of gold or gilded silver. The windows were grilled and covered with curtains. The *mashwâr* isn't described, but based on what took place there and the way it took place there, we understand that it was an elongated space facing the domed room. It was certainly enclosed by a wall. At the other end, symmetrically facing the domed room was a portal that closed the *mashwâr*. A tree-lined street extended the *mashwâr*. We know that there was also a mosque, in all likelihood located in the same area, perhaps directly accessible from the palace and the *mashwâr*.

At Mâli City, Ibn Battûta attended ceremonies, several of which he classified as audiences. In the strict sense, only those meetings where the sultan himself sat in the domed room warrant this appellation. On the days "[w]hen he is sitting they hang out from the window of one of the arches a silken cord to which is attached a patterned Egyptian kerchief. When the people see the kerchief drums are beaten and trumpets are sounded." It was the signal for a precise arrangement that Ibn Battûta observed from the *mashwâr*, where he took his place among the other residents of the city who whispered to him the meaning of this or that gesture. Three hundred armed men, some carrying bows, others lances and shields, came forth from the palace and lined up on either side of the esplanade. This was the king's slave bodyguard. Then two saddled and bridled horses were introduced, along with two rams and the sultan's lieutenant, his stand-in, so to speak. This was the king's symbolic entrance. Next came the traditional chiefs and Muslim religious leaders, that is, the "civil" notables. Soldiers, on foot and on horseback, were ranged outside the *mashwâr*, each company behind its emir. The men bore "lances and bows, drums and trumpets. Their trumpets (*bûq*) are made out of elephant-tusks and their [other] musical instruments are made out of reeds and gourds and are played with a striker (*sattâ'a*) and have a wonderful sound." The eunuchs and foreigners were also assembled there. A curiously dressed man stood at the gate of the *mashwâr*. Ibn Battûta, who met him at the very beginning of his sojourn in Mâli, says that this was the sultan's interpreter; his name was Dûghâ. On that day, "[he was wearing] fine garments of silk brocade . . . and other materials, and on his head a turban with fringes which they have a novel way of winding. Round his waist he has a sword with a golden sheath and on his feet boots and spurs. No-one but him wears boots on that day. In his hand he has two short lances, one of gold and the other of silver, with iron tips."

Audiences took place in the following fashion. One of the king's simple subjects comes to make a request; we do not know *what* he asks, but we know *how* he asks: he takes off his clothes, dons rags, and crawls toward the sultan. When the king speaks to him, the man goes down on his knees. When the king finishes speaking, the suppliant grabs dust from the ground and tosses it on his head and back. Next is a man of the highest rank who comes to boast of his merits; if someone agrees with his boasts, he makes it known by the twang of his bowstring. If the sultan makes a speech, everyone removes his turban. Finally it's the turn of a jurist who comes from a distant province to bear witness to injustice. He is a wise man. Locusts, he says, have descended upon the land. A holy man, an ulama,* was sent to investigate and the locusts spoke to him: "God sends us to the country in which there is much oppression in order to spoil its crops." No one would have dared to make such a public criticism, but was anyone going to reproach the locusts?

The spatial arrangement and the proceedings of the royal audiences in Mali reveal a curious aspect: they kept the king hidden. Let's start by saying that this is a feature of royalty that we recognize up until the nineteenth and twentieth centuries in many African kingdoms, especially those of the Sahel. To say that what we see here is an indication of a sacred monarchy is to speak too quickly. For the king was not hidden from view in all he did or on every occasion. Furthermore, he was not absent; on the contrary, he was eminently present, his physical occultation accentuating his royalty. At Mâli City, his presence is affirmed in multiple ways: by the curtains drawn over the windows, the kerchief passed through the window grille, the music, the stand-in, the royal animals, and the entire ceremonial that showcased the humility of those who dared to brave the royal presence. There is nothing here of divine kingship, but rather the affirmation, remarkable for the sophistication of its mise-en-scène, of the presence of a political body that augmented as far as it concealed the individual body that personified it.

However, the king was not always removed from sight. There were other public ceremonies where everyone could see him; each Friday he went to the mosque and prayed with the faithful. On many other occasions, the people—Muslim or non-Muslim, distinguished or of low birth, aggrieved or satisfied—could see him exercise his kingship. All in all, it was only during audiences that the man who exercised sovereignty was hidden from the eyes of his fellow human beings. On those days, the asymmetry of gazes combined with an asymmetry of verbal exchange, which saw an authoritative way of speaking respond to a humble, measured, allegorical one and imposed on everyone, from paupers to the powerful, performances of the most striking debasement. It was not a dialogue, still less a deliberative assembly. It was a strange speech circulation system. Let's take a closer look: petitioners didn't address the sultan directly; they addressed a man who stood below the windows of the domed room. It was he who transmitted the case or request made in the dust outside to the sultan in his domed room; it was he who received the response and transmitted it toward the *mashwâr*, before the dignitaries who formed the sultan's council. Should we call him the spokesman, the public crier? For all that, he was not the centerpiece of the system. That was Dûghâ, whom Ibn Battûta called the interpreter because he spoke Maninka and Arabic and could translate from one language to the other, but also, and perhaps especially, because he was the man who *formulated* the demands addressed to the sultan as well as the royal decisions in response. "Anyone who wishes to address the sultan addresses Dûghâ and Dûghâ addresses that man standing [under the windows] and that man standing addresses the sultan." As long as it concerns something political, as is the case in such circumstances, speech has to be made public in a loud and clear voice.

No secrets, no demands murmured in low voices, no opinions influenced by favoritism. During these audiences where the sultan judged, honored, decreed—in short, governed—the requests and the decisions they elicited were publicly pronounced by Dûghâ. This flesh-and-blood man was, as it were, the minister of the word. The one who, on those days and in that place, was the ultimate source of law, remained invisible and silent.

BIBLIOGRAPHICAL NOTE

All citations from Ibn Battûta's description of Mâli are taken from Nehemia Levtzion and J.F.P. Hopkins (eds.), *Corpus of Early Arabic Sources for West African History* (Princeton, NJ: Markus Wiener, 2000), pp. 286–294 (slightly modified on one occasion, about the curdled milk). On Ibn Battûta's voyage to Mâli and the doubts that can be brought to bear on the subject, and on the journey's narrative logic, see the article Bertrand Hirsch and I have written on the topic: "Voyage aux frontières du monde. Topologie, narration et jeux de miroir dans la *Rihla* de Ibn Battûta," *Afrique & Histoire* 1 (2003): 75–122, which can be accessed online: https://www.cairn.info/revue-afrique-et-histoire-2003-1-p-75.htm. See also my article "Ibn Battuta, Muhammad ibn Abdullah," in John Middleton and Joseph C. Miller (eds.), *New Encyclopedia of Africa* (Detroit: Thomson/Gale, 2008), 3:2; and my chapter "Trade and Travel in Africa's Golden Global Age (700–1500)," in Dorothy Hodgson and Judith Byfeld (eds.), *Global Africa into the Twenty-First Century* (Berkeley: University of California Press, 2017), pp. 17–26. The most accepted—and the most reliable, in my view—hypothesis for the location of the capital described by Ibn Battûta is that of John O. Hunwick of a location in present-day Mali, somewhere between Bamako and Niamina; it is presented in "The Mid-Fourteenth Century Capital of Mali," *Journal of African History* 14 (1973): 195–206. But it should also be stressed that no discovery on the ground has as yet confirmed this hypothesis. Some still believe that the fourteenth-century capital of Mâli was at the site of Niani in Guinée-Conakry, which has been excavated by a Polish-Guinean team; see Władysław Filipowiak, *Études archéologiques sur la capitale médiévale du Mali* (Szczecin: Muzeum Narodowe, 1979). On the reservations one should have regarding the interpretation of these excavations, see my articles "Niani Redux: A Final Rejection of the Identification of the Site of Niani (Republic of Guinea) with the Capital of the Kingdom of Mali," *Palethnology* 4 (2012): 235–252, http://blogs.univ-tlse2.fr/palethnologie/en/2012-10-fauvelle-aymar/, and "African Archaeology and the Chalk-Line Effect: A Consideration of Mâli and Sijilmâsa," in Toby Green and Benedetta Rossi (eds.), *Landscape, Sources and Intellectual Projects of the West African Past: Essays in Honour of Paulo Fernando de Moraes Farias* (Leiden: Brill, in press). For an illustration of the vision that a merchant from the Islamic tradition, in this case a Jew from al-Andalus, had of ninth-century Europe, and the doubts that persist regarding the toponym AQSH, in which may possibly be recognized a city by the name of Aix (of which there are many in France and Germany), see André Miquel, "L'Europe occidentale dans la relation arabe d'Ibrâhim b. Ya'qûb (Xe s.)," *Annales. Économies, sociétés, civilisations* 21 (1966): 1048–1064.

CHAPTER 30

The Production of Eunuchs in Abyssinia

Ethiopia and Somaliland, around 1340

Of all the kings ruling over parts of Abyssinia, the lord of Amhara, whom we're accustomed to calling the *negus* of Ethiopia, had long exercised suzerainty over his neighbors, perhaps by virtue of an ancient lineal privilege; yet the king of Amhara was Christian while some of the others were Muslims. On the face of it, this situation was desirable for the sovereign of Ethiopia. Several Ethiopian manuscripts in the Ge'ez language preserve the account of the campaign led in 1332 by the king Amda Seyon (r. 1314–1344) against a coalition of "infidels" (Muslims) led by the sultan of Ifât. This sultan, Sabraddin, the account tells us, turned against the Christian king and said, "I will be king over all the land of Ethiopia; I will rule the Christians according to my law, and I will destroy their churches." The rest of the story demonstrates that this arrogant pronouncement was wrong. Raids, battles, lists of lands conquered and enemies put to the sword, treasons, decisive confrontations: the account of Amda Seyon's campaign is narrated as if it was an irresistible march toward the territorial, political, and religious "integration" of the Ethiopian Empire.

But it would be hard to understand the durability of the Islamic principalities of Abyssinia, as united as they could sometimes be, if we relied only on the written testimonies made by the Christian royal party. For here indeed one should remember that the tale of Amda Seyon's victorious wars was not only the expression of the Christian point of view on Christian-Muslim relations; it was also a propaganda tool used to demonstrate the king's martial prowess and his role as the torchbearer of the monkish evangelizers. Consequently, how much faith should we put in this discourse of holy war when the words attributed to Sabraddin are evidently nothing more than ventriloquism?

In one of the rarities of African history, we have at our disposal a document written at the same time, but from the opposite point of view. It allows us to better understand, as if from a reverse shot, the nature of the interactions between Christian and Muslim Abyssinians around 1340.

Our informant is again al-Umarî, former secretary of the Mamluk sultan, who was living in Damas after being driven from office. Writing in the 1340s, he remembered that a delegation of Muslim religious dignitaries from Zeyla (↦14), port of the sultanate of Ifât, modern Somaliland, came to Cairo for a curious diplomatic mission. "The learned jurist Abd Allah ez-Zeilâi," he wrote, "was actively pleading with the sultan in Cairo to put pressure on the patriarch [i.e., the head of the Coptic Church] to write a letter that forbade the king to commit abuses in Muslim lands and to seize their most precious goods when an ambassador from the sovereign of Amhara arrived there. The patriarch was ordered to do so, and wrote an eloquent, effective letter condemning these acts and forbidding anyone to commit them; his exhortations were excellent, but this incident is characteristic of the situation." It is indeed: the head of the Ethiopian Church was a metropolitan* named by the Coptic patriarch of Cairo, himself subject to an Islamic state. The Christian king of Ethiopia was thus forced to acknowledge a metropolitan whose credentials had been conferred by a foreign, Muslim monarch (↦4). The Abyssinian Muslims understood this well; they seized upon the arrival of a Christian ambassador to dispatch their own representatives to Egypt and obtain, under pressure from the sultan, a written injunction from the patriarch to the king of Ethiopia.

Truth be told, we don't need to shed light on the diplomacy surrounding this letter to demonstrate that Abyssinia's religious communities gave less priority to holy war than the narrative of Amda Seyon's campaigns would suggest. Al-Umarî's description of Muslim Abyssinia mentions seven Islamic kingdoms, "of frail construction and little wealth"; indeed, the sheik of Zeyla regretted "their weakness and their scattered authority." But he accorded the close proximity of these Islamic polities to the Christian kingdom and their common cultural foundations the status of an absolutely unproblematic self-evident fact, by no means a reprehensible one. Abyssinian Muslims, al-Umarî tells us, ate *tef*, a local variety of cereal; they ate raw meat; they produced butter and honey; they chewed shoots of *khat*, a stimulant and mood-enhancing drug. We could think we were on the Christian Ethiopian highland today. No doubt born of the same cultural matrix, Muslims and Christians did not consider themselves natural enemies. What's more, setting aside the vindictive sermons launched by the church or the mosque against the infidel, everything indicates that, in this time before the destructive sixteenth-century religious wars, the Christians and Muslims of Abyssinia thought of themselves as communities bound together by history and a common destiny. Muslims and Christians would later change their strategy: to fight to the death, it would be necessary to invent separate identities.

For the moment, the two religious communities were yoked together by converging economic interests. The Islamic states of Abyssinia procured gold from a kingdom in the interior called Dâmût. It was a powerful pagan kingdom (if by "pagan" we mean people who were labeled as such by outsiders, but of whose religion we are ignorant). We don't know precisely where it was located, but we do know that it was also a neighbor and an old enemy of the Christian kingdom. But we mustn't rule out the possibility that a political and economic rivalry over access to the production zones of this pagan kingdom's exportable goods lay behind the religious competition between Islam and Christianity. The most sought-after "product" was certainly the slave. Hadiya, the westernmost Islamic sultanate of Abyssinia and likely the closest to the Christian kingdom, made importing slaves from the "land of the infidels" (literally "disbelievers," a designation that could apply to both pagans and Christians) into a specialty.

The problem was that Hadiya wanted to export eunuchs; Abyssinian eunuchs had an excellent reputation on the slave market of the Islamic world. For centuries they were found in the harems of Egypt or Iraq. But the Christian king, though not averse to slavery, condemned castration, which he considered abominable. Thus it was necessary to bring a third partner into the exchange. The slaves—whether purchased in the Christian kingdom or elsewhere—were transported to a city called Washlû (Wašlū), most likely some unsavory free zone between Christian and Islamic territory. There, we are told, lived "a mixed population without religion," needless to say, without morals; furthermore, weren't the people of Washlû, according to al-Umarî, "the only ones in the whole land of Abyssinia [who] dare to act in this way"? It was they who practiced the castration that greatly increased the slaves' commercial value. Then the merchants quickly resumed their route with their merchandise, for the survivors had to be treated. At Hadiya, "they passed under the razor a second time to reopen the urinary canal that happens to be blocked by the pus. Afterwards they are treated . . . until they are healed." But more people died from the transfer to Hadiya and the consequences of the operation than survived. Like us, al-Umarî was astonished that the treatment was carried out at a different location from the castration itself. It seems that the inhabitants of Hadiya specialized in these traumatic treatments since the people of Washlû knew only how to wield the razor. It's a safe bet that this unusual division of labor was motivated less by economic rationality than by the common hypocrisy that allowed Christians and Muslims to collaborate in a practice whose operation they preferred not to see.

BIBLIOGRAPHICAL NOTE

The account of Amda Seyon's wars has been edited and translated into English by G.W.B. Huntingford, *The Glorious Victories of 'Āmda Ṣeyon, King of Ethiopia* (Oxford: Clarendon Press, 1965). The cited passage is on page 54. The edition (in Ge'ez and Italian) by Paolo Marrassini, *Lo Scettro e la croce. La campagna di 'Amda Ṣeyon I contro l'Ifāt (1332)* (Naples: Istituto Universitario Orientale, 1993), is the critical edition of reference. On the relationship between the king and the Ethiopian monastic communities, especially in the context of the extension of the royal domain, see Marie-Laure Derat, *Le domaine des rois éthiopiens (1270–1527)* (Paris: Publications de la Sorbonne, 2003). Though in many respects superseded by Derat, Taddesse Tamrat, *Church and State in Ethiopia, 1270–1527* (Oxford: Oxford University Press, 1972), remains the most convenient and accessible book on medieval Ethiopia published in English. See also Samantha Kelly (ed.), *A Companion to Medieval Ethiopia* (Leiden: Brill, forthcoming). Al-Umarî's description of the Muslim kingdoms of Ethiopia has been published in Ibn Fadl Allah al-'Omarī, *Masālik el absār fi mamālik el amṣār, I—L'Afrique moins l'Égypte*, trans. Maurice Gaudefroy-Demombynes

(Paris: Paul Geuthner, 1927), chaps. 8–15. The cited passages (in French) come from pp. 2–3, 16–17. By convention, I use the term "Ethiopia" for the Christian kingdom and "Abyssinia," in the sense given to it by the Arab sources, for the larger geographic area made up of other political and religious formations. On the "economy" of eunuch production in the Islamic world, and especially the obligation to "outsource" in view of the prohibition of this practice in the Dar al-Islam, see Jan Hogendorn, "The Hideous Truth: Economic Aspects of the 'Manufacture' and Sale of Eunuchs," *Paideuma* 45 (1999): 137–160, or, by the same author, "The Location of the 'Manufacture' of Eunuchs," in Tōru Miura and John Edward Philips (eds.), *Slave Elites in the Middle East and Africa: A Comparative Study* (London: Kegan Paul International, 2000), pp. 41–68.

CHAPTER 31

Inventory at
Great Zimbabwe

Present-Day Zimbabwe, Fourteenth to Fifteenth Century

Going by what has been said about them, these are the ruins of an ancient Phoenician, Egyptian, or Arabic trading post. Or perhaps the ruins of the capital city of the land of Ophir (↦18) or of the queen of Sheba. In any case, according to these diverse opinions, it was a great commercial city, a royal fortress, or a ceremonial center. We aren't lacking for hypotheses. And although a lot of different things are still being said about them, it is today acknowledged that these are the ruins of a complex created and occupied by Africans. As for their precise function, it would be best to reserve judgment for the time being.

We are in the eastern part of the Zimbabwe plateau, on the site called Great Zimbabwe. Monumental ruins made from blocks of granite sit atop two hills abutting a small valley. The walls running along the contour lines still reach seven meters in height, and up to four to five meters in width. We can walk the narrow, open-air passages; climb the stairs; penetrate the big, open spaces surrounded by defensive walls; and make out the presence of outbuildings. In comparison with other domestic enclosures, which constituted the dwelling unit in large parts of Africa, it is a veritable fortress. A conical tower is located in the complex. It is filled in—that is, the interior is inaccessible. For lack of a functional explanation, it is sometimes described as "ritualistic," a handy term that says everything and nothing. During the Europeans' first visits to the site, in the last quarter of the nineteenth century, when it was still home to wattle-and-daub huts and overrun with creepers, several monolithic soapstone steles topped with a sculpted bird of prey were found. The steles were described as "symbolic," once again a term as handy as it is useless. Most of the site was then excavated by people who cleared out centuries of accumulated sediment to get at its objects with little regard to their stratigraphic position; we thus have a plethora of "finds" of which it is more or less possible to say what sector of the site they come from, but much more difficult to say what archaeological phase. Regardless, we can affirm that the monumental ruins of Great Zimbabwe, which themselves sit on the site's previous occupations, date from the fourteenth century and the first half of the fifteenth.

Many other *zimbabwe*, or "houses of stone" (in the local Shona language), are found on the plateau. There are also some in neighboring Botswana, and smaller numbers of them are found on the coastal plain extending to Mozambique. Great Zimbabwe is the most important of them all; it gives the country its name. The kingdom of which Great Zimbabwe was the capital dominated vast regions and owed its power to control over the gold supply destined for the Swahili coast (↦18, 19). But perhaps, here again, we should put quotation marks around "kingdom": we know almost nothing about the social and political organization of this space. Should we see in it a kingdom with a hierarchical power structure or one with as many seignorial fiefdoms as *zimbabwe*? Consequently, let's also put quotation marks around "capital." The vast majority of the fragments of imported ceramics found on the plateau come from Great Zimbabwe, which could be an indication of its high status. This is true, but opinion on the subject would be somewhat different if some other *zimbabwe* had been the object of so much attention for so long.

In July 1903, one group of ruins at Great Zimbabwe, Renders Ruin, was excavated. It is a cluster of circular compartments linked by walls; it is impossible to distinguish which spaces were once open or closed, or even the ground levels or some structure that could bear witness to a spot's function or use. But at least we know that here, in Enclosure 1, a varied group of objects, precious enough to have constituted a treasure, had been found among the ruins of various structures and the sedimentary history cleared in a jumble. To begin, let's try to reconstruct it based on the inventory of objects discovered during the excavation campaigns of 1902–1903. Fortunately the inventory recorded where on the site the objects were found (the numbers are the entry numbers in the original inventory). Commentary made possible by other information given in the reports is added in brackets: 74: copper finger rings [two], snake pattern;

76: single iron gong; 77: large piece of coral [or rather coral limestone]; 84: soapstone amulet or seal (?); 85: block of solid copper; 86: iron striker found with gong; 92: soapstone with gravitating holes; 97: iron spoon, 98: iron lamp and stand [conjectured]; 101: twisted iron wire in coils [7 to 8 kg in total, the wire is precut for bracelets]; 104: bundle of brass wire bangles [including 2 to 3 kg of flat, twisted wire rolls, 2 to 3 kg of round, twisted wire, 4 dozen of bracelets and a large quantity of fragments]; 108: [bronze] spearhead; 110: collection of specimens of hoes, assegai-heads, arrow-heads, axes and ironwork found in ruins [around a hundred kilos of them from Renders Ruin]; 115: two small bronze bells; 117: collection of copper ingots, copper bars, copper wire, copper bangles and cakes of copper [various origins are indicated, including Renders Ruin]; 118: copper band 12 feet 6 inches long [3.75m] and 1 inch wide [2.5cm]; 119: box of Nanking china [i.e. Chinese porcelain], sections showing plates of various sizes and designs [coming from "most of the ruins"]; 121: glazed pottery, with conjectured post-Koranic lettering, [i.e. pseudo-Arabic letters] [which include around ten fragments of an exceptional enameled bowl with blue and gold painted decoration on a white background]; 122: fragments of Venetian glass [dark green in color]; 123: fragments of antique glazed earthenware, showing potter's wheel marks; 124: 3 fragments of antique pottery, glazed [one with green glaze: Chinese greenware]; 125: 12 feet [3.60m] of fine copper chain; 126: pottery nozzle of blow-pipe; 127: fused brass wire [by corrosion]; 128: two iron instruments; 130a: part of young lion's jaw; 130b: large lumps of resin; 130c: warthog tusk; 130d: two sections of glass prism; 131: remains of antique copper box.

All these objects had been found, so it seems, in the "thick layer of sediment" interposed between a modern occupation level (at the top of the sequence) and the bedrock (at the bottom of the sequence). But the excavation reports have not preserved for us the arguments, apart from the opinion of the excavator, that would allow us to confirm that these objects came from a single group that would correspond to a unique archaeological deposit. Some of the objects were indeed found in contact with the bedrock, others throughout the thickness of the sediment, which gives the archaeologist the impression that it had built up from the slope located uphill from the site. In short, this arrangement seems at first glance to encourage us, here again, to put quotation marks around the word "treasure," for if some objects did indeed constitute "batches" that owed nothing to chance, others could very well have been brought together in the same place as a result of various sedimentary processes. At best, we can say with some certitude that the archaeological ensemble from which we have isolated the above inventory could have been built up *around* one (or several) treasure(s) in a relatively short span of one to two centuries.

To the fuzzy contours of this treasure let's add some batches and objects that seem to be part of it, but for unexplained reasons weren't put in the inventory. We list them here by letters: a: two pints [one liter] of small yellow and green glass beads, "unknown to present natives"; b: a pint [half a liter] of similar beads of larger size, equally "unknown to present natives"; c: (at least) 100 ribbed, porcelain beads sea-green in color, also unknown locally; d: cowrie shells [several kilos]; e: two very damaged elephant tusks; f: about 20 fragments of beaten gold, several broken gold wire bracelets, and several golden beads, the whole weighing 3 ounces [about 90 grams]; g: two fragments of an Islamic glass cup with flower decoration, pink, blue and white; h: a large steatite bowl; i: 200 ivory and glass beads, apparently from a different batch than the ones already counted before; j: two pairs of double iron gongs [apparently different from specimen 76]; k: crucibles for melting copper.

Richard Hall, a journalist by profession, and one of the site's first archaeologists, felt that this treasure testified to the existence of an "Arab trading centre." For him, it was certainly "the stock in trade" of a community of medieval Muslim merchants. That, then, is how the "Orientalist" perspective on Great Zimbabwe was expressed—the same perspective that called the largest and highest perched enclosure the "acropolis" and considered the archaeological remains "Middle-Eastern." The presence of Islamic ceramics and glass, including some amazing Persian items, Chinese porcelains, and a large number of glass-paste beads "unknown to the natives"—in other words, imported—made the following scenario plausible for Hall and others like him: men from a great nation of traders and travelers established trading posts here; they traded the luxury goods of their world for gold and ivory. Let's add two arguments that Hall would have found important: cowries* (↦27) were collected in large quantities only in the Maldives; and the assemblage, especially the blue and green drawn glass beads, betrays an Indo-Pacific* origin. But we must admit that it could just as well be concluded from the same inventory that the treasure of Renders Ruin constituted the wares of a Swahili or local merchant. From one nation or another, a merchant or peddler would open his stall here; he traded a few of the remarkable, but rare, dishes he owned for a small amount of gold and ivory; above all, he bought everyday iron items here and resold them there to ordinary customers and retailed pieces of metal. On the basis of ethnographic comparisons, one of the site's most recent exegetes, Thomas Huffman, thought he could see royal emblems in some of the objects (especially the gongs); the indication of a regalian privilege in the abundance of metal (especially the collection of hoes); and the confirmation of the prestige attached to the exercise of royalty in the imported objects. Here, he thought, was where the king's first wife resided, under whose watchful eye the treasure was kept.

The search for the identity of the owner of the Renders Ruin treasure is far from finished. Each of the above hypotheses has merit; but all lack the decisive argument. Above all, they will remain heavily mortgaged by our ignorance of this assemblage's makeup over time. As for the uncertainty over the pieces' representativeness, especially the most uncommon ones, it can be used to support all sorts of speculations: perhaps they traveled far and wide as part of a merchant's stock, or, alternatively, perhaps they stayed put in the royal enclosure. Let's just say that the treasure of Great

Zimbabwe—if it wasn't what we'd like it to be: the relics of a particular individual (a merchant or king)—was the result of an unintentional, discontinuous collection of activities that engaged different segments of a vast oceanic and continental commercial network, though not necessarily all at once. Hence the treasure shifts in meaning with every glimmer shed by the light of inquiry.

BIBLIOGRAPHICAL NOTE

Innocent Pikirayi, *The Zimbabwe Culture: Origins and Decline of Southern Zambezian States* (Walnut Creek, CA: Altamira Press, 2001), pp. 123–155, offers an excellent recent synthesis on Great Zimbabwe. Richard N. Hall and W. G. Neal, *The Ancient Ruins of Rhodesia* (London: Methuen, 1904), and R. N. Hall, *Great Zimbabwe* (London: Methuen, 1905), constitute the reports of early excavations. An appendix to the latter, pp. 442–448, inventories the principal finds made during the campaigns of 1902–1903; I have quoted from its list. I have also added observations encountered on pages 126–134, 386–388, 436 in square brackets and in a second list with letters. Every effort has been made to cross-check the various lists and descriptions, but I cannot claim with certainty to have sufficiently clarified the confusion brought on by the imprecision of its descriptions. Hall's reflections on the "Arab trading centre" are borrowed from pages 132–133. Peter Garlake, "The Value of Imported Ceramics in the Dating and Interpretation of the Rhodesian Iron Age," *Journal of African History* 9 (1968): 13–33, has also attempted a reconstruction of the treasure. His lavishly illustrated *Great Zimbabwe* (London: Thames and Hudson, 1973) has excellent black-and-white and color photographs of the site and the objects discovered there. Thomas Huffman's *Snakes and Crocodiles: Power and Symbolism in Ancient Zimbabwe* (Johannesburg: Witwatersrand University Press, 1996), which relies excessively on ethnographic comparison and "cognitive" archaeology, should be read with caution. A very useful critique of this approach may be found in David Beach, "Cognitive Archaeology and Imaginary History at Great Zimbabwe," *Current Anthropology* 39 (1998): 47–72; the article is followed by a sample of the debates on the topic. Regarding Indo-Pacific* beads, the indispensable reference is Peter Francis Jr., *Asia's Maritime Bead Trade* (Honolulu: University of Hawai'i Press, 2002).

CHAPTER 32

Next Year in Tamentit, or the (Re)discovery of Africa

*Tuat Oasis, Central Algeria,
Second Half of the Fifteenth Century*

The letter, written in 1447, is addressed to Giovanni Marioni, a Genoese merchant and the representative on Majorca of the Genoese firm—
"multinational" would be anachronistic but more apt—Centurione. It is in
Latin. It had been sent from Tuat, the oasis in west-central Algeria, which
delineated a chain of ksour* at the edge of the Great Occidental Erg.*
Written at Tamentit, the principal urban center and economic capital of
Tuat, the letter, in order to reach its recipient, had to be carried north
through the valley of the Saoura Wadi, Sijilmâsa (↦16), and Fez, or perhaps more likely through Tlemcen, while following the caravan routes.
Having reached a port on the African coast, it was then sent to the Balearic Islands. Its author was also Genoese; he signed the letter MBLFNT,
a clear cryptogram for Antonio Malfante. He tells us that he is the first
Christian to find himself in these places, and that is certainly true; but
let's add two qualifications: he was the first *free* (for there must have been
some Christian slaves taken in the Mediterranean) and *Latin* (for there
must have been some Arab followers of African or Eastern Christianity)
Christian. "It is true," he wrote, "that on my first arrival they were scornful
of me, because they all wished to see me, saying with wonder 'This Christian has a countenance like ours'—for they believed that Christians had
disguised faces." The first free Latin Christian to have ventured so far into
the Sahara, he was also the first to give news about it. A century earlier,
the only information that reached Europe was transmitted by the Jewish
communities of North Africa (↦28).

Malfante was certainly not there just by chance: the context and the
content of the letter indicate quite clearly that he had been dispatched as
a commercial agent of his company, and that his mission was to gather
as much information as possible on the region's commercial conditions
and business prospects. The company was especially interested in trade
with the lands beyond the Sahara, and first and foremost, of course, in the
gold trade. Tuat, he says, is where merchants from the Maghreb or Egypt
buy the precious metal transported from the south. It was the place to

be if one worked for the Centurione family, patricians, bankers, and big spice merchants who had just imposed the gold standard on the European rules of exchange. As for inquiring into the gold's origins, Malfante did so, though without much subtlety: "I often enquired where the gold was found and collected; my patron always replied 'I was fourteen years in the land of the Blacks, and I have never heard nor seen anyone who could reply from definite knowledge. That is my experience, as to how it is found and collected.'" And the informant added, "What appears plain is that it comes from a distant land, and, as I believe, from a definite zone." That's what's called stonewalling. For let there be no doubt, as imprecise as the opinion of this man—whose brother was the most important merchant in Timbuktu—may have been, he had quickly understood that it was a good idea to not be too forthcoming with the Genoese.

Malfante also informs us about the sociological and economic conditions of trans-Saharan trade. Arab merchants from the Mediterranean coast came here with grain that they sold on-site. (Only dates were available locally.) They also brought copper ($\mapsto$27) and salt that would be used to pay for gold. It's not known, he says, what the "Blacks" did with it, but their need was so great ($\mapsto$25) that what the caravans carried to their lands was never enough. Egyptian merchants, via another route, also sold copper, as well as camels and cattle—up to half a million at a time (annually? We do not know)—a number, Malfante tells us, "which is not fantastic in this region." It's these merchants, the North Africans, who returned from the Land of the Blacks with gold powder. But the buying and selling at Tuat was not done by mutual agreement; it had to pass through intermediaries who recorded the deposits, bore the exchange risks, and signed the debt instruments drawn up in Marseille, Tunis, or Cairo. Only the Jews were able to carry out these services owing to the existence of a diaspora network and of commercial links relying on family ties ($\mapsto$15, 16). Thus the commissions of the Jews would need to be added to the 100 percent profit margin demanded by the Muslim merchants. Malfante thought it right to inform his hierarchy about it, since it was not without repercussions: "I have lost, Laus Deo! on the goods I brought here, two thousand *doubles* [understand *dinars**]." In the cruel world of big business, there is no room for the naive.

The Jews of Tuat, as rich and influential as some of them might be, lived "under the protection of the several rulers, each of whom defends his own clients." Malfante is here describing the special status of the *dhimmî* that applied in Muslim countries to all the communities of the "people of the Book" (Jews and Christians, mostly). The status of *dhimmî*, literally the "protected ones," granted protection to a community and the maintenance of its religion in return for its formal submission to Islamic authority and acceptance of an inferior legal status that imposed a certain number of obligations, especially the payment of a capitation tax, the *jizya*. This status didn't apply to the traveler from beyond the lands of Islam, such as our Genoese, who was probably granted safe-conduct. Yet he benefited from a similar patronage system: his protector was one of the neighborhood bosses, probably the sheik of one of the tribes that lived together in the ksar* of Tamentit. These bosses, eighteen in number, constituted the oligarchic government of the city. "Each ruler of a quarter protects his followers," that is, his clients. "[T]hus merchants enjoy very great security, much greater, in my opinion, than in the kingdoms such as Themmicenno [Tlemcen in today's Algeria] and Thunisie [Tunis]."

In the mid-fifteenth century, Tamentit was the southernmost Maghrebian trading post in the Sahara. Some six hundred kilometers southeast of Sijilmâsa—a city that had played this role up until the previous century, but which now found itself reduced to the less enviable role of caravan stop—Tamentit was simultaneously pioneer city, port, and entrepôt. In the surrounding desert "dwell the Philistines, who live like the Arabs, in tents," and who "hold sway over the land of Gazola from the borders of Egypt to the shores of the Ocean." Incomparable riders, they consumed only milk, meat, and rice and covered the bottom of their face with a veil.

They were Berber nomads. They inhabited the land of "Gazola," a hitherto unknown and mysterious name that Malfante gave to the desert that we call the Sahara. Perhaps his situation forced him to become a geographer, and he just didn't have the talent for it. In Majorca or Genoa secretaries and cartographers would certainly have to think long and hard about Malfante's list: from Tamentit, therefore, they could get to lands or localities with more or less recognizable names: Teghida, most likely the Takedda of the Arabic sources, which might correspond to a group of sites in the Azelik region in Niger where evidence of copper and salt working has been found, some fourteen hundred kilometers away as the crow flies; Chuchiam, in all probability Kûkiyâ on the Niger, downstream from Gao; Thambet, Timbuktu; Geni, present-day Djenné; Meli, Mâli, capital of the kingdom of the same name (↦29); Oden, perhaps Ouadane, in the Adrar of Mauritania, fifteen hundred kilometers away; and so on. One thing is clear: the information sweeps the horizon from east to west. Then, in the background, at a distance some two thousand kilometers away, some jumbled names: Dendi, Sagoto, Bofon, Igdem, Bembo, "[A]ll these are great cities, capitals of extensive lands and towns under their rule." We can scarcely get our bearings: Sagoto seems to be Sokoto, and this second list could in that case refer to the new Hausa cities, at the borders of Niger and Nigeria. And then, beyond: "To the south of these are innumerable great cities and territories, the inhabitants of which are all blacks and idolaters, continually at war with each other in defense of their law and faith of their idols. Some worship the sun, others the moon, the seven planets, fire, or water; others a mirror which reflects their faces, which they take to be the images of gods; others groves of trees, the seats of a spirit to whom they make sacrifice; others again, statues of wood and stone, with which, they say, they commune by incantations." The slaves who are sold at Tuat for a very low price, "two doubles a head," come from these lands, seized during their internal wars. Why wouldn't they force these captives into slavery, he must have thought, when they were rumored to engage in incest and cannibalism?

The geographical picture Malfante gives us, his "human geography," one might say, makes us smile. He is said to be the "discoverer" and "explorer" of the Tuat oasis, which is doubly false. First, because it is always false if the places "discovered" were already inhabited and were not isolated from the wider world; second, because as a merchant discovering for himself new landscapes from the back of his camel, he was merely following in the footsteps of his predecessors, the Muslim as well as Jewish merchants who had frequented the area for centuries. In any event, his "discovery" reveals to us a baroque picture of sub-Saharan Africa that mixes some useless and indirect echoes of traditional religions with the first snapshots, good stories, and moral justifications that will be successful in European travel literature in the following centuries.

However, his description is new, because the political landscape that we make out through his description was new. If Tuat was certainly an old palm grove, its role as a trans-Saharan port of commerce seems recent, dating back two centuries perhaps, and its domination in this role more recent still. It could only be tied to the economic ascendance of the part of the Sahel that encompassed the Niger Bend, to which Tuat is joined by the most direct route. With a jump of thirteen hundred kilometers, one reaches Kûkiyâ, mentioned here for the first time, cradle of the Songhai kingdom that, at the time Malfante was recording, had retaken Gao from a declining Mâli and asserted itself as the new regional power. On the other shoulder of the Niger Bend, attesting to the transfer of commercial activity to the central Sahel, Timbuktu, also freed from the suzerainty of Mâli and passing once more to the Masûfa Berbers, asserted itself as the greatest Sahelian crossroads, replacing Oualata. And in the central Sahel, the Islamic city-states of the Hausa world had already appeared.

But Malfante's letter is also valuable, and perhaps most of all, because of what its very existence reveals to us. That a merchant from the northern side of the Mediterranean—not a slave taken by Barbary pirates but a freeman, not a René Caillié disguised as an Arab but an avowed

Christian—found himself in the middle of the Sahara, daring to do business there and making plans, illustrates the push of Europe's political and economic powers to the south. The kingdoms of Aragon and Castile, at the same time they were waging the Reconquista, had had designs on the Maghreb since the thirteenth century; if their plans weren't immediately implemented, they nevertheless reveal an economic appetite that managed to sate itself through agreements allowing Christian merchants— Iberians and Italians—to settle in the major cities of the Maghreb. In 1415, Portugal took Ceuta, a Moroccan port across from Gibraltar. This first foothold foreshadowed, from the end of the fifteenth century, the creation of a series of Iberian enclaves on Morocco's Mediterranean coast; but it was also the starting point of the Atlantic route that from the middle of the century bypassed Morocco. When Malfante arrived in Tuat, the Portuguese already had a trading post on the island of Arguin off the Mauritanian coast (↦33). Our Genoese merchant wasn't only a diligent *observer* of trans-Saharan commerce; he was an *actor* playing a role in what we would today describe as the opening of a line of business to competition. Was it the cause or the consequence? In the second half of the fifteenth century, the economic and political imperialism of Christian Europe went hand in hand with the political fragmentation of the Maghreb. Morocco, in particular, was also disrupted by the influx of Jews expelled from Christian Spain and Muslim "refugees" chased from the last bastions of al-Andalus by the Reconquista. The Maghrebian societies responded to this crisis with bursts of religious reformism, indeed religious fundamentalism.

In the middle of the twentieth century, the Jews who still lived in the Saharan oases ended the Passover seder with the formula "Next year in Tamentit," instead of the traditional "Next year in Jerusalem." The substitution commemorates Tamentit's Jewish community, prosperous in Malfante's day thanks to its role as a hinge between the Maghrebian and Saharan segments of the gold trade, a community that was destroyed and dispersed a few decades after he sent his letter. The architect of this destruction was a Muslim scholar named Muhammad al-Maghîlî. He had perhaps studied at Tuat under the *cadi*, the judge of the oasis, in his youth, but he had certainly settled there by 1477–1478. Concerned by the tepid religious observance and crumbling morality he felt he was witnessing in the Maghreb, he was particularly shocked by the condition of the Jews of the Saharan oases, especially those of Tuat, who seemed to him to be unduly raised above the status—submission—reserved for them by Islamic law. The payment of the *jizya* was irregular and was not accompanied, as some jurists recommended it should be, by a ceremony of public humiliation. As far as al-Maghîlî was concerned, it was nothing more than a kind of prebend collected by complacent sheiks. The Jews of Tuat found some defenders among the merchants or other Muslim clerics, one of whom asserted that the mass of Jews were poor and oppressed. But the populace, whipped up by calls to spill the blood of the Jews and the "infidels" who defended them, and attracted by the reward of seven gold dinars* offered for each victim, destroyed the synagogue and butchered the Jews. The massacre took place around 1492, the same year the kingdom of Granada fell to the Castilians and the Jews were chased from Spain.

Al-Maghîlî was the prototype of the wandering ulama* seeking the patronage of a king or community. He is mentioned in Gourara, another western Algerian oasis, where it seems he provoked a new pogrom; he was dismissed from Fez by the sultan. Then he crossed the Sahara. His trail leads to Takedda in the Aïr Massif. He spent several years at Kano, a Hausa city-state; he left descendants there and wrote a treatise on government for the country's Muslim sovereign. Later we run into him at Katsina, also in the Hausa. Finally, we find him in Gao around 1497. The religious geography was decidedly merchant geography. At Gao he served as a legal adviser to the Songhai sovereign, the *askyia* Muhammad, who had only recently (1492, again) taken possession of a kingdom that had absorbed Timbuktu and Djenné. He wrote a treatise in the form of a dialogue with the monarch. Al-Maghîlî's rigorous Islam certainly helped to strengthen his patron's dubious legitimacy. The "pagan" epic associated with the empire's formative period had to be forgotten; a climate of justice suitable to restoring trade had to arise. When he learned of the death of his son at the hands of a faction at Tamentit primarily made up of Jewish survivors, he had all the merchants from Tuat in Songhai territory arrested and vowed to confiscate the goods of those who did business with the Jews. A judge at Timbuktu set them free. The outcome: al-Maghîlî left to die at Tamentit. His dreams and his victories were the hallmarks of the epoch: There's no great span of time between the first sighting of a Christian merchant at Tuat and the destruction of the Jewish community in the same place.

BIBLIOGRAPHICAL NOTE

The "Letter from Tuat" was discovered by Charles de La Roncière, then curator at the Bibliothèque nationale de Paris, in 1918, in a fifteenth-century manuscript also containing copies of the letters of Cicero and Prester John. A brief description of this discovery may be found in *Comptes-Rendus des Séances de l'Académie des Inscriptions et Belles-Lettres* 62 (1918): 221. The letter (in Latin) was edited (without a translation) and commented on by its discoverer in "Découverte d'une relation de voyage datée du Touat et décrivant en 1447 le bassin du Niger," *Bulletin de la Section de Géographie* [of the Comité des Travaux historiques et scientifiques] 33 (1918): 1–24, then (with a facsimile, translation, and updated commentary) in *La découverte de l'Afrique au Moyen Âge*, 3 vols. (Cairo: Société royale de géographie d'Égypte, 1925–1927) (the letter appears on 1:143–160, but vol. 3 also presents documents that are useful for illuminating Malfante's life and activities). Unfortunately, these references' critical apparatus is obsolete by today's standards and has not been updated. The extracts cited or paraphrased in this chapter follow the English translation of G. R. Crone in *The Voyages of Cadamosto and Other Documents on Western Africa in the Second Half of the Fifteenth Century* (London: Hakluyt Society, 1937), pp. 85–90. The literature on the Jews of the Saharan oases, especially the Jews of Tuat, is vast. However, it evinces a tendency to extrapolate from the chronological and geographical data. As space precludes a proper introduction of the historiographical and critical "dossier" that the subject deserves, it's best to limit ourselves to the fundamental work of Haim Zeev Hirschberg, *A History of the Jews in North Africa*, vol. 1, *From Antiquity to the Sixteenth Century*, 2nd rev. ed. (Leiden: Brill, 1974), and, for the Jewish community of Tuat, to the remarkable essay by John Hunwick, *Jews of a Saharan Oasis: Elimination of the Tamantit Community* (Princeton, NJ: Markus Wiener, 2006), a no-frills synthesis whose essence had already been presented in a more accessible article: "Al-Maghîlî and the Jews of Tuwât: The Demise of a Community," *Studia Islamica* 61 (1985): 155–183. The expression that became this chapter's title was borrowed from the first chapter of *Jews of a Saharan Oasis*, which itself had borrowed the formula from Robert Capot-Rey, *Le Sahara français* (Paris: Presses universitaires de France, 1953), pp. 189–190. On al-Maghîlî's relationship with the Songhai monarch, see also John Hunwick, *Sharī'a in Songhay: The Replies of al-Maghīlī to the Questions of Askia al-Ḥājj Muhammad* (Oxford: Oxford University Press, 1985); it is a critical edition of the "Response" al-Maghîlî gave to the sovereign. The discovery of a Hebrew funeral inscription dedicated to a Monispa (the reading is not certain), daughter of Amr'an, who died in childbirth in the year 5089 of the Jewish calendar, or 1329 in the Gregorian calendar, provides a moving material contribution to our knowledge of this medieval Jewish community: see Philippe Berger, "Une inscription juive du Touat," *Comptes-Rendus des Séances de l'Académie des Inscriptions et Belles-Lettres* 47 (1903): 235–239. On Takedda and its identification with one or another of the archaeological sites in the region of Azelik, one must first read the articles by Henri Lhote, "Recherches sur Takedda, ville décrite par Ibn Battouta et située en Aïr," *Bulletin de l'Institut fondamental d'Afrique noire* 34 (1972): 429–470; and Suzanne Bernus and Pierre Gouletquer, "Du cuivre au sel. Recherches ethno-archéologiques sur la région d'Azelik (campagnes 1973–1975)," *Journal des africanistes* 46 (1976): 7–68, in order to familiarize oneself with a chaotic dossier. Regarding the history of the Songhai kingdom, the best reference remains the long introduction to Paulo F. de Moraes Farias, *Arabic Medieval Inscriptions from the Republic of Mali: Epigraphy, Chronicles, and Songhay-Tuāreg History*, Fontes Historiae Africanae, new series (Oxford: Oxford University Press, 2003).

CHAPTER 33

Africa's New Shores

*The Coasts of Present-Day Mauritania,
Senegal, and Gambia, 1455*

On 22 March 1445, Alvise Ca' da Mosto rounded Cape St. Vincent, off the Sagres Point of the province of Algarve in southern Portugal. At the time, when someone intended to visit the African coast, he needed to have a commission from the infante (prince) of Portugal, Henry the Navigator. This was the case for the Venetian often called Cadamosto (as his Italian name is often transcribed in other languages), a down-on-his-luck aristo- crat keen to rebuild his fortune and rehabilitate his image. He invested his unique inheritance in this business: his membership in a nation of merchants.

Cadamosto first stopped in Madeira. Discovered a century earlier by Italians, the archipelago, located about six hundred kilometers off the Moroccan coasts, was uninhabited. The main island, Madeira itself, was covered by a thick forest. Its rare woods had been exploited since 1420, when the Portuguese took possession of the island and settled colonists there. Wheat and oats were grown there to feed the metropole; livestock raised there were slaughtered to resupply the passing caravels. A famous product from the harvest was "dragon's blood," a bright-red medicinal resin extracted from a plant. Most important of all, sugarcane cultivation was introduced from the former Islamic islands of the Mediterranean.

After Madeira, Cadamosto reached the Canaries. Perhaps familiar to ancient sailors, these islands, indisputably African—the easternmost, Fuerteventura, is only one hundred kilometers off the Moroccan coast— had been visited many times during the fourteenth century. At the very beginning of the fifteenth century, a Frenchman, Jean de Béthencourt, lord of Grainville in Normandy, would attempt to carve out a fiefdom for himself under the suzerainty of the king of Castile. It must be said that this archipelago offered sources of wealth that no other African Atlantic island could offer: orchid lichen, a variety of lichen that was used to make an ex- pensive purple dye, and, most of all, slaves. In Cadamosto's day, European navigators still ventured forth to raid "idolatrous" villages and capture the Guanches, the islands' indigenous Berber inhabitants.

After having returned to African coastal waters, Cadamosto sailed south for the "sandy country," which was on the left-hand side. He imagined it would take "well-mounted men fifty to sixty days to cross" this vast desert; he was right. The desert is, of course, the Sahara, separating what was then called "Barbary," a term in which there was nothing pejorative, to the north, from "Ethiopia," an ancient Greek term designating all of black Africa, to the south. Around the middle of this "white, arid, and all equally low-lying" coast, endless dunes that jut into the ocean, Cadamosto rounded the Cabo Blanco, "which is so called because the Portuguese who discovered it saw it to be sandy and white, without signs of grass or trees whatsoever." This prominent cape embraces a gulf that encloses a small island, Arguin, which would be of little interest were it not for its inestimably precious resource: fresh water. The Portuguese had a castle there, or what can more aptly be called a "fortified boutique," and some stone huts, where their factor* negotiated with the inhabitants. As in the Canaries, slaves had once been hunted on the beaches. But by the time Cadamosto arrived there, the slave "trade" (i.e., business) was more profitable and raids were prohibited by the infante.

It had been almost fifteen years since the first vessel landed on this coast; now Portuguese caravels arrived there all year round. Good merchant that he was, Cadamosto quickly understood the terms of regional trade. The Arabs he met in Arguin were nomads and Muslims; it was from these men, "very hostile to Christians," but pragmatic merchants all the same, that the Portuguese got information about Taghâza (↦25), Timbuktu, and even Kûkiyâ. They had a city, Ouadane, six days by camel in the hinterland, and circulated easily between Barbary and the Land of the Blacks. From the north, they brought copper, silver, horses, and silks made in Granada or the Maghreb that they traded for slaves and gold in the south. The price of a horse? Ten to fifteen slaves. Arguin was the portal through which the Portuguese entered into this trade: they sold wheat, silver, and fabrics of all kinds to the Arabs; in turn they purchased black slaves, gold, and Melegueta pepper. So efficient and profitable was this trade in those years that between eight hundred and a thousand slaves were taken from Arguin per annum.

Let's pursue the route taken by the Portuguese "discoverers" and the Venetian who followed in their wake. The journey remained long: there was still half a Sahara to cross; along the route Arabs became few and far between, replaced by "Azengues" (i.e., Sanhâja Berbers), who followed the custom of covering their mouths and noses with a veil. They were strong, thin people with an unsophisticated culture, who covered their hair with fish grease. They used "porcellana" (i.e., cowries*) as currency, and their weaponry consisted of darts and leather shields. The descriptive headings (physical appearance, clothes, arms, etc.) of every subsequent travelogue are already present here. "There are no lords among them, save those who are richer: these are honoured and obeyed to some degree by the others." Here also are the first signs of ethnographic curiosity. Every three or four years, their land was subject to the ravages of locusts.

Then came the mouth of the Senegal River, "discovered" only a decade before. The current border between Mauritania and Senegal, the river marked the ancient boundary between two sharply different natural and cultural milieus. Cadamosto was stunned by the change that occurred within a few dozen leagues: to the south, "men are very black, tall and big, their bodies well formed; and the whole country green, full of trees and fertile"; to the north, "the men are brownish, small, lean, ill-nourished, and small in stature: the country sterile and arid." It is hard to imagine a bigger contrast between two countries and their people separated only by the mouth of a river.

From the Senegal River stretched a long chain of societies that would be met with all along the coast of sub-Saharan Africa. Here, everything was new, everything worthy of being observed and talked about: ingenuously, travelers were surprised to see women go topless before even being shocked about it; they found it odd that cows were not red and that dogs barked just as they did in Portugal. It was the first encounter between Europeans and Africans that was not the product of the long history of the slave trade. The merit of Cadamosto's fresh, honest description is all the greater for it.

Between the Senegal and Gambia Rivers lay the kingdom of Jolof, whose king ruled over other kings, his vassals. But "this king," said Cadamosto, who tried as best he could to capture the originality of what he saw and heard, "is lord of a very poor people, and has no city in his country, but villages with huts of straw only." Besides, their kingdoms were not hereditary: royal authority depended, so it seems, on exchanges of services and tribute between lords and kings. A king could have as many wives as he wanted and owned slaves who cultivated his domain. It was while staying with a coastal lord, the "Bodumel"—actually *buur damel,* the Wolof title of the sovereign of Kajor—that the Venetian refined his anthropology of power: the major figures of this country were not kings because of the size of their domains, the power of their castles, or their hereditary status. "Such men are not lords by virtue of treasure or money, for they possess neither, nor do they expend any money: but on account of ceremonies and the following of people they may truly be called lords; indeed they receive beyond comparison more obedience than our lords." Even beyond the African case that is here under scrutiny, these are thorough reflections on the nature of power: it cannot be explained by a mere list of attributes; it has to do with symbols and social perception.

Here wealth was counted in imported horses, harnesses, livestock, and slaves. The latter were sold to Sanhâja Muslims, but also, from this point on, to Christians. Cadamosto received one hundred slaves in exchange for his horses. And as the delivery was overdue, he stayed for a month with the king, who provided support—enough time for a trusted traveler to observe the local mores and practices. What resembled a hamlet was actually a royal residence: "In the village where I was . . . there were from forty to fifty grass huts close together in a circle, surrounded by hedges and groves of great trees, leaving but one or two gaps as entrances. Each hut has a yard divided off by hedges, and thus one goes from yard to yard, and from house to house. In this place Budomel had nine wives: and likewise in his other dwellings." Cadamosto had already noted the presence of Moorish "priests" (i.e., ulamas*) in the king's entourage. They were Arabs as well as Sanhâja and stayed close to his side. It was through their influence that "[t]he chiefs adhere to the tenets of the Muhammadans." But this adherence, as far as it is possible to judge from Cadamosto's account, didn't have much of an effect on daily life. So loosely rooted was Islam that the king amused himself by pitting the Christian and Muslim religions against one another. And here is the Christian among the Moors, required by his host to speak, becoming bold: "On many grounds I proved his [the king's] faith to be false and our faith to be true and holy—thus getting the better of his learned men in argument." The king laughed; he was wise enough to make sure that it was he alone who announced the moral of the story to the small audience of religious zealots of both faiths: the Muslim religion would not be worse than the Christian religion if God was just. And if God is just, since he has given such a bounty to whites here on earth, then he would give paradise to the blacks in the hereafter. "In this," concluded the Venetian, a good loser, "he showed good powers of reasoning and deep understanding."

"Desirous of seeing the world and things never before seen by our nation, . . . I hoped also to draw from it honour and profit." That is how Cadamosto described his motivations for exploring the African coast. It is to this desire to see the world—a desire that was far from universal among voyagers—that we owe his meticulous description of the landscapes and societies of this new Africa. He rounded Cape Verde, the continent's westernmost point, and was one of the first to discover some of the neighboring islands. It was the most beautiful coast the Venetian had ever seen. Next his caravel entered the Gambia River; the local population, who had never seen a white man, appeared hostile, and the Portuguese sailors refused to go any farther. Cadamosto was not an explorer; he prudently turned the ship around.

Trade along Africa's new shores was not carried out haphazardly. It was a system whose need to assure its profitability meant that it adhered to the habits and regularities of a gigantic marketplace. Merchants did business on one shore or another, and each had its specialty: Iberian fabrics were delivered to Arguin; Barbary horses bought in Morocco were sold in Senegal. On either side of this thin margin of beaches, two worlds faced each other. One was the continental hinterland, where regional trade networks existed, such as in the Sahara. Just as a branch circuit derives its electricity from being attached to a principal circuit, so too did each of the trading posts modeled after Arguin receive their resources from these regional networks: slaves first, with gold following soon thereafter. The other was the sea. The coveted archipelagos played the role of way stations. At Madeira, the exploding sugar industry required slaves to cultivate the crop. Here, in microcosm, was the triangular trade that would be found in all of Africa's Atlantic archipelagos from the fifteenth century onward, and later in the Americas.

BIBLIOGRAPHICAL NOTE

All direct or indirect citations from Cadamosto's account are from G. R. Crone's translation in *The Voyages of Cadamosto and Other Documents on Western Africa in the Second Half of the Fifteenth Century* (London: Hakluyt Society, 1937), pp. 1–84. The work of reference on the Senegal region in the late Middle Ages is Jean Boulègue, *Le Grand Jolof (XIIIe–XVIe siècle)* (Blois: Façades, 1987). The expressive turn of phrase "fortified boutique" ("boutique fortifiée") was coined by Théodore Monod in the preface to his edition of *Voyage d'Eustache Delafosse sur la côte de Guinée, au Portugal et en Espagne, 1479–1481* (Paris: Chandeigne, 1992), p. 7. For the gold trade at Arguin, see Duarte Pacheco Pereira, *Esmeraldo de Situ Orbis. Côte occidentale d'Afrique, du Sud marocain au Gabon*, translation and notes by Raymond Mauny (Bissau: Centro de Estudos da Guiné Portuguesa, 1956), pp. 40–43. A considerable literature exists on the creation of an Atlantic economy in the second half of the fifteenth century. On this vast subject, the note by Vitorino Magalhães Godinho, "Création et dynamisme du monde atlantique (1420–1670)," *Annales. Économies, sociétés, civilisations* 5 (1950): 32–36, remains essential reading in that it outlines the program of this field of study in terms that remain no less significant. For a historical vision of the place and role of Africans in the Atlantic world that took shape in the subsequent centuries, see John K. Thornton, *Africa and Africans in the Making of the Atlantic World, 1400–1800*, 2nd ed. (Cambridge: Cambridge University Press, 1998). On the role of the sugar economy in Madeira, see especially Sidney M. Greenfield, "Madeira and the Beginnings of New World Sugar Cane Cultivation and Plantation Slavery: A Study in Institution Building," *Annals of the New York Academy of Science* 292 (1977): 536–552.

CHAPTER 34

Vasco da Gama and the "New World"

Indian Ocean, 1498

The first leg of the expedition retraced the route taken by the Portuguese voyages of exploration in the first half of the century. Having departed on 8 July 1497, the squadron passed by Lanzarote, one of the Canaries, on the fifteenth; by the twenty-seventh it was at Santiago in the Cape Verde archipelago, where it stocked up on meat and water. It took only twenty days to cover a distance that had taken several decades to first explore. Here the squadron split up. Some continued to the Gulf of Guinea; their destination was a Portuguese trading post on the coast of present-day Ghana where ships would now sail to and dock any time of the year: the Castle of Saint George, called Elmina, the "mine." Cargoes of gold and slaves were already being sent to Portugal from there. The others veered boldly out to sea, penetrating into the immensity of the Atlantic. One hundred and sixty men crewed three caravels and a supply ship. The captain was Vasco da Gama.

During the second leg, the ships' sails were filled with the winds that circled around the South Atlantic High. It lasted exactly three months, with no sign of land or ship. It was the first time that the Portuguese risked this operation, the *volta*, which consisted of making a gigantic loop in the unknown waters of the South Atlantic, a loop that had the potential to bring them back to the tip of the continent: a considerable detour in space, but a shortcut in time, that avoided having to sail against the northward winds which blow along the African coasts south of the equator. These lands—including the allied kingdom of Kongo, already nominally Christian—had been regularly visited since the 1480s. But they were not the goal of the squadron, which, on 4 November, landed on South Africa's Atlantic coast. It took an additional month and a half to round the Cape of Good Hope and pass the farthest point reached by the Portuguese ten years before. Bartolomeu Dias, suspecting a passage to another world, had indeed entered the waters of the Indian Ocean. But his frightened crew had forced him to turn around and go back home.

As soon as they made landfall, and for weeks afterward—the third leg of the expedition—Vasco da Gama and his crew watched for signs. On 11 November, the captain disembarked and showed the Africans whom he met on shore—Khoisan pastoralists probably intrigued by these strange visitors—cinnamon, cloves, mother-of-pearl, and gold, all of which they seemed not to know. Around mid-December, they felt that the land was improving: the coast got more pleasant; the vegetation became denser, the villages more numerous, and the women, as the sailors missed no opportunity to point out, more beautiful. None of this was a coincidence, they felt. On 11 January 1498, probably around the Natal region in eastern South Africa, a crew member, Martim Afonso, was sent ashore. He had spent time in Kongo. And wouldn't you know it: Afonso understood the local lord's welcome. A linguistic miracle had occurred during an adventure where one usually had to make do with barter and gesticulations: the languages of the East African coast belong to the Bantu language family; they are related to the Kongo language. Of course, no one could have known it, but such an event could only mean that the Portuguese were nearing their goal—a feeling that was confirmed on 25 January, probably around the mouth of the Zambezi River, where they stayed for about a month to repair the masts and refresh their bodies. Now they were sure: they had entered a New World, one that Europeans had dreamed of and longed for for centuries. Even if the lands "discovered" in the Caribbean during the first two voyages of Christopher Columbus were technically new, the "Americas" were not yet a new world of their own in the cartography and mental geography of the time.

The Africans here were friendly people who did business in their pirogues, apparently not at all surprised to see foreigners. Local notables came to meet the Portuguese: one lord wore a turban lined with silk, another a satin cap; a young man signaled with hand gestures that he'd already seen ships like that. The whole crew was enthusiastic, because "we were nearing what we so much desired." They named the local river

Rio dos Bon Sinais, or "River of the Good Signs" in Portuguese. Heading north now, on 2 March, they saw sailboats for the first time, coming out of a channel. It was the Island of Mozambique. The Portuguese approached the island and dropped anchor in the lagoon; they were met by boats and pirogues. Were they hostile, as would be expected of a first encounter? Quite the opposite. They sounded their trumpets, and copper-skinned men, "of the Mahometan religion" and speaking Arabic, boarded without hesitation and invited the newcomers to trade. The Portuguese had just entered the Islamic commercial domain of the Indian Ocean.

If no one was surprised to see the Portuguese burst in *from the south*, it was probably because no one in these waters had any reason to know what Portugal was in the first place, a microscopic kingdom in the far west of Christendom as distant from these shores as Japan. Moreover, no one had any reason to know that this kingdom had sent an insignificant flotilla to launch an assault on their world, or that they planned to do so by bypassing Africa, or that bypassing Africa was even possible. Furthermore, the Portuguese didn't call themselves Portuguese, but Christians. It was as such that they began to sail north along the East African coast, on a quest to find gold and spices, a pilot who would lead them to India, and other Christians if any lived in the environs.

Their journey in the Indian Ocean was the fourth leg of the expedition. In order to enter into discussions with the merchants of Mozambique, a crew member who had been a captive of the Moors in the Mediterranean acted as a spokesman. They learned that the merchants of this coast traded with the Arabs whose boats were still docked, loaded with fabrics, pepper, ginger, jars of cloves, mother-of-pearl, and gems. At first, the local sultan was welcoming, but then inexplicably became hostile. Several skirmishes, a few hostage exchanges, and the capture of two or three merchant pirogues filled with cotton, baskets, scented water in glass jars, and books in Arabic followed suit. Why this about-face? Was it because they suddenly understood who these newcomers were? That's what the Portuguese thought. Yet, just as they were about to depart, an Arab from Mecca, accompanied by his son, stowed aboard without fear, wishing to take advantage of the shuttle that would bring him closer to the Red Sea.

The Portuguese left Mozambique (in 1507, an armada would return to take the city and set up a small fort). On 4 April, they passed Kilwa in present-day Tanzania (↦21) without managing to make a stopover there; they were told that the Christians who lived there faced Muslim hostility. The city would be sacked in 1505. By the evening, they dropped anchor just off the island of Mafia; two pirogues brought oranges, and again Arabs who were heading north invited themselves on board—a strange and very imprudent familiarity. On 7 April, the squadron sailed between the continent and the islands of Zanzibar and Pemba. That evening it dropped anchor at Mombasa, in today's Kenya. Here, too, they were told, lived Christians. Someone was sent ashore to meet them: he came back saying that they worshipped a picture of the Holy Spirit painted on a sheet of paper. The stopover, however, turned out badly: after the customary gifts (oranges, citrons, sheep) were offered to the foreign visitors, the sultan of Mombasa proved to be uncooperative, and the Portuguese even suspected treachery. In a moment of panic, several Muslims jumped overboard to escape; two of them who stayed were tortured to divulge details of the plot. They escaped the next night. It was time for the Portuguese to set sail. Mombasa would be bombarded and set aflame within a few years, following the sack of Kilwa.

On 14 April, the squadron, weakened by fatigue and illness—only a hundred men were still alive—was anchored at Malindi: the captain and the sultan exchanged gifts at a distance; then a meeting took place at sea, sambuk* on one side, rowboat on the other. Both sides, of course, were armed. Sensibly, neither party gave the other an opportunity to commit violence, which would inevitably have pushed them over the fine line between business and piracy. And the exchange, minimal and symbolic, was established: the captain freed some prisoners captured the day before, and the sultan left his son as a hostage; jousts took place on the beach; cannons fired from the ships. Then the Portuguese learned that four ships belonging to Indian Christians were anchored in the bay. Here on the East African coast branches of the Christian family separated since apostolic times met once more; when some of these Indian Christians came on board, they were shown an altarpiece of the Virgin at the foot of the Cross. When the Indian cousins bowed low, the faces of the Portuguese lit up. The Indians feasted on board their ship and launched rockets. And they advised the Portuguese not to disembark. At this point, a little nervous, Vasco da Gama was starting to get irritated that he had not been given the pilot he expected; he captured one of the sultan's favorites and immediately got a pilot, a Christian again, so he thought. The squadron set sail on 24 April; on 20 May, it reached Calicut, on the coast of Kerala in southwestern India. The expedition had attained its goal; Vasco da Gama and his crew had experienced India's existence and proved that it was possible to sail there. After a three-month stay, Vasco da Gama set sail once again. It would take him a year to return to Portugal. A few months later, Pedro Álvarez Cabral would follow the same route, with thirteen caravels and fifteen hundred men. It was an army that came to dictate treaties of "friendship," set up factors,* and bombard the recalcitrant powers. The Portuguese Empire was born.

But why, we may wonder, were the Islamic powers who were met along the African coast during the first voyage of a Christian fleet in the Indian Ocean so considerate and indulgent toward the Portuguese (save the reciprocal small raids that were the rule in what was decidedly not a gentleman's world)? Why was the existence of other "Christians" evoked numerous times in regard to regions and cities where there had never been any (excluding the Eastern Christian communities scattered from Socotra to India)? Why was it once again a "Christian" pilot who led the Portuguese to Calicut?

The answer came on their arrival in Calicut. Only then can we under-stand what the Portuguese didn't: that they hadn't been deliberately and belligerently deceived or prevented from trading; that they hadn't been seen as enemies or acknowledged as the glorious conquerors they thought they were.

In Calicut the log provides the first written portrait of these "Christians" mentioned in several instances in the Indian Ocean and finally encoun-tered in their own land: "The city of Calecut [Calicut] is inhabited by Christians. They are of tawny complexion. Some of them have big beards and long hair, whilst others clip their hair short or shave the head, merely allowing a tuft to remain on the crown as a sign that they are Christians. They also wear moustaches. They pierce the ears and wear much gold in them. They go naked down to the waist, covering their lower extremities with very fine cotton stuffs. But it is only the most respectable who do this, for the others manage as best they are able." Hindus! The chronicler describes a "church"; it was actually a Hindu temple. The people of India the Portuguese took, or so ardently desired to take, for Christians, were neither simply Christians nor Indian Christians. They were Indian Hin-dus. Similarly, those whom the East African Muslims had been implying for months were other "Christians," because they of course had no idea what Christians really were, were not Christians either. They too were Indian Hindus. The misidentification is telling: it reveals that the signif-icant, incredible bypassing of Africa by the Portuguese went unnoticed in this Indo-Oceanic world that it would transform only a few years later. The sudden appearance of Latin Christians could be formulated only in the cultural and religious terms of the world that was the Indian Ocean. The little Portuguese squadron certainly owed its success in part to this, even though their miserable first adventure in the Indian Ocean would soon be regilded with all the color of an epic saga; perhaps it wouldn't have completed its expedition if the Muslims of Mozambique, Tanzania, or Kenya had known from what impossible horizon it had come.

Yet two men in Calicut immediately realized the journey's significance. As soon as his squadron arrived near the coastal city, Vasco da Gama had sent ashore one of the convicts kept on board to perform a dangerous task: establishing first contact with people who might or might not be hostile. The man was put in a rowboat and led toward the shore. He met two Muslims from Tunis who spoke Castilian and Genoese. As merchants, they had already encountered Christians in the ports of the Mediterranean. Meeting a Christian on the shores of India, perhaps seeing him as an omen of the end of an era, they immediately spoke in terms that betrayed incredulity and anger: "May the Devil take thee! What brought you hither?"

BIBLIOGRAPHICAL NOTE

The account of the voyage of Vasco da Gama followed here is generally attributed to Alvaro Velho, a participant and eyewitness. The citations are from *A Journal of the First Voyage of Vasco da Gama, 1497–1499*, translation and notes by E. G. Ravenstein (London: Hakluyt Society, 1898). On Vasco da Gama and the historical significance of the first Portuguese expedition in the Indian Ocean, see the work of Sanjay Subrahmanyam, *The Career and Legend of Vasco da Gama* (Cambridge: Cambridge University Press, 1997). The accounts of the sacks of Kilwa and Mombasa are available in the collection of documents brought together in G.S.P. Freeman-Grenville, *The East African Coast* (Oxford: Clarendon Press, 1962). For a remarkably well-documented archaeological monograph on Elmina Castle, built in 1482, see Christopher R. DeCorse, *An Archaeology of Elmina: Africans and Europeans on the Gold Coast, 1400–1900* (Washington, DC: Smithsonian Institution Press, 2001). On the history of Kongo, see John K. Thornton, "The Origins and Early History of the Kingdom of Kongo, c. 1350–1550," *International Journal of African Historical Studies* 34 (2001): 89–120, among many other works by the same author. On the subject of the much-debated identity of the pilot Vasco da Gama obtained at Malindi, see the clarification by Charles Verlinden, "Problèmes d'histoire de l'expansion portugaise," *Revue belge de philologie et d'histoire* 68 (1990): 802–816. Finally, on the significance of Bartholomeu Dias's circumnavigation of Africa, see my article "La croix de Dias. Genèse d'une frontière au sud de l'Afrique," *Genèse* 86 (2012): 126–148.

ACKNOWLEDGMENTS

Numerous individuals and institutions have supported me throughout the writing of this book. I would like to thank (in alphabetical order) Ladan Akbarnia, Francis Anfray, Colin Baker, Sophie Berthier, Claire Bosc-Tiessé, Pierre Cathala, Monique Chastanet, Emmanuel Fritsch, Annabelle Gallin, Laurence Garenne-Marot, Detlef Gronenborn, Jean-Loïc Le Quellec, Bertrand Poissonnier, Stéphane Pradines, Serge Robert, Caroline Robion-Brunner, Karim Sadr, Wolbert Schmidt, Marina Steyn, Fahmida Suleman, Balázs Tamási, Sian Tiley, Robert Vernet, and Magdalena Wozniak, who provided me with information, clarifications, or bibliographical and iconographical material. I would also like to thank the colleagues and students who attended my seminar on the archaeology and history of ancient Africa at the University of Toulouse. I have benefited from the attentive readings, suggestions, and encouragement of Claire Bosc-Tiessé, Bertrand Hirsch, Romain Mensan, Yann Potin, and Robin Seignobos. François Bon, Marie-Laure Derat, Bertrand Poissonnier, and Julien Loiseau patiently read the entire manuscript and gave me valuable and judicious comments. They permitted me to correct numerous errors and should not be held responsible for those that remain. Several of this book's chapters could not have been written without the support of the French Center for Ethiopian Studies (CFEE) in Addis Ababa, the Centre Jacques-Berque in Rabat, and the French Center in South Africa (IFAS) in Johannesburg, three research institutes under the aegis of the French National Center for Scientific Research (CNRS) and the French ministry of foreign affairs, as well as the University of Witwatersrand in Johannesburg, the Mapungubwe Museum at the University of Pretoria, and the Bibliothèque de recherches africaines of the University of Paris I Panthéon-Sorbonne. I am very grateful to Patrick Boucheron, Catherine Argand, and Jean-Maurice de Montremy for having believed in this book from the beginning. Sadly, this book lacks a reader who died in 2011: Jean Boulègue, professor of ancient African history at the University of Paris I Panthéon-Sorbonne, whose sensibility, precision, and exigence in the reading of sources have been a guide for me since my time as his student; I dedicate this book to his memory.

The English edition owes much to Martine Bertéa. Brigitta van Rheinberg, History Editor at Princeton University Press, gave it an enthusastic welcome. The two anonymous reviewers for the Press offered valuable comments that pushed me to substantially rewrite the introduction. I thank Troy Tice for his remarkably sensitive translation and for the continuous conversations that led me to reformulate and deepen several passages. My thanks also to Amanda Peery at Princeton Univerity Press; to Lauren Lepow, whose copyediting was always very judicious; and to Chris Ferrante for his graphically slick design. For his part, Troy Tice would like to thank Amélie Chekroun, Julien Loiseau, and Sam Nixon, who kindly provided extra documents and information for this edition, as well as Elizabeth A. R. Brown for translation advice.

GLOSSARY

banco: West African architectural term for a mixture of earth (which may be of varied composition) and natural temper (sand, gravel, straw, etc.). This mixture is shaped into bricks (sun-dried, never baked) and used for construction. Along with wattle and daub* and rammed earth,* it is one of the construction techniques that use raw earth as a building material.

Bantustan: During South Africa's apartheid regime (1948–1994), the word for the rural enclaves or "reserves" where the majority of the country's black population was forced to live. Except for miners and domestic workers, who were allowed (under strict conditions) to live in urban areas, the rest of the black population was considered nonproductive and unworthy to live in the part of the country reserved for whites.

coin weights: Glass tokens precisely the same weight and shape as various coins. In the Islamic world, the token often bore an inscription with the name of a sovereign. Inalterable, these objects could serve as standards of weight or units of account.

cowrie (pl. cowries): Name for several varieties of marine gastropod mollusks or sea snails sometimes called "porcelains." Two very small varieties, *Cypraea moneta* and *Cypraea annulus*, endemic to the tropical latitudes of the Indian and Pacific Oceans, were at the center of a vast exchange system across the Islamic world, starting from the region where they were almost exclusively collected: the Maldives archipelago. In many places in Africa, cowrie shells served as currency, decorative items, and divination objects.

dinar: Gold coin of the bimetallic (gold/silver) Islamic monetary system.

dirham: Silver coin of the bimetallic Islamic monetary system, valued at a fraction of the dinar.*

erg: Duned desert (as opposed to rocky desert).

factor: Firm clerk, under royal or private commission, who carried out business for the firm and in its name, sometimes as the head of an overseas establishment dedicated to this function, also called "trading post."

Indo-Pacific (beads): Term referring to the geographical distribution (around the Indian and Pacific Oceans) of sites where little glass-paste beads spun of diverse colors, sometimes called "trade-wind beads," were produced. During antiquity and the Middle Ages, these beads came from several ateliers situated on the southeast coast of India, Malaysia, the Indochinese Peninsula, and Indonesia.

ksar (pl. ksour): Generic term, borrowed from Maghrebi Arabic, designating a fortified, generally rectangular, village of North Africa or the Sahara. Before the modern era, a ksar often constituted a political unit.

metropolitan: Initially the title of a bishop of a provincial capital, the term came to designate, in Eastern Christianity, the head of a church canonically dependent on a mother church. The metropolitans of the Nubian and Ethiopian Churches, for example, were consecrated by the Coptic patriarch at Alexandria, and later at Cairo.

mihrâb: Arabic term. Wall niches in mosques that indicate to the faithful the direction of Mecca. Typically, in North and West Africa, the mihrâbs are oriented toward the east or southeast; in Ethiopia and along the east coast of Africa, they are oriented to the north.

mithqâl: Measure corresponding to around 4.25 grams, considered the standard weight for the dinar* in the first centuries of Islam. Sometimes used as a synonym for dinar.

mopane: Characteristic tree (*Cholophospermum mopane*) of the arboreal savannas of southern Africa. It has rot-resistant wood and is host to an edible caterpillar, the mopane worm.

rammed earth: Architectural term (equivalent to French *pisé* and Arabic *tabiya*) for a mixture of earth (which may be of varied composition), temper (sand, gravel, pebbles, etc.), and lime, poured and compacted in a wooden form to raise walls. Along with banco* and wattle and daub,* it is one of the construction techniques that use raw earth as a building material.

sambuk: Arabic term for small, triangular-sailed boats with teakwood hulls that have sailed back and forth across the western Indian Ocean from antiquity up to the present day.

shea tree: Tree (*Vitellaria paradoxa*) native to the savanna of western and central Africa, it produces a kernel from which a fatty substance is extracted (traditionally by grinding). This "shea butter" is used in food preparation and medicinal ointments, and as a luxury additive in coating for banco* walls, notably in present-day Mali.

township: In twentieth-century South Africa, the neighborhoods on the cities' peripheries reserved for nonwhites. These neighborhoods were characterized by a lack of infrastructure and utilities.

tumulus: Burial structure in which a tomb—or multiple tombs—is incorporated into an artificial mound made from blocks of rock or from earth.

ulama: Arabic term. Muslim scholar, preacher, jurist, and theologian all at once. From the Sahara to the Sahel, the ulamas were the agents of Islamization.

wattle and daub: Architectural term for a mixture of earth and temper (straw, grass, etc.) daubed smooth, generally over a trellis of branches, to form the walls and partitions of houses. Wattle and daub is widely used for traditional African dwellings. Along with banco* and rammed earth,* it is one of the construction techniques that use raw earth as a building material.

FURTHER READING

I have tried to indicate in the notes to each chapter the specific works I have used as well as the fundamental sources and references, recent publications, and, if necessary, the most accessible ones. The literature on this topic is vast and most of the time not readily accessible. Nevertheless, the following pages offer an annotated guide to the most useful source collections, general works of synthesis, and reference works on the African Middle Ages.

Austen, Ralph A. *Trans-Saharan Africa in World History*. Oxford: Oxford University Press, 2010. The most accessible synthesis on the Sahara as both barrier and "highway" over the longue durée.

Derat, Marie-Laure. *Le domaine des rois éthiopiens (1270–1527). Espace, pouvoir et monachisme*. Paris: Publications de la Sorbonne, 2003. Reference work on the Solomonic (thirteenth- to fifteenth-century) era of medieval Ethiopia.

General History of Africa. Paris: UNESCO, various publication dates. This voluminous work has been published in several languages. Among the collection's eight volumes, the two most pertinent to medieval African history are vol. 3, *Africa from the Seventh to the Eleventh Century* (1990) and vol. 4, *Africa from the Twelfth to the Sixteenth Century* (1985), but the contributions are highly heterogeneous in quality and sometimes considerably outdated.

Horton, Mark, and John Middleton. *The Swahili: The Social Landscape of a Mercantile Society*. Malden, MA: Blackwell Publishers, 2000. Work of synthesis that portrays Swahili society as an urban and commercial interface between Africa and the Indian Ocean. Because of this, it privileges the great hallmarks of the whole of Swahili civilization over historical dynamics. To be read in comparison with Pouwells.

Insoll, Timothy. *The Archaeology of Islam in Sub-Saharan Africa*. Cambridge World Archaeology. Cambridge: Cambridge University Press, 2003. Reference book that approaches the question of Islamization and the presence of Islam in precolonial African societies from an archaeological perspective.

Levtzion, Nehemia. *Ancient Ghana and Mali*. London: Methuen, 1973. The canonical reference on the medieval Sahelian kingdoms. More recent work has slightly modified, but not overthrown, its conclusions. No one has since attempted a similar synthesis integrating the written sources, archaeology, and oral traditions.

Levtzion, Nehemia, and J.F.P. Hopkins (eds.). *Corpus of Early Arabic Sources for West African History*. Princeton, NJ: Markus Wiener, 2000 (reprint of the original edition, Cambridge University Press, 1981). Collection of external Arabic sources related to medieval West Africa, with introductions and annotations.

Levtzion, Nehemia, and Randall L. Pouwels. *The History of Islam in Africa*. Athens: Ohio University Press, 2000. A collection of articles by specialists on all aspects of the ancient and contemporary history of Muslim societies in Africa.

Masonen, Pekka. *The Negroland Revisited: Discovery and Invention of the Sudanese Middle Ages*. Helsinki: The Finnish Academy of Science and Letters, 2000. A very good study of the birth and development of Western historiography on Sahelian Africa and the intellectual "construction" of medieval political formations.

Mauny, Raymond. *Tableau géographique de l'Ouest africain au Moyen Âge, d'après les sources écrites, la tradition et l'archéologie*. Dakar: Institut fondamental d'Afrique noire, 1961. The first report of all research on medieval West African history. Although other studies have superseded the work in some respects, its encyclopedic compendium of the various aspects of the field (archaeological remains, ethnographic observations, etc.) remains unequaled. Likewise unequaled is its successful integration of the heterogeneous data from written sources, oral and ethnographic sources, and archaeology.

McIntosh, Susan Keech (ed.). *Excavations at Jenné-Jeno, Hambarketolo, and Kaniana (Inland Niger Delta, Mali), 1981 Season*. Berkeley: University of California Press, 1995. The comprehensive publication resulting from the excavation of medieval Djenné and still one of the best examples of an archaeological monograph in the West African Sahel.

Monod, Théodore. *Méharées. Explorations au vrai Sahara*. Arles: Actes Sud, "Babel," 1994 (1st ed. 1937). More than just an introduction to Saharan studies; an introduction to archaeological fieldwork itself.

Moraes Farias, Paulo F. de. *Arabic Medieval Inscriptions from the Republic of Mali: Epigraphy, Chronicles, and Songhay-Tuāreg History*. Fontes Historiae Africanae, new series. Oxford: Oxford University Press, 2003. This summit of erudition revitalizes the approach to the Arabic funerary epigraphy of sub-Saharan Africa to produce a history of the relationship between the Tuareg and Songhay in modern Mali, while posing important epistemological questions on the respective contributions of the different types of sources.

Oliver, Roland, and Anthony Atmore. *Medieval Africa, 1250–1800*. Cambridge: Cambridge University Press, 2001 (1st ed. 1981). Good overview of "medieval" African history conceived as precolonial in the widest sense.

Phillipson, David W. *African Archaeology*. 3rd ed. Cambridge: Cambridge University Press, 2005. Now in its third edition, this work is the "reference manual" for African archaeology. While it does not cover the medieval period in great depth, the book does offer the best archaeological panorama of Africa from prehistory to colonization.

Pikirayi, Innocent. *The Zimbabwe Culture: Origins and Decline of Southern Zambezian States*. Walnut Creek, CA: Altamira Press, 2001. The best archaeological and historical synthesis of the societies of the Zambezi basin, especially Great Zimbabwe, and of their interactions with their neighbors, particularly the coastal societies. One of the book's great qualities is that the Zambezi basin is presented as central and not as a mere periphery of the Swahili world; another of its strengths is that it places medieval developments in the longue durée that persisted until the eve of colonization.

Pouwells, Randall L. *Horn and Crescent: Cultural Change and Traditional Islam on the East African Coast, 800–1900.* Cambridge: Cambridge University Press, 1987. A book by a historian that clearly addresses the formative phase of Swahili culture and the profound transformations it underwent over the course of its history. Although dated in some respects, it remains a very good illustration of the difficulties associated with weaving a narrative from archaeological, linguistic, written, and oral data.

Welsby, Derek A. *The Medieval Kingdoms of Nubia: Pagans, Christians and Muslims along the Middle Nile.* London: British Museum Press, 2002. The essential work on medieval Nubia. It skillfully blends history and archaeology while principally following (contrary to its title) the narrative thread of the Christian kingdoms, from their rise in antiquity to their collapse in the fifteenth century.

INDEX

cattle, 138, 172, 224

celadon. *See* greenware

Centurione, 223–24

Chakrabarty, Dipesh, 11

Charles V, king of France, 191

check, 51, 53–55

China, 17–21, 26

Chittick, Neville, 145

Christianity: in Abyssinia, 210–13; churches of Lalibela, 155–58; early appearances of, in Africa, 223, 227–28; in Ethiopia, 40–41, 90, 95–98, 155, 210–13; Muslims' relations with, in Abyssinia, 210–13; in Nubia, 29–30, 37–42; Portuguese exploration of Africa and, 242–47. *See also* Coptic Christianity

city-dwellers, on caravans, 178–79

coin hoards, 96–97

Columbus, Christopher, 242

commerce. *See* trade

concubines, 107

conversions, 70–73

copper, 54, 58, 224

Coptic Christianity, 30, 38–42

cowries, 84, 86, 127, 139, 146, 185–87, 220

Cresques, son of Abraham, 192

dakākīr. See idols

Daniel (author of Ethiopian inscriptions), 90–92

Davidson, Basil, 10

Debre Damo monastery, 95–98

Desplagnes, Louis, 83

Devisse, Jean, 52

dhimmî (protected ones), 225

Diafounou, 78–79

Dongola, 29–32, 34, 40

Dûghâ (sultan's interpreter), 205–7

Du Huan, 17–18

Dulcert, Angelino, 192

Dyula (traders), 122

Egypt, 30–34, 39–42, 161

Ethiopia: Christianity in, 40–41, 90, 95–98, 155, 210–13; decline of, 14; inscriptions from, 90–92; treasures of Debre Damo in, 95–98; tumuli in, 82

ethnoarchaeology, 128

eunuchs, 212–13

Faras, 38

Fouché, Leo, 137

fundamentalism, religious, 228–29

funerary practices, 85–87

Gama, Vasco da, 6, 242–47

Gao, 70

George II, king of Nubia, 37, 39–42

Ghâna (medieval), 7, 52, 57–61, 65–68; capital of, 59–61; funerary practices in, 86–87; gold in, 58, 65–66, 120–21, 197; as Muslim kingdom, 66–67, 70; two instantiations of, 66–68

Ghana (modern), 57

glass beads, Indo-Pacific, 86, 137, 139, 145, 220

global Middle Ages: Chinese-African contacts in, 20–21; concept of, 11–12

Global Positioning System (GPS), 184

gold: from Aoudaghost, 54; from Ghâna, 58, 65–66, 120–21, 197; Mapungubwe and, 139; mines for, 126–29; Mûsâ's association with, 191, 196–97; in the Sahel, 76, 113, 120–24; trade in, 121–24, 139, 212, 223–24, 228; from Zimbabwe, 217

Gold Coast, 57

golden rhinoceros of Mapungubwe, 10, 137–40

Great Zimbabwe, 216–21

Greefswald farm, 136–38

greenware, 139, 145

Guanches, 233

Reconquista, 228
religion. *See* Christianity; Islamic religion; traditional religion
religious fundamentalism, 228–29
Robert, Denise and Serge, 52
rocs, 150
Roger II, king of Sicily, 101
royalty, myths of origin/succession of, 162–68

Sabraddin, sultan of Ifât, 210
Sâfî (slave), 106–7
Sahara, 51–54, 170; caravans in, 176–81, 184–88; customs of tribes in, 79; exploration of, 45–48; trade in, 48, 51, 53–55, 113, 116, 120, 171–73, 193, 223–24
Sahel: conversions in, 70–73; documentary sources about, 6; enslaved inhabitants of, 48; gold in, 120–24
al-Sâhilî, Abû Ishâq, 194
Salek ould Guejmoul, 184
salt, 53–54, 58, 170–73, 224
Sanhâja nomads, 51–52, 76–77
al-Sarakhsî, 115
Senegal, 84
serpents, 78, 178–79
Shiism, 47
Sijilmâsa, 48, 51, 53–54, 76, 112–17, 120, 176–77, 193, 225
Silla, 70
skins. *See* animal skins
slavery: Abyssinia and, 212–13; Berbers as victims of, 45–46; Nubia and, 30, 32–33; trade associated with, 30, 32–33, 212–13, 226, 233, 236
snakes. *See* serpents
Sofala, 24–25, 132–34
Solomon, king of Jerusalem, 126
Somalia, 19–20
Somaliland, 107
Soninke, 78

South Africa, 136–38
sperm whales, 23
Sûdân. *See* Land of the Blacks
Sulaymân, sultan of Mâli, 201
Sunnism, 46–47, 114
Swahili civilization/language, 24–25, 151, 153

Taghâza, 170–73
Takrûr, 70
Tamentit, 223–30
Tankâminîn, 57–59
Tanzania, 14
thirst, 176–77
throne-base, 90–92
Timbuktu, 170–71, 193–94, 227
Tî-n-Yarûtân, 51
trade: in ambergris, 23–24, 26; archipelagos and, 238; with China, 18–21, 26; family-based, 115–16; funerary practices reflecting, 86; in gold, 121–24, 139, 212, 223–24, 228; Great Zimbabwe's role in, 219–20; with India, 107, 139; in ivory, 26; Jews involved in, 106–7, 112–14, 193, 224, 228; Kilwa's role in, 144–47; Majorca's role in, 193; Mapungubwe's role in, 139–41; Mogadishu's role in, 151–52; Portuguese entry into, 228, 234–35; in the Sahara, 48, 51, 53–55, 113, 116, 120, 171–73, 193, 223–24; in salt, 171–72; Sijilmâsa's role in, 48, 51, 53–54, 76, 112–17, 120, 176–77, 193, 225; in slaves, 30, 32–33, 212–13, 226, 233, 236; system/market for conducting, 121–24, 238; Taghâza's role in, 171; Tuat's role in, 223–24, 227; Zanj/Qambalû and, 25–26. *See also* caravans
traditional religion, 58, 70–73
treasures, 10
treaty. See *baqt*
troglodytic dwellings, 158
Tuaregs, 58, 79